Dennis D. Curry
1005 W Leland Ave Apt B
Springfield, IL 62704

D1567520

FENTON ART GLASS

Hobnail Pattern

IDENTIFICATION & VALUE GUIDE

Margaret & Kenn Whitmyer

COLLECTOR BOOKS

A Division of Schroeder Publishing Co., Inc.

Front cover:
No. 3303-25" Gone with the Wind lamp, Willow Green Opalescent, introduced 2001, discontinued 2003, $250.00 – 275.00. No. CV273 Cranberry
Spiral Optic Tulip vase, produced for QVC in 1999, $85.00 – 95.00. No. 389-
5" Covered Jar, Green Opalescent, introduced 1940, discontinued 1941,
$400.00 – 500.00. No. 3761 Handled Decanter, Red Carnival, made for a spe-
cial order customer in the early 1990s, $325.00 – 375.00.

Back cover:
No. 3700 Covered Slipper Candy Box, Blue Marble, introduced 1971, discontinued 1974, $40.00 – 50.00. No. 1167, 3-piece Fairy Light, Rose Magno-
lia w/Sea Mist Green trim, produced for QVC in 1999, $60.00 – 70.00. No.
3863 Cruet and Stopper, Spruce Green Iridized Overlay, produced for QVC
in 1999, $60.00 – 70.00. No. 3303 Pitcher and Bowl Set, Blue Slag ("Almost
Heaven"), produced in 1988, $385.00 – 425.00. No. 3805 Vanity Set, Milk,
with tray, introduced 1955, discontinued 1965, $295.00 – 325.00.

Cover design by Beth Summers
Book design by Lisa Henderson

COLLECTOR BOOKS
P.O. Box 3009
Paducah, Kentucky 42002-3009

www.collectorbooks.com

Copyright © 2006 Margaret & Kenn Whitmyer

The current values in this book should be used only as a guide. They are not
intended to set prices, which vary from one section of the country to another.
Auction prices as well as dealer prices vary greatly and are affected by condition
as well as demand. Neither the authors nor the publisher assumes responsibility
for any losses that might be incurred as a result of consulting this guide.

Searching For A Publisher?

We are always looking for people knowledgeable within their fields. If you
feel that there is a real need for a book on your collectible subject and have a
large comprehensive collection, contact Collector Books.

CONTENTS

Blue Opalescent large handled mug made as a sample or whimsey from the tall footed swung vase mold. 7½" tall, 8" diameter. Value undetermined.

Green Opalescent flared rim large comport made as a whimsey from the tall footed swung vase mold. 7¼" tall, 6¾" diameter. Value undetermined.

DEDICATION

To

Frank M. Fenton

a generous man
with the foresight to
preserve the past

ACKNOWLEDGMENTS

Fenton Art Glass Hobnail Pattern has evolved through the efforts of the many faithful collectors and dealers who have been willing to share their knowledge and information with us. We want to thank all of the readers of our previous books about Fenton Art Glass who have sent us pictures and other information which have helped to verify the existence of the many pieces listed in this book. Due to the volume of mail, we have not been able to respond personally to all of your letters, but we have tried to answer as many as possible. We apologize if you have written to us and have not received an answer. However, we want you to know your letter has been read and the information or suggestions in it have been appreciated.

The contributions of Carrie and Gerry Domitz, Caroline and Woody Kriner, and Jackie Shirley are especially appreciated. Without the thoughtfulness and dedication of these individuals many exciting pieces would be lacking from this volume.

Several auction houses and antique malls graciously allowed us to photograph items in their possession. We are extremely grateful for the cooperation of Berner's Auction and the Heart of Ohio Antique Center of Springfield, Ohio. Jeffrey's Antique Gallery of Findlay, Ohio, was also a wonderful resource.

We are also very grateful to the following people who either helped with pricing or supplied us with much needed information: Henke and Anne van Bemmelen, Dennis Bialek, Joyce and Parke Bloyer, Sam and Becky Collings, Bill Cottenmyre, William Hatchett, Audrey and Joseph Humphrey, Kevin Kiley, Lorrie Kitchen and Mark Hunter, Lorraine and David Kovar, Joseph Lockard, Nancy and Jim Maben, Fred McMorrow, Tom Smith, David Shupp, Dick Tabor, Rick and Ruth Teets, Dan and Geri Tucker, and Delmar and Mary Lou Youngen.

Hopefully we have included everyone, but if someone's name has mysteriously been lost in our mountain of papers, please understand that we are not unappreciative of your cooperation. We do try to keep track of where the information is coming from, but sometimes finding names at the moment you need them is a problem.

PRICING

The prices in this book represent average retail prices for mint condition pieces. Pieces that are chipped, cracked, or excessively worn should only bring a fraction of the listed price. Also, collectors should be aware that certain currently rare items that are now valued at a high dollar amount may prove hard to sell if a large quantity of these items is discovered. A few items that have been found listed in the company catalogs, but are not known to be available, may not be priced in the listings.

A price range is included to allow for some regional differences. This book is only a guide and is not intended to set or establish prices.

Prices are for each piece unless a set is indicated in the description. Candleholders are priced individually. Salt and pepper shakers were listed in the Fenton price lists as sets and are priced in this book as sets. The prices listed are those we have seen collectors pay and prices collectors have told us they would be willing to pay.

REISSUES

Periodically, when Fenton determines that market conditions are appropriate, old molds may be reused to produce items for the regular line. The managers of Fenton are well aware of the collectibility of their older glassware. As a result certain steps have been taken to ensure that newer issues will enhance the collectibility of Fenton glassware and preserve the value of the older collectibles.

Many of the older molds that are brought out of retirement are used for special purposes, such as the Family Signature Series, the Connoisseur Collection, or the Historic Collection. These special series usually feature pieces in colors that were not made previously.

Beginning in 1970, molds were marked with an oval Fenton logo. This process was completed by about 1974. All items made after this date for the regular line will be marked on the bottom with the oval logo. As production has progressed through each successive decade, a small number has been added to the logo. The 1980s decade has an "8" and the 1990s production bears a "9." Production after 2000 has a "0."

Over the past several decades Fenton has purchased numerous molds from companies that have ceased production. In recent years production from molds used from this source has been marked with a script "F" encased in an oval.

HISTORY OF THE FENTON ART GLASS COMPANY

Brothers Frank L. and John W. Fenton opened The Fenton Art Glass Company as a cutting and decorating shop in July 1905, in Martins Ferry, Ohio. The business began as a decorating shop that used blanks supplied by various glass manufacturing companies. Not long afterwards, brother Charles H. gained employment with the firm.

As the firm prospered it became evident to the Fentons that their suppliers either could not or would not meet their increasing demands for more glassware. Therefore, it was an almost inevitable decision that to survive and prosper, they would have to produce their own glass. A decision was made to purchase a site and build a plant in Williamstown, West Virginia. The first glass from the new Fenton Art Glass plant was produced on January 2, 1907.

In late 1907, the officers of the company included John as president and Frank as general manager. Charles was still with the company as head of the decorating department and brother James E. joined the force as maintenance supervisor in late 1908. John left the Williamstown operation in 1909, and went to Millersburg, Ohio, to found a glass plant there. In 1910, older brother Robert C. was brought in to assist Frank L., who had assumed the presidency vacated by John. At this time Frank L. also retained the positions of treasurer and general manager.

The first plant manager was Jacob Rosenthal, a seasoned veteran of the glassmaking business. He had learned his skills in over 25 years of working at the various glasshouses around the country. He brought with him many secret formulas, and his knowledge of color was soon tested by the fledgling Fenton operation. Colored glassware in opalescents, Persian Blue, and Chocolate was soon pouring from the plant. Upon Jacob's retirement, his son Paul became plant manager and glassware continued to be produced with the same unique formulas.

Early glassware also included pressed glass pieces in Green, Crystal, Topaz Opalescent, Blue Opalescent, Ruby, and Amethyst. Iridescent glassware soon became the rage and the Fenton plant produced vast amounts of carnival glass. Patterns were numerous, production expanded, and the company prospered. In 1912, the company was back into the decorating business. By 1918, the volume in the cutting shop peaked and then gradually declined until Fenton finally phased out the cutting operation in the early 1930s.

The general appeal of pressed pattern carnival glass began to recede during the early 1920s. Thus, Fenton countered with another type of iridescent glass — stretch glass. Also another line of new colors was introduced about this time. These were solid opaque colors called Jades in green, yellow, blue, and moonstone. Sales of the new types of glass reached lofty heights.

The economies of the Great Depression forced Fenton to produce "necessary" products. Tableware lines such as Lincoln Inn and Georgian were born, and more production focused on essentials such as lamps, mixing bowls, and reamers. With the end of prohibition Fenton welcomed the thirsty public by providing decanter and beverage sets to all who needed them.

As unreal as it may sound, a small Hobnail cologne bottle was responsible for rescuing Fenton from the doldrums following the Great Depression. In 1938, Fenton's Chicago representative, Martin M. Simpson, used his contacts with a perfume company to facilitate a market test of a Hobnail cologne bottle that was produced by Fenton. The test results were phenomenal and Fenton's fortunes improved dramatically. In 1939, Fenton stepped up production of the No. 289 Hobnail cologne bottle for Wrisley. At times there were as many as eight to ten shops making this piece and sales to Wrisley approached 30 percent of the total company sales. However, the honeymoon with Wrisley was short-lived. By 1941, the greater economies of machine-made glassware were more appealing, and the Wrisley contract was lost to Hocking.

In 1940, the Hobnail pattern was introduced into the general line in Blue Opalescent, French Opalescent, Green Opalescent and Cranberry colors. During mid-1941, Topaz Opalescent replaced Green Opalescent. Topaz Opalescent was discontinued at the end of 1943. Hobnail in Rose Overlay was also made during 1943. After World War II, Hobnail in Blue Opalescent, French Opalescent, and Cranberry continued in production.

Milk Hobnail entered the line in 1950. This new color became very popular and the line was expanded continuously. Hobnail was made in Blue, Green, and Pink Pastel during the mid-1950s. Blue Pastel only remained in the line for one year. Green Pastel and Rose Pastel fared slightly better. Green Pastel remained in production for two years and Rose Pastel was discontinued at the end of 1957. Blue Opalescent Hobnail, which had been in the line continuously since 1940, was discontinued in December 1954.

Hobnail made a brief appearance in overlay colors during the early 1960s. Apple Green Overlay, Coral, Honey Amber, Powder Blue Overlay, and Wild Rose were cased colors with opal interiors. Only about five or six items were made in each color. Apple Green Overlay, Coral, and Powder Blue Overlay were only made for one year, and Wild Rose Hobnail lasted two years. Hobnail in Honey Amber was discontinued at the end of 1963, with the exception of the lavabo, which continued in production through 1966. In 1968, Fenton experimented with marketing Hobnail in crystal. However, it made a quick exit, only lasting one year.

Eleven items in Blue Marble Hobnail were introduced in January 1970 and an ashtray set in this color was added the next year. Production of all pieces of Blue Marble was discontinued by the end of 1973. Fenton's Hobnail candle bowl was packaged with assorted colored candles and a colored plastic flower ring and marketed as a decorative candle arrangement. The style and color of these arrangements was changed for the spring and fall seasons until this bundled assortment was abandoned in the middle of the decade. In 1971, Fenton began decorating items in milk glass Hobnail with hand-painted designs. The Blue Bell decoration designed by Louise Piper was offered from 1971 through 1972. Special milk glass Holly decorated pieces were offered in the July catalog from 1971 through 1976 for the Christmas season. In 1972, Hobnail entered the line in transparent ruby. This popular color continued in the line into the 1980s. Toward the end of the decade, Blue Opalescent made a third appearance in the Fenton line with the introduction of 10 different shapes. Eight of these shapes had not been made in this color previously. Also, eight items in Hobnail were selected to be made in Cameo Opalescent. Most pieces were discontinued by the end of 1980, but the 10" bud vase was made through mid-1982.

During the 1980s the Fenton general line featured numerous pieces of Hobnail in Milk and Ruby. New to the line were Hobnail pieces in carnival. In 1980, a 14-piece assortment of Topaz Opalescent Hobnail was made for The Levay Distributing Company. In 1982, Fenton also made Hobnail for Levay in Blue Opalescent, Cranberry, and Aqua Opalescent Carnival. An assortment of Hobnail in Plum Opalescent was made for Levay in 1984. The 1988 limited edition Collectors Extravaganza Offering featured the numerous items in Pink Opalescent Hobnail. Most items in Hobnail, with the exception of lamps, were phased out of the line by the end of the decade. Fenton formed an association with television network QVC near the end of the 1980s. Numerous items were designed and decorated especially for sale through this outlet. A number of Hobnail items were sold through QVC as the marketing relationship matured through the 1990s and continued into the next century.

During the early 1990s Hobnail limited edition collections were made in Gold Pearl, Persian Pearl, and Rose Magnolia. Milk Hobnail returned for another showing between 1991 and 1996. Attractive, colorfully trimmed baskets were made for Easter and a few even entered the general line. Cranberry returned to the line for three years during the mid-1990s. With the exception of the production of lamps for the general line and special items for QVC, Hobnail production was not a priority toward the end of the decade.

In 2000, eight items in Hobnail returned to the regular line in a pink opalescent iridescent color dubbed Champagne. Production of Champagne was discontinued after a year, but the Hobnail pattern remained in the line. Cranberry returned to the line after an absence of several years. In addition Hobnail assortments in two new colors — Willow Green Opalescent and Pink Chiffon Opalescent — were introduced. These two colors remained in the line for two years. Several items in Cranberry were still in production during 2005.

PATTERN AND SHAPE IDENTIFICATION

Prior to July 1952, Fenton identified patterns or shapes with a mold number. For example, the number "389" was used to represent the entire Hobnail pattern. All pieces of this pattern were identified by this number and a further description was necessary to identify an individual item.

After July 1952, Fenton switched to a ware number system. With this new system each item in regular line production was assigned a four-digit number followed by a two-letter code. The numerals represent the pattern and shape and the letters indicate the color or hand-painted decoration. As an example, examine Ware No. 3760 MI:

The first two numbers: 37 — represent the Hobnail pattern;
The second two digits: 60 — represent a pitcher vase;
The two letters: MI — represent Fenton's opaque milk color.

With very few exceptions, each item has a unique ware number. There have been instances where numbers and letters have been reused; however, most of the time there has been a significant time gap between the two occurrences and there should not be any confusion about the description.

IDENTIFICATION OF EARLY SHAPES

One of the more confusing aspects of collecting Fenton's Hobnail pattern is identifying the shapes of pieces made prior to the introduction of ware numbers in July 1952. Ware numbers standardized Fenton's product line, with each ware number representing a specific shape in a pattern. Prior to that time all items in the Hobnail pattern were identified by using the No. 389 pattern number. Adding to the confusion are the slight differences in size for the same item that may have been listed in the Fenton catalogs over the period of years. For example, the 8½" flat double crimped vase from the early 1940s is listed at 8" in the late 1940s. Also, terminology changed over the years. A shallow bowl listed as a nappy one year might be listed as a bonbon the next year. It is, therefore, sometimes difficult to differentiate numerous shapes of the same type of item that were made during this period. The shapes of the various covered candy jars, bowls, and vases seem to be the most confusing. Remember that many of the pieces made during this era from the same mold were often finished with a different crimping. Therefore, pieces from the same mold that are finished in a different fashion may vary considerably in size.

KEY TO ABBREVIATIONS

DC	double crimped
HP	hand-painted
Irid	iridescent
MOP	mother-of-pearl iridescence
Opal	opalescent
UND	undetermined

Two letters in parentheses indicate Fenton's color code.

COLOR CODES AND COLOR DESCRIPTIONS

During the 1940s and into the 1950s, all Fenton Hobnail was identified by mold numbers. Original numbers were No. 289 for the cologne bottle produced for Wrisley, No. 489 for "Burred" Hobnail, and No. 389 for the remainder of the Hobnail line. Beginning in July 1952, Fenton implemented a two-letter color code that was used in combination with ware numbers to identify each item in the line. With a few exceptions, each color made by Fenton after July 1952 is identified by a unique two-letter or letter and number combination. The following color and decoration codes are associated with the Hobnail pattern made from 1952 to the present. Years of manufacture in the listing below only apply to the Hobnail pattern. These colors may have been used to produce items in other patterns during various other time periods.

Color	Code	Years of Manufacture	Description
Amber	AR	1959 – 1982	Transparent amber was called Antique Amber prior to 1963. In 1963, this color became known as Colonial Amber (CA) and both the AR and CA designations were used as codes for transparent amber that year. After 1963, the CA code was used to signify amber.
Antique Amber	AR	1959 – 1964	Transparent amber became known as Colonial Amber after 1964.
Apple Green Overlay	AG	1961	Apple Green pieces have a light green exterior layer of glass applied over a milk glass interior. This color was only made in 1961, although examples were still illustrated in the 1962 catalog.
Aquamarine Iridescent, hand-painted	9N	2000	This decoration code was used for a hand-painted boot made for QVC and signed by Frank M. Fenton.
Aquamarine Satin, hand-painted	J4	2000	This decoration code was used for a hand-painted No. 3668 candy box produced for QVC.
Aqua Opalescent Carnival	IO	1982	This marigold spray over a blue opalescent base was used for a limited production for The Levay Distributing Company.
Azure Blue Carnival	MM	2000	An Azure Blue iridized mini epergne was made for QVC.
Black	BK	1962 – 1975	Black was also called Ebony at various times. This color was used for items in many of the patterns in Fenton's line during this period. Some Hobnail items in this color were made for the Fenton Gift Shop and for the florist industry.
Black and White	BW	1962 – 1966	The black and milk color mixture was used for a salt and pepper shaker combination.
Black Carnival	XB	1990 – 1991	A 7-piece water set and a syrup jug were made for QVC.
Black Rose	RZ	1992	Black Rose is a cased glass with an ebony crest. The cased glass consists of a gold ruby inner layer and a milk exterior layer. In the 1950s the color code was BR. This later Hobnail example consisted of a basket with Frank M. Fenton's signature, produced for QVC.
Blue	BG	1975 – 1977	A No. 3872-6" candle bowl and 6" footed vase were made in this glossy opaque medium blue color.
Blue Marble	MB	1970 – 1974	This color is created by adding opal to molten light blue opaque glass. The resulting product features interesting opal swirls.

Color	Code	Years of Manufacture	Description
Blue Opalescent	BO	1940 – 1955 1959 – 1965 1978 – 1983	This color code was used for Fenton's original transparent blue opalescent color used with the Hobnail pattern. Shades may run from aqua to a deep medium blue. Blue Opalescent Hobnail was also made for The Levay Distributing Company in 1982.
Blue Pastel	BP	1954	This is a light blue colored opaque glassware.
Blue Royale	KK	1988 – 1990	This is a dark, almost cobalt, transparent blue color.
Blue Satin	BA	1971 – 1984	This is a medium blue opaque satin glassware.
Blue Slag	UND	1989	This dark blue and milk swirl color was dubbed "Almost Heaven" by Bill Fenton. The color was used for items produced for the Fenton Gift Shop.
Blue Topaz	SY	2002 – 2003	Blue Topaz is a light blue iridized color developed at the start of the twenty-first century.
Blue Topaz Opalescent	I2	2003 – 2004	Fenton made a Blue Topaz Opalescent vanity boxtle as a part of the 2003 Museum Collection for QVC.
Blue Topaz Overlay	L7	2003	The No. 3856-6" vase was made in this blue overlay color as a QVC.com exclusive.
Burmese	BR	1971 – 1972	Burmese is an opaque custard-colored glassware with a rose blush. During the 1950s, this color code was used for Black Rose.
Cameo Opalescent	CO	1979 – 1983	Cameo Opalescent is a translucent, pinkish-amber colored glassware with silky opal edges.
Carnival	CN	1970 – Present	An overspray of metallic salts on a deep amethyst base produced the colorful iridescence of Fenton's new line of carnival glass introduced in 1970. These later issues of carnival glass have the embossed Fenton logo.
Champagne	PY	1998 – 2001	Champagne is an iridescent pink opalescent color.
Champagne Satin Iridescent with light Plum trim	LJ	2000	A Champagne Satin pitcher with light Plum crest and handle was made for QVC.
Champagne Satin Opalescent with Violet trim	P9	2000	A Champagne Satin wave Hobnail bell with a violet edge was made for QVC.
Chocolate	CK	1982	A slipper was made in this opaque brown color for The Levay Distributing Company. Earlier, this heat-sensitive opaque color was used in the Bicentennial assortment for seven shapes in the general line.
Cobalt	KN	1998	Cobalt is a transparent dark blue glassware. Tumblers were made in this color to complement pitchers produced for QVC in Cobalt Blue Overlay.

Color	Code	Years of Manufacture	Description
Cobalt Blue Overlay	AB	2001	This is a cased glassware with cobalt blue glass applied over an interior layer of milk. A water set was made for QVC and a miniature lemonade set was made for Doris Lechler in the 1980s.
Cobalt Iridescent with milk insert and trim	7V	2001	A Cobalt Iridescent Hobnail three-piece, 9" footed fairy light with a milk glass edge and insert was made for QVC.
Cobalt Marigold Carnival	NK	1984	This glassware featured an iridescent marigold spray applied over cobalt blue.
Colonial Amber	CA	1964 – 1980	Fenton's transparent amber was called Antique Amber prior to 1964.
Colonial Blue	CB	1964 – 1980	This is a deep, transparent peacock blue color. Hobnail was first made in the color beginning in 1964.
Colonial Green	CG	1964 – 1977	Fenton's transparent olive green color was dubbed Colonial Green. Hobnail was made in this color starting in 1964.
Colonial Pink	CP	1967 – 1969	Fenton's Colonial Pink is a transparent deep rose color. A Hobnail slipper was made in this color in the late 1960s.
Coral	CL	1961	Coral is a cased orange exterior color over milk glass.
Cranberry Opalescent	CR	1940 – Present	Cranberry is an opalescent color produced by casing gold ruby with with a French Opalescent exterior.
Crystal	CY	1940 – 1942, 1968	Hobnail in Crystal was made in the early 1940s and again in 1968. Poor sales limited production of this color.
Crystal Satin Iridescent	WH	1992	An 8" candle bowl was produced in this color for QVC.
Custard	CT	1973 – 1977	Candle arrangement bowls, florist items, and Fenton Gift Shop items are most commonly found in this glossy opaque pale yellow color.
Custard Satin	CU	1972 – 1978	This satin version of custard was used for two Hobnail pieces produced for the Fenton general line during the 1970s.
Decorated Blue Bell	BB	1971 – 1973	Thirteen pieces of milk Hobnail were decorated with a hand-painted Blue Bell pattern in the early 1970s.
Decorated Holly	DH	1971 – 1976	Holly decorated milk Hobnail pieces were offered from July through December during the 1970s.
Decorated Roses	RW	1974 – 1976	Nine pieces of milk Hobnail were hand painted with a dainty pink rose decoration during the mid-1970s.
Dusty Rose	DK	1984 – 1988	This is a transparent pink color that was used for many items in the Fenton line during the last half of the 1980s. Only a few items in Hobnail were made in this color.

Color	Code	Years of Manufacture	Description
Dusty Rose Carnival	DN	1993, 1995	Several Hobnail pieces were made in this iridescent rose color for QVC.
Dusty Rose Carnival w/Teal trim	DO	1988	An iridescent rose pitcher and bowl set with a teal pitcher handle and bowl edge was made for QVC.
Dusty Rose Carnival, hand-painted	K8	1997	This decoration code was used for a 2-piece Hobnail fairy light made for QVC. The iridized Dusty Rose background was adorned with a hand-painted pink and white glass fruit pattern.
Dusty Rose Stretch	DL	1989	A 10" epergne was made in iridized Dusty Rose for QVC.
Emerald Green Carnival	EY	2002	Fenton's No. 3600 Butterfly finial candy lid was made in this color for QVC.
Empress Rose Iridescent	CV	1998, 2000	The No. 3778-10" candle bowl was made in 1998 for QVC in this rose iridized color. The No. 3704, 2-piece epergne was made for QVC in 2000.
Empress Rose Iridized Overlay w/Violet trim	CH	1999	Fenton produced its No. 3656-5½" vase in this pink iridescent overlay color with a violet edge for QVC.
Federal Blue	FB	1984 – 1986	Fenton produced this transparent steel blue color during the mid-1980s. Only a few items in Hobnail were made in this color.
French Opalescent	FO	1940 – 1965	This popular crystal opalescent glassware was made in many shapes and was in the general line for 25 years.
French Opalescent Iridescent	FS	2002	The No. 3778-8" iridized opalescent candle bowl and No. 3902 covered sugar and creamer were made for QVC.
French Opalescent Iridescent w/Azure Blue trim	FC	1997	A 4-piece Hobnail epergne set was made for QVC with an iridescent French opalescent base trimmed with an Azure Blue edge around the bowl and the tips of the horns.
French Opalescent w/Dusty Rose trim	FD	1993, 1994	This color code was used for several Hobnail baskets made for Easter 1993, and the general line in 1994. These baskets had French opalescent bodies with Dusty Rose handles and edges.
French Opalescent Iridized w/Empress Rose edge	IF	1991	This color combination, an Iridized French Opalescent base decorated with an Empress Rose Edge, was used for a miniature epergne set.
French Opalescent with Autumn Gold trim	FT	1994	Hobnail baskets were made for the general line in French Opalescent with an Autumn Gold trim edge and handle.
French Opalescent Iridized w/Dusty Rose trim	IH	1993 – 1995	In the mid-1990s, several sizes of baskets were made in French Opalescent with Dusty Rose trim for the Easter season. Later, in 1997, a 10½" basket was made for QVC.
French Opalescent with Sea Mist Green trim	IM	1995	French Opalescent baskets decorated with this color green trim were made for the general line.

Color	Code	Years of Manufacture	Description
French Opalescent with Twilight Blue trim	F3	1993	Two sizes of Hobnail baskets were made in iridized French Opalescent with Twilight Blue trim for the Easter season.
French Opalescent with Sea Mist Green trim	FR	1994	This color code was used for several baskets made for the general line. These baskets had lightly iridized French Opalescent bodies with Sea Mist Green handles and edges.
Gold Iridescent	GJ	1999	A gold iridized 6" cornucopia hand vase was made for QVC.
Gold Pearl	GP	1992 – July 1992	This is an iridescent topaz color created for a limited edition offering from a formula using cerium and titanium.
Green Carnival	GZ	1991	A 14-piece, 7-quart punch set was made in this green iridescent color for QVC.
Green Opalescent	GO	1940 – 1941, July 1959 – July 1961, July 1985 – 1986	Early Green Opalescent Hobnail was usually a light or yellow green color. Green Opalescent made in the 1960s was a deep blue-green. The Green Opalescent Hobnail made in 1985 for the Connoisseur Collection was more like the original shade.
Green Pastel	GP	1954 – 1956	This is a pale opaque green colored glassware.
Holiday Green Carnival, hand-painted	8H	1992	This Green Carnival cat slipper has a hand-painted burgundy and white rose pattern. It was produced for QVC.
Honey Amber	HA	1961 – 1968	Honey Amber is a cased glassware that was produced by combining an exterior layer of amber with an interior layer of milk glass.
Ice Blue Iridized with Violet trim	O9	2002	An Ice Blue Iridized Hobnail basket with a wave design between the Hobnail pattern was made for QVC. This basket has a Violet double crimped crest and rib twisted handle.
Iridescent French Opalescent	FM	2002	An iridized French opalescent footed cake plate was made for QVC.
Jonquil Yellow	JO	1968	This translucent yellow color is similar to Fenton's early Chinese Yellow. Hobnail items were sampled in this color and some pieces were sold through the Fenton Gift Shop.
Light Green	LG	1952 – 1954	Fenton's No. 3996-6" and No. 3994-4½" jardinieres were made in light transparent green for the florist trade during the early 1950s.
Lime	LM	1975 – 1977	Lime is a glossy opaque medium green color that was used for the No. 3872-6" candle bowl and the No. 3956-6½" vase in the general line. Other Hobnail pieces in this color were made for the Fenton Gift Shop and for the florist industry.
Lime Opalescent	LO	1952 – 1955	This green opalescent color is produced by casing dark green inside a French Opalescent exterior.

Color	Code	Years of Manufacture	Description
Lime Sherbet	LS	1973 – 1979	The No. 3984, 3-footed covered candy box and No. 3608, 2-piece fairy light were the only items in the Fenton general line in this opaque satin green color.
Milk	MI	1950 – 1989 1991 – 1996	Milk is an opaque white color that became a bestseller for Fenton in the Hobnail pattern during the 1950s.
Milk, hand-painted	9N	2000	A milk No. 3995 slipper signed by Shelley Fenton with a hand-painted fuchsia decoration was made for QVC.
Milk Glass Royale	SC	1995	An assortment containing several items in opaque white Hobnail with a crystal edge and handles was made for one year.
Misty Blue Opalescent Iridescent	LK	1997, 1999	Baskets and an epergne set were made for QVC in this light blue iridized opalescent color.
Ocean Blue Carnival	OZ	1994	An iridized deep blue Hobnail mini epergne was made for QVC.
Opal	OP	1969	This translucent, heat-resistant milk formula was used for a boudoir lamp and 2-piece fairy light.
Opaline Iridescent	TY	1997	A blue-green iridized Hobnail mini epergne set, a No. 3804, 3-piece fairy light and a 22½" student lamp with prisms. were made for QVC.
Opal Satin, hand-painted	V7	2000	Fenton's No. 3700 Opal Satin Hobnail covered slipper candy box was hand painted with a purple grape decoration for QVC.
Opal Satin, hand-painted	8M	1992	Fenton's No. 3700 Hobnail pink accented Opal Satin covered slipper candy box was hand painted for QVC with a mauve and burgundy floral decoration on the toe and heel.
Opaque Blue Overlay	OB	1962 – 1964	These pieces have a Colonial Blue exterior and opal interior. The name of this color was changed to Colonial Blue Overlay in 1967 when Roses pattern lamps were made in this color.
Orange	OR	1964 – 1978	Orange is a transparent red-amber color. Some pieces may have a yellow cast in random highlighted areas.
Peach Blow	PB	1952 – 1957	Peach Blow is an overlay color consisting of a layer of milk glass over a gold ruby interior. The interior appears pink and the exterior is white — often with a slight pink cast.
Peaches 'n Cream	UO	1988 – 1990	This was Fenton's name for its soft pink opalescent color made in the late 1980s.
Pekin Blue II	BJ	1968	This translucent blue color was sampled during the late 1960s. Pieces of Hobnail that were produced were sold through the Fenton Gift Shop.
Persian Pearl	XV	July 1992 – 1993	This is an iridized green opalescent color that was made for a limited time for the Historic Collection.

Color Codes and Color Descriptions

Color	Code	Years of Manufacture	Description
Pink Chiffon	XT	2000 – 2002	In 2000, a 3-piece vanity boxtle was made for QVC in this iridized pink opalescent color. The color was used in the general line in 2001 and 2002.
Pink Chiffon Iridescent w/Violet trim	X7	2001	Fenton produced a Pink Chiffon Opalescent Iridized Hobnail cruet for QVC. This cruet has a saddle crimp spout with a violet notched handle and violet stopper.
Pink Chiffon Opalescent	YS	2001 – 2003	This is a soft iridescent pink opalescent glassware.
Pink Opalescent	UO	1988 – 1989	Hobnail pieces in pink opalescent were included in the 1988 Collector's Extravaganza assortment. Some pieces in this color were also available through the Gracious Touch catalog.
Plum Opalescent	PO	1959 – 1962, 1984	This is a deep purple opalescent, heat-sensitive color that was obtained by pressing items made with the Cranberry Gold Ruby formula. Hobnail items were in the general catalog from 1959 to 1962. Some Hobnail pieces were made for The Levay Distributing Company in 1984.
Plum Opalescent Iridescent	IP	1999, 2001	In 1999, the No. 3634 oval handled basket was made for QVC. In 2001, Fenton's 8½" scalloped fan vase and No. 3350-5" vase with a tea light insert were made for QVC.
Powder Blue Overlay	BV	1961	The code is the same as that used for the earlier Blue Overlay color. An opal interior layer of glass is combined with a light blue exterior.
Provincial Blue Opalescent	OO	1987 – 1990	Most Hobnail pieces in this deep blue opalescent color were made for Fenton's Gracious Touch division.
Purple Slag	PS	1981	A limited number of Hobnail items were produced for The Levay Distributing Company in opaque marbleized purple.
Rosalene Iridescent	RJ	1994	Rosalene is an opaque pink glass combined with swirls of white to produce a soft pink glass with varying swirls. An iridescent Rosalene epergne was made for QVC.
Rosalene Satin, hand-painted	6R	1993	Fenton made a No. 3995 Rosalene Satin Hobnail cat head slipper with hand-painted pink roses for QVC.
Rosalene Satin, hand-painted	H2	1994	A No. 3995 Rosalene Satin Hobnail cat head slipper with hand-painted roses was made for QVC.
Rose Magnolia	RV	1993 – July 1993	Hobnail pieces were made in the first half of 1993 for the Historic Collection in this rose opalescent color produced with the rare earth element neodymium.
Rose Magnolia Opalescent Iridized w/Sea Mist Green trim	1Q	1994	Fenton made a footed 3-piece fairy light in iridized opalescent Rose Magnolia for QVC. The top edge of the base was decorated with a green crest and the light came with a green candle insert.

Color	Code	Years of Manufacture	Description
Rose Opalescent Iridized	NI	2002	Fenton's No. 3902 covered sugar and creamer were produced in this pink iridescent color for QVC.
Rose Overlay		1943 – 1948	Rose Overlay is an opaque cased glass consisting of a layer of pink glass over a layer of milk glass.
Rose Pastel	RP	1954 – 1957	This is a light pink colored opaque glassware.
Ruby	RU	1966 – 1990	Ruby is a transparent, heat-sensitive glass that achieves a true red color through a reheating process. Uneven reheating often results in an amberina color.
Ruby Carnival	RN	1992 – 1995	Ruby iridescent glassware is made by spraying ruby glass with hot metallic salts.
Ruby Satin	RA	1982	A very limited number of Hobnail pieces were made in satin ruby glass for The Levay Distributing Company.
Sapphire Blue Opalescent	BX	1988 – 1990	This is a deep blue opalescent color. Numerous items in Hobnail were made for the Gracious Touch party division in this color.
Sea Mist Green Iridescent w/Cobalt trim	UG	1995	A No. 3834 basket was made for QVC in this iridescent green color. The basket was part of the Museum Collection. It had a cobalt twist handle and crest.
Shell Pink Iridescent w/Salem Blue trim	YK	1990	Fenton made a pitcher and bowl set for QVC in this iridescent pink color. The bowl had a blue crest and the pitcher had a blue crest and a blue ribbed handle.
Springtime Green	GT	1977 – 1978	Springtime Green is a transparent emerald green color that replaced Colonial Green in the Fenton line.
Spruce Green Carnival	SI	1995	A Hobnail mini epergne was made for QVC in this iridescent dark green color.
Spruce Green Carnival Overlay	OV	1999	This is a cased color with an interior layer of milk and an outer layer of Spruce Green with an iridized finish. A No. 3863 cruet was made for QVC.
Spruce Green Carnival Satin	SJ	1995	Fenton's No. 3664-70 oz. ice lip jug was made for QVC in this iridized deep green satin color.
Sunset Iridescent	SD	2003	Fenton made a Sunset iridized 2-piece No. 3704 Hobnail epergne for QVC.
Sunset Overlay Iridescent w/black edge	1W	2002	A Sunset Overlay Iridescent Hobnail 8¼" double crimped vase with black crest was made for QVC.

Color	Code	Years of Manufacture	Description
Topaz Opalescent	TO	1941 – 1944, July 1959 – 1961, 1980, 1983	Topaz opalescent Hobnail replaced Green Opalescent Hobnail in the Fenton line during 1941. This color was discontinued at the end of 1943. From July 1959 through December 1960, Hobnail was again made in this color for the general line. A few small assortments of Topaz Opalescent Hobnail were made for The Levay Distributing Company in 1980 and 1983.
Topaz Opalescent	TS	1997	This iridized version of Topaz Opalescent was used for pieces produced for Fenton's 1997 Historic Collection.
Topaz Opalescent w/cobalt handle	T3	1997	A No. 3834 basket was made as a special-order with a Topaz Opalescent body and a cobalt handle. A special order No. 3761 decanter was made in 2005; it had a Topaz Opalescent body, a Cobalt handle, and a Cobalt stopper.
Topaz Opal Irid Satin, hand-painted	H2	1997	A yellow opalescent iridized, hand-painted floral decorated No. 3995 slipper was made in this color for QVC.
Turquoise	TU	1955 – 1959	Turquoise is a light blue-green colored opaque glassware.
Twilight Blue Carnival	TZ	1992	The No. 3801 epergne set, No. 3967 pitcher and No. 3949, 9 oz. tumblers were made for QVC in the iridized deep blue color.
Twilight Blue Carnival, hand-painted	9T	1992	Fenton's No. 3995 slipper was painted with a purple and pink rose decoration for QVC.
Violet	OQ	2000 – 2002	Several iridized violet Hobnail items were in the Fenton line.
Violet Opalescent	EJ	2002	A deep purple opalescent squat jug and the No. 3861 rose bowl were made for QVC.
Wild Rose	WR	1961 – 1962	This is cased glassware with ruby exterior and milk glass interior.
Willow Green Opal	GY	2000 – 2003	A number of Hobnail pieces were included in an iridized green opalescent assortment in the general line. A few items were also made for QVC.
Willow Green Opalescent w/Empress Rose trim	GW	2000	A Willow Green Opalescent Iridized Hobnail 10½" basket with an Empress Rose crest was made for QVC.
Woodland Frost	FM	2001, 2002	A Hobnail footed cake plate was made in this iridized French Opalescent color for the Christmas season in 2001. It was also made for QVC the next year.

Unfortunately, we do not always know years of introduction and/or years pieces or colors were discontinued in the Hobnail line. If we were unsure of a date, we left the column blank. Although we feel like we could make an educated guess on many of these, we do not wish to give incorrect information to our readers.

ASHTRAYS AND SMOKING ACCESSORIES

NO. 3648 BALL ASHTRAY

A ball-shaped ashtray was made for several years during the latter part of the 1970s. The ashtray is 4" high and 4¾" wide.

No. 3648 Ashtray	Introduced	Discontinued	Value
Colonial Amber	1977	1979	$18.00 – 20.00
Colonial Blue	1977	1979	$22.00 – 25.00
Milk	1977	1979	$28.00 – 35.00
Orange	1977	1978	$14.00 – 18.00
Ruby	1977	1979	$20.00 – 25.00
Springtime Green	1977	1979	$22.00 – 27.00

Colonial Amber

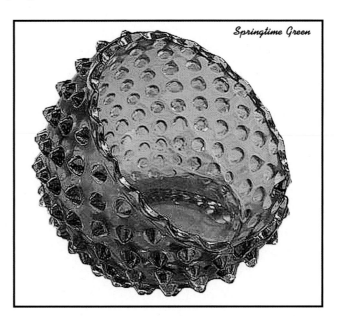

Springtime Green

NO. 3872 FAN-SHAPED ASHTRAY

Fenton's small opalescent fan-shaped Hobnail ashtray was introduced into the line in 1941. The ashtray measures 4" wide by 5½" long. This ashtray is the same shape as the larger version that is used as an underplate for the 5-piece condiment set.

No. 3872 Ashtray	Introduced	Discontinued	Value
Blue Opalescent	1941	1955	$18.00 – 22.00
French Opalescent	1941	1955	$18.00 – 20.00
Topaz Opalescent	1941	1944	$25.00 – 28.00

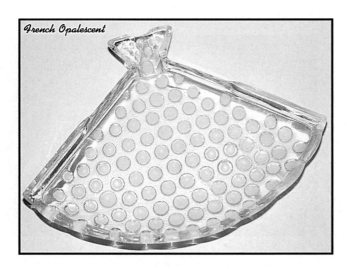

French Opalescent

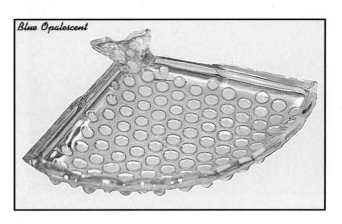

Blue Opalescent

NO. 3810 OCTAGONAL 3-PIECE ASHTRAY SET

Three sizes of octagonal-shaped ashtrays were produced. The smallest of these eight-sided ashtrays is 4" in diameter. Fenton's ware number for this piece is No. 3876. The No. 3877 medium ashtray measures 5¼" and the large No. 3878 ashtray is 6½" across. These ashtrays stack conveniently for easy storage. The amber ashtray set was first produced for one year in 1954. This set was again in the line for another year beginning in 1959. The Pekin Blue II and Jonquil Yellow ashtrays were samples made in the late 1960s. These colors in Hobnail were not in the regular Fenton line, but some pieces were sold through the Fenton Gift Shop.

4" Ashtray	Introduced	Discontinued	Value
Colonial Amber	1959	1960	$4.00 – 5.00
French Opalescent	1954	1956	$18.00 – 20.00
Jonquil Yellow	1968	1968	$18.00 – 22.00
Milk	July 1954	1977	$6.00 – 8.00
Pekin Blue II	1968	1968	$18.00 – 20.00

5¼" Ashtray	Introduced	Discontinued	Value
Colonial Amber	1959	1960	$5.00 – 6.00
French Opalescent	1954	1956	$20.00 – 22.00
Jonquil Yellow	1968	1968	$20.00 – 22.00
Milk	July 1954	1977	$8.00 – 10.00
Pekin Blue II	1968	1968	$20.00 – 22.00

6½" Ashtray	Introduced	Discontinued	Value
Colonial Amber	1959	1960	$6.00 – 8.00
French Opalescent	1954	1956	$22.00 – 25.00
Jonquil Yellow	1968	1968	$20.00 – 25.00
Milk	July 1954	1973	$10.00 – 12.00
Pekin Blue II	1968	1968	$20.00 – 25.00

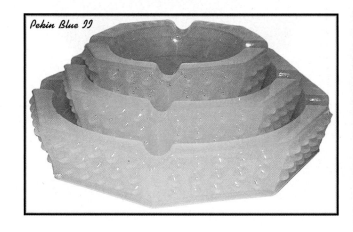

Pekin Blue II

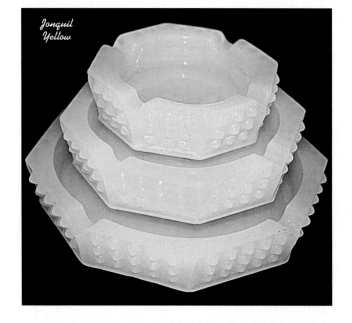

Jonquil Yellow

Milk

NO. 3873 OVAL ASHTRAY

This shallow oval ashtray first appeared in Fenton catalogs during the early 1940s. Colors produced were Blue Opalescent, French Opalescent, and Topaz Opalescent. The ashtray measures 4" long by 3¼" wide.

Oval ashtray	Introduced	Discontinued	Value
Blue Opalescent	1941	1955	$15.00 – 18.00
French Opalescent	1941	1957	$15.00 – 18.00
Topaz Opalescent	1941	1944	$25.00 – 28.00

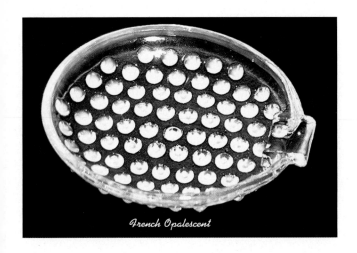

French Opalescent

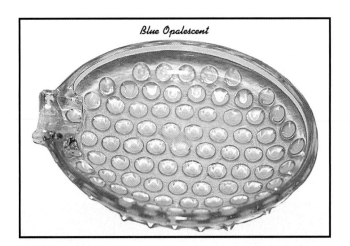

Blue Opalescent

NO. 3773 PIPE ASHTRAY

Fenton's Hobnail pipe ashtray was only in the general line in the milk color. This item was only made for for five years. The ashtray is 6½" in diameter and has an embossed dogwood-style flower in the center.

Pipe ashtray	Introduced	Discontinued	Value
Milk	1963	1968	$40.00 – 45.00

Milk

NO. 3610 ROUND 3-PIECE ASHTRAY SET

Fenton's round 3-piece No. 3610 ashtray set was introduced into the regular line in 1964. The set was produced by combining three different sizes of ashtrays that stacked together. The small No. 3972 ashtray is 3½" in diameter; the medium No. 3973 ashtray is 5" across; and the large No. 3776 ashtray measures 6½". This ashtray was produced in milk glass for the greatest number of years.

3½" Ashtray	Introduced	Discontinued	Value
Blue Marble	1971	1973	$8.00 – 10.00
Blue Opalescent	1978	1979	$6.00 – 8.00
Colonial Amber	1964	1977	$3.00 – 5.00
Colonial Blue	1964	1977	$5.00 – 8.00
Colonial Green	1964	1977	$3.00 – 5.00
Crystal	1968	1969	$2.00 – 3.00
Milk	1964	1985	$4.00 – 6.00
Orange	1965	1970	$3.00 – 5.00
Ruby	1976	1979	$7.00 – 9.00
Springtime Green	1977	1978	$4.00 – 6.00

5" Ashtray	Introduced	Discontinued	Value
Blue Marble	1971	1973	$14.00 – 16.00
Blue Opalescent	1978	1979	$12.00 – 14.00
Colonial Amber	1964	1977	$2.00 – 4.00
Colonial Blue	1964	1977	$8.00 – 10.00
Colonial Green	1964	1977	$5.00 – 8.00
Crystal	1968	1969	$3.00 – 4.00
Milk	1964	1985	$6.00 – 8.00
Orange	1965	1970	$6.00 – 8.00
Ruby	1976	1979	$9.00 – 11.00
Springtime Green	1977	1978	$6.00 – 8.00

6½" Ashtray	Introduced	Discontinued	Value
Blue Marble	1971	1973	$18.00 – 20.00
Blue Opalescent	1978	1979	$16.00 – 18.00
Colonial Amber	1964	1977	$5.00 – 8.00
Colonial Blue	1964	1977	$12.00 – 14.00
Colonial Green	1964	1977	$5.00 – 8.00
Crystal	1968	1969	$4.00 – 5.00
Milk	1964	1985	$8.00 – 10.00
Orange	1965	1970	$10.00 – 12.00
Ruby	1976	1976	$10.00 – 12.00
Springtime Green	1977	1978	$8.00 – 9.00

Milk

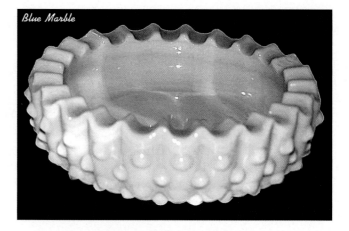

Blue Marble

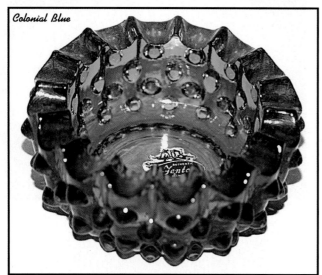

Colonial Blue

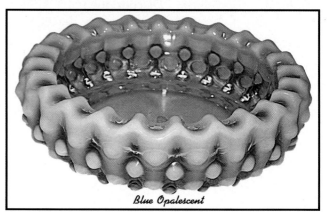

Blue Opalescent

NO. 3693 RECTANGULAR ASHTRAY

Fenton's Milk Hobnail rectangular ashtray was introduced into the regular line in the early 1960s. The ashtray was produced for over a decade before it was discontinued. This ashtray is 3" wide and 4¼" long.

Rect. ashtray	Introduced	Discontinued	Value
Amber	1967	1971	$5.00 – 7.00
Milk	July 1962	1976	$10.00 – 12.00

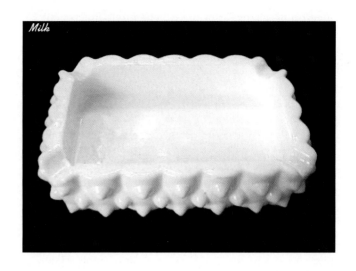

NO. 389 ROUND 3" ASHTRAY

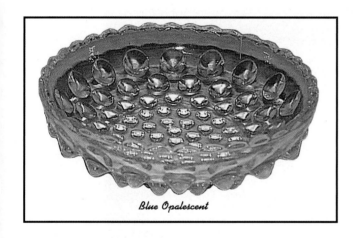

Blue Opalescent

This small round, 2⅞" diameter, shallow cupped ashtray was made in the early 1940s in Blue Opalescent, French Opalescent, and Topaz Opalescent. It was listed in early catalogs as part of a six-piece cigarette set. The set included four of these ashtrays, a #1 hat, and a #2 hat. For more information see the cigarette set illustrated on page 23.

3" Ashtray	Introduced	Discontinued	Value
Blue Opalescent	1941	1944	$20.00 – 22.00
French Opalescent	1941	1944	$18.00 – 20.00
Topaz Opalescent	1941	1944	$30.00 – 32.00

NO. 3679 SQUARE 5" ASHTRAY

Fenton produced this 5" square ashtray for the regular line in Milk. The ashtray was made for about 15 years beginning in 1961.

5" Sq. ashtray	Introduced	Discontinued	Value
Milk	1961	1978	$18.00 – 20.00

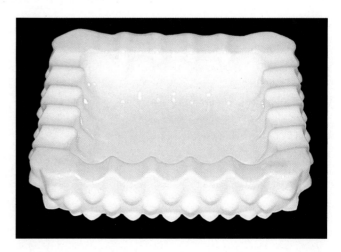

NO. 3778 ASHTRAY, CHIP 'N DIP, OR CANDLE BOWL

Fenton proclaimed this piece to be multi-functional. This 8" wide bowl has a large 3" diameter raised center and 12 scallops around the top. It could be used as a candleholder, an ashtray, or to serve chips or vegetables with dip. This ashtray was made in the regular line in milk during two different production periods. It was first introduced in 1971 and discontinued at the end of 1989. The ashtray then returned to the general line in 1991. This item was also part of a special Christmas assortment produced in ruby from July 1987 through December 1987. Ruby ashtrays were also offered to Gracious Touch customers in the June 1987 catalog supplement. The ashtray was also made for QVC in four different colors. It was sold on the November 1992 show in Crystal Satin Iridescent (WH) and on a November 1998 show in Empress Rose Iridescent (CV). Later on a September 2002 show this multi-purpose ashtray was marketed in Blue Topaz Iridescent (SY) and French Opalescent Iridescent (FS). This ashtray combination candle bowl is similar to the larger No.

3748 candle bowl and chip 'n dip that Fenton made in milk from 1973 through 1975. See page 77 for an example of this larger piece. This ware number was also used for a milk punch bowl base made during the late 1950s.

No. 3778 Ashtray	Introduced	Discontinued	Value
Blue Topaz			
Iridescent	2002		$35.00 – 40.00
Crystal Satin			
Iridescent	1992		$22.00 – 27.00
Empress Rose			
Iridescent	1998		$30.00 – 35.00
French Opalescent			
Iridescent	2002		$30.00 – 35.00
Milk	1971	1990*	$20.00 – 25.00
Ruby	July 1987	1988	$22.00 – 25.00

*Also made from 1991 to 1994.

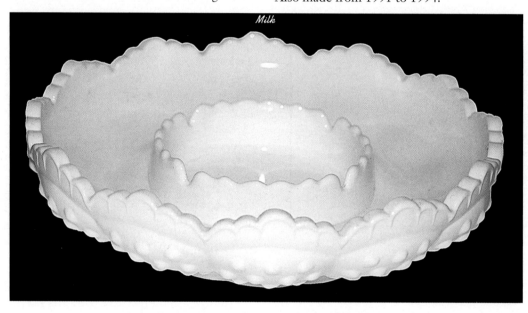

Milk

NO. 3685 CIGARETTE BOX

Fenton's Hobnail covered cigarette box is 4¼" square and 3¼" high. The lid has four rows of hobs, a scalloped edge, and a square knob. This box was also sold with the No. 3603 cigarette set. The set also included a No. 3692 cigarette lighter and three No. 3693 rectangular ashtrays.

No. 3685 Cigarette box	Introduced	Discontinued	Value
Colonial Amber	1967	1971	$30.00 – 35.00
Milk	1961	1972	$25.00 – 30.00

Milk

NO. 3692 CIGARETTE LIGHTER

This cube-shaped lighter is 2¼" square and 2¼" tall. The sides of the body are covered with hobs and the interior hollowed area contains a removable chrome lighter. The lighter was made in milk and in Fenton's Colonial colors.

Colonial Blue

No. 3692 Cigarette lighter	Introduced	Discontinued	Value
Colonial Amber	1965	1971	$12.00 – 15.00
Colonial Blue	1965	1969	$18.00 – 20.00
Colonial Green	1965	1969	$12.00 – 15.00
Milk	July 1962	1978	$18.00 – 22.00
Orange	1965	1969	$16.00 – 20.00

NO. 3603 CIGARETTE SET

Colonial Amber

The No. 3603 cigarette set was comprised of one No. 3685 square covered cigarette box, a No. 3692 cigarette lighter, and three rectangular No. 3693 ashtrays.

No. 3603 Cigarette set	Introduced	Discontinued	Value
Colonial Amber	1967	1971	$57.00 – 65.00
Milk	July 1962	1978	$75.00 – 100.00

NO. 389 CIGARETTE SET

Fenton marketed two variations of cigarette sets during the early 1940s. The 6-piece version included a #1 hat, a #2 hat, and four round ashtrays. The 5-piece set was composed of a #2 hat and four round ashtrays. See the hats and ashtray listings in this section for more information about these individual pieces.

No. 389 Cigarette set	Introduced	Discontinued	Value
Blue Opalescent	1941	1944	$125.00 – 145.00
French Opalescent	1941	1944	$90.00 – 105.00
Topaz Opalescent	1941	1944	$190.00 – 200.00

Topaz Opalescent

NO. 389 #1 HAT

This small 1¾" tall by 2⅛" wide hat was introduced into the Fenton regular line in opalescent colors during 1941. This hat was included as part of a 6-piece cigarette set that was comprised of four small round ashtrays and the larger size #2 hat.

No. 389 Hat	Introduced	Discontinued	Value
Blue Opalescent	1941	1944	$22.00 – 25.00
French Opalescent	1941	1944	$14.00 – 18.00
Topaz Opalescent	1941	1944	$60.00 – 70.00

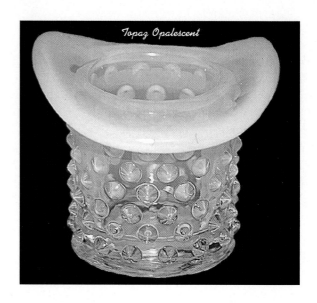
Topaz Opalescent

NO. 3991 #2 HAT

Fenton's 2¾" tall by 3½" diameter hat was initially produced in opalescent colors beginning in 1941. During these early years this size hat was included in the 6-piece cigarette set that was also made up of four small round ashtrays and a smaller size hat. In January 1950 a No. 489 Burred Hobnail version of this size hat entered the regular Fenton line in milk. The Burred Hobnail pattern is a small modification of the regular Hobnail pattern. There are small burrs around the base of each hob. During the 1960s this hat was made with plain hobs. When the hat was reissued in 1987, it returned to the line with burred hobs.

No. 3991 Hat	Introduced	Discontinued	Value
Blue Opalescent	1941	1954	$25.00 – 30.00
French Opalescent	1941	1954	$22.00 – 27.00
Milk	1950	1969*	$14.00 – 16.00
Topaz Opalescent	1941	1944	$40.00 – 50.00

*Reissued in 1987.

Milk

Closeup of Milk Hobnail Hat Showing Burrs

BASKETS

NO. 6832-4¼" BASKET

This small contemporary Hobnail pattern basket was introduced into the Fenton line in the year 2000 in Champagne (PY). During the next several years this basket was made in Violet (OQ), Willow Green Opalescent (GY), Blue Topaz (SY), and Pink Chiffon Opalescent (YS). The basket is 4" high and 4¼" wide. This petite basket was made in Iridized Spruce Green Opalescent with a French Opalescent handle (SA) for the QVC Miniature Basket Collection during 2000.

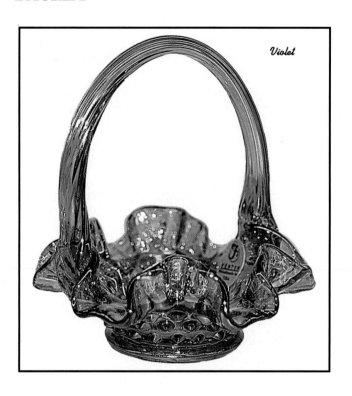

Violet

No. 6832 Basket	Introduced	Discontinued	Value
Blue Topaz	2002	2003	$22.00 – 27.00
Champagne	2000	2001	$25.00 – 30.00
Green Opalescent	2000	May 2000	$20.00 – 25.00
Iridized Spruce Green Opalescent	2000	2000	$32.00 – 37.00
Pink Chiffon Opalescent	2001	2003	$22.00 – 25.00
Violet	2000	2003	$22.00 – 25.00
Willow Green Opalescent	2001	2003	$22.00 – 25.00

NO. 3335 BASKET

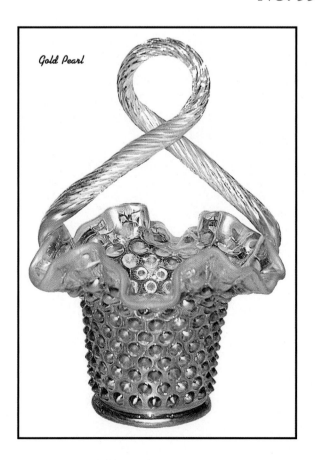

Gold Pearl

Fenton's No. 3335 double crimped basket is 8" high and 2" wide at the base. The basket that was produced for the Fenton limited edition collections has a looped handle with a spiral design. This style basket was originally made in topaz opalescent for Levay in 1983. The Levay basket does not have a looped handle. In 1988 the basket was a part of the Pink Opalescent Collector's Extravaganza series. It was introduced into the regular Fenton line in milk in 1992 and was also made in the limited edition Gold Pearl color at this time.

No. 3335 Basket	Introduced	Discontinued	Value
Milk	Feb 1992	1995	$27.00 – 30.00
Gold Pearl	1992	July 1992	$45.00 – 55.00
Pink Opalescent	1988	1989	$45.00 – 55.00
Topaz Opalescent	1983	1983	$80.00 – 90.00

NO. 3834-4½" BASKET

This small Hobnail basket was introduced into the regular Fenton line in 1940 and the shape is still being made today. French Opalescent, Blue Opalescent, and Cranberry baskets were made from 1940 until the mid-1950s and are found most commonly on today's secondary market. Violet Opalescent and Rose Overlay colors were made during the mid-1940s. These colors are very difficult to obtain today. The blue opalescent basket was also made for Levay in 1982. This basket will have the Fenton logo embossed on the underside. Fenton made this basket in Aqua Opalescent Carnival for Levay during 1982. Ruby baskets were also offered to Gracious Touch customers in the June 1987 catalog supplement. Versions of the basket were also produced for QVC during the 1990s. The ware number for these baskets is preceded by the letter "C." An Iridescent Sea Mist Green basket was made for QVC in 1995. This basket has a cobalt rope style twisted handle and a cobalt edge. The basket reappeared in the QVC line in Iridescent Misty Blue Opalescent during 1997 and in Iridescent Willow Green Opalescent during the year 2000. Beginning in 1997, the basket was produced in Topaz Opalescent with a cobalt handle for Rosso. The basket also appeared in limited edition special colors such as Rose Magnolia, Pink Opalescent, and Persian Blue Opalescent. Production of baskets in these colors was limited and they are not easily found today.

No. 3834 Basket	Color Code	Introduced	Discontinued	Value
Aqua Opalescent Carnival	IO	1982	1982	$40.00 – 50.00
Blue Opalescent	BO	1940	1955	$40.00 – 50.00
Blue Opalescent (Levay)	BO	1982	1982	$37.00 – 42.00
Blue Pastel	BP	July 1954	1955	$45.00 – 50.00
Blue Slag		1988	1988	$65.00 – 75.00
Cranberry	CR	1940	1957	$55.00 – 65.00
French Opalescent	FO	1940	1956	$30.00 – 35.00
French Opalescent w/Autumn Gold trim	FT	1994	1994	$35.00 – 40.00
French Opalescent w/Dusty Rose trim	FD	1994	1994	$35.00 – 40.00
French Opalescent w/Sea Mist Green trim	FR	1994	1994	$35.00 – 40.00
Green Opalescent		1940	1941	$95.00 – 120.00
Green Pastel	GP	1955	1956	$35.00 – 40.00
Iridescent Misty Blue Opalescent (QVC)	LK	August 1997	1997	$30.00 – 40.00
Iridescent Willow Green Opalescent (QVC)	GY	April 2000	2000	$30.00 – 40.00
Lime Green Opalescent	LO	1952	1955	$125.00 – 150.00
Milk	MI	1950	1990	$20.00 – 25.00
Persian Blue Opalescent	XC	July 1989	1990	$27.00 – 32.00
Pink Opalescent	UO	1988	July 1988	$27.00 – 32.00
Rose Magnolia	RV	1993	July 1993	$30.00 – 35.00
Rose Overlay		1943	1945	$75.00 – 100.00
Rose Pastel	RP	July 1954	1957	$30.00 – 40.00
Ruby	RU	July 1987	1989	$27.00 – 32.00
Ruby Overlay	RO	1968	1969	$45.00 – 55.00
Sea Mist Green Iridescent w/Cobalt trim	UG	1995	1995	$25.00 – 30.00
Topaz Opalescent	TO	1941	1944	$125.00 – 145.00
Topaz Opalescent Iridescent		1975	1975	$50.00 – 60.00
Topaz Opalescent w/cobalt handle	T3	1997	1997	$25.00 – 30.00
Turquoise	TU	1955	1959	$30.00 – 35.00
Violet Opalescent		1942	1945	$90.00 – 110.00
Wisteria Opalescent		1942	1944	$90.00 – 110.00

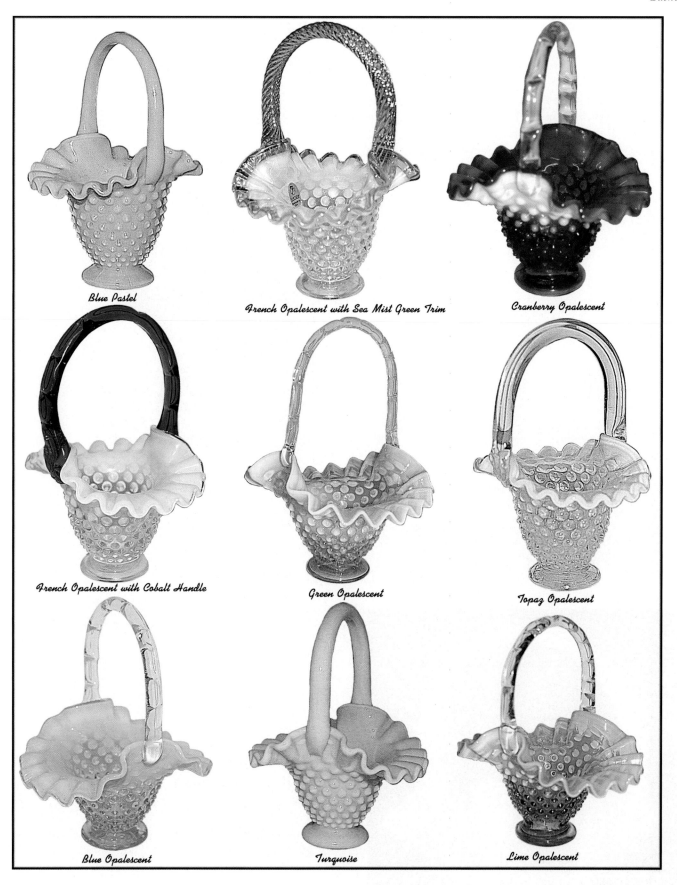

Blue Pastel

French Opalescent with Sea Mist Green Trim

Cranberry Opalescent

French Opalescent with Cobalt Handle

Green Opalescent

Topaz Opalescent

Blue Opalescent

Turquoise

Lime Opalescent

NO. CV214-4½" BASKET

This 4½" wide by 6" high Cranberry Opalescent Spiral Optic Hobnail basket was made for QVC in 1998. A larger 7" basket in this style was produced for QVC in 1993 and a 5½" squat basket was made in 1997. Numerous other Cranberry Spiral Optic Hobnail pieces were also made for QVC. Included in this production were various sizes of vases, a fairy light, a small handled jug, and a cruet with a stopper.

No. CV214 Basket	Produced	Value
Cranberry	April 1998	$70.00 – 80.00

NO. 3735-5½" BASKET

Milk

Fenton's small double crimped No. 3735 handled basket was introduced into the regular line in milk in 1971. This basket is about 5½" in diameter and 6" tall. Later, in 1984 this basket was made in plum opalescent for Levay. This ware number was used for a 9" cupped bowl made in milk and Topaz Opalescent during the early 1960s.

No. 3735 Basket	Introduced	Discontinued	Value
Milk	1971	1985	$27.00 – 32.00
Plum Opalescent	1984	1984	$125.00 – 140.00

NO. CV186-5½" BASKET

This shallow style 5½" diameter and 6" tall Cranberry Opalescent Spiral Optic Hobnail basket was made for QVC in 1997.

No. CV186 Basket	Produced	Value
Cranberry	October 1997	$90.00 – 110.00

NO. 3835-5½" BASKET

Fenton introduced this low profile, 5½" diameter crimped basket into the line in late 1949. The original colors were Blue Opalescent, French Opalescent, and Cranberry. This basket was also made in Peach Blow beginning in July 1952. The basket was discontinued in all colors by the beginning of 1956. Today, collectors are having moderate difficulty finding this basket.

No. 3835 Basket	Introduced	Discontinued	Value
Blue Opalescent	Oct. 1949	1955	$110.00 – 135.00
Cranberry	Oct. 1949	1956	$135.00 – 150.00
French Opalescent	Oct. 1949	1955	$65.00 – 75.00
Peach Blow	July 1952	1956	$75.00 – 85.00

NO. 1159-6" BASKET

Fenton's attractive No. 1159-6" basket was made for Easter 1995. The colors produced were French Opalescent with Dusty Rose trim (IH), French Opalescent with Sea Mist Green trim (IM), and French Opalescent with cobalt trim (IQ).

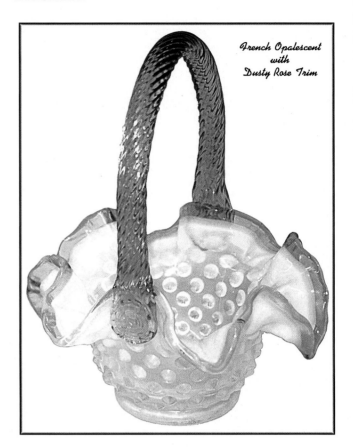

French Opalescent with Dusty Rose Trim

No. 1159-6" Basket	Introduced	Discontinued	Value
French Opalescent w/Dusty Rose trim	1995	1995	$30.00 – 40.00
French Opalescent w/Sea Mist Green trim	1995	1995	$35.00 – 40.00
French Opalescent w/Cobalt trim	1995	1995	$40.00 – 45.00

NO. 3634-6" OVAL BASKET

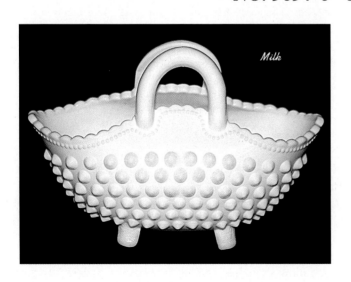

Milk

Fenton's No. 3634 oval basket is 6" long, 4" wide, 4" high, and has four feet. It was introduced into the regular Fenton line in milk glass in 1963 and remained in production through the end of 1967. The milk glass version of this basket enjoyed two more one-year production periods in 1979 and 1987. These later issues will have the Fenton logo embossed on the bottom. Later, in 1999, this basket was made for QVC in Plum Opalescent Iridescent. A blue opalescent example exists in the Fenton Art Glass Museum collection.

No. 3634-6" Oval basket	Introduced	Discontinued	Value
Blue Opalescent			UND
Milk	1963	1968*	$25.00 – 30.00
Plum Opalescent Iridescent	1999	1999	$60.00 – 65.00

*Also reissued in 1979 and 1987.

NO. CV229-6" BASKET

This low profile basket was produced in milk for QVC in 1998. The basket is 6" high and has a crimped edge and a twisted ribbed handle. In early 1999, this basket was made for QVC in Misty Blue Opalescent (LK).

No. CV229 Basket	Produced	Value
Milk	June 1998	$35.00 – 45.00
Misty Blue Opalescent	March 1999	$50.00 – 55.00

NO. 389-6¼" FOOTED BASKET

Fenton introduced this 6¼" diameter tall slender footed basket into the regular line in July 1941. The basket has a crystal crimped handle and measures about 9" high. It was made through the mid-1940s in French Opalescent, Topaz Opalescent, and Blue Opalescent.

No. 389 Basket	Introduced	Discontinued	Value
Blue Opalescent	July 1941	1947	$65.00 – 90.00
French Opalescent	July 1941	1947	$45.00 – 55.00
Topaz Opalescent	July 1941	1944	$110.00 – 125.00
Violet Opalescent	1942	1945	$150.00 – 175.00

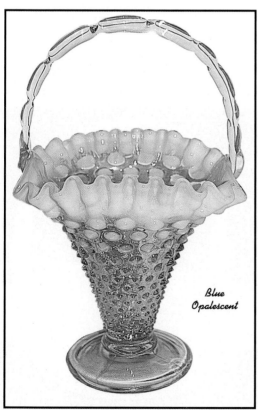

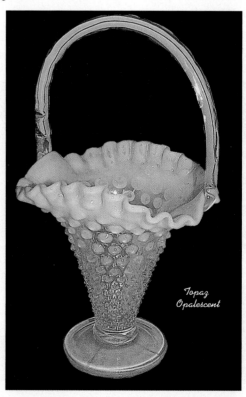

NO. 3336-6½" BASKET

This small double crimped basket first appeared in the regular Fenton line in February 1992. The basket was made in milk and is 5¾" tall and 6½" wide.

No. 3336 Basket	Introduced	Discontinued	Value
Milk	Feb. 1992	1995	$25.00 – 30.00

NO. 3736-6½" BASKET

This shallow double crimped basket is 6½" tall and 7½" in diameter. The basket entered the line in 1958 in milk. In the 1970s it was made in Blue Marble and milk with a hand-painted Blue Bell decoration. The basket was discontinued in milk at the end of 1984. It was reissued in milk in 1992. The basket was made for Easter in 1993 in French Opalescent with Dusty Rose trim (FD) and French Opalescent with Twilight Blue trim (F3).

No. 3736 Basket	Introduced	Discontinued	Value
Blue Bell decorated	1971	1973	$90.00 – 110.00
Blue Marble	1970	1974	$45.00 – 55.00
Blue Slag	1988	1988	$90.00 – 100.00
French Opalescent w/Dusty Rose trim	1993	July 1993	$40.00 – 45.00
French Opalescent w/Twilight Blue trim	1993	July 1993	$45.00 – 55.00
Milk	1958	1985*	$30.00 – 35.00

*Reintroduced 1992.

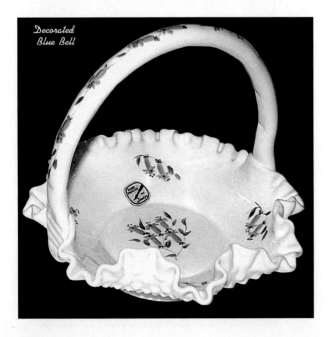

Decorated Blue Bell

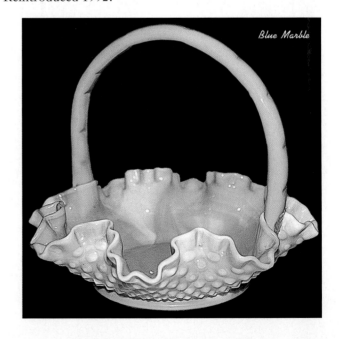

Blue Marble

NO. 3838-6½" OVAL BASKET

This Fenton oval milk glass basket is 6½" long, 4½" wide, and 2¼" high. The basket has ribbed handles that curve upward toward the center from the sides.

No. 3838 Basket	Introduced	Discontinued	Value
Milk	1960	1969	$25.00 – 30.00

NO. 3837-7" BASKET

This size and shape basket has been one of Fenton's most popular. This basket has a pie crust crimped edge and is 7" in diameter and 7½" tall. It first appeared in the line in 1940 and has been produced in a multitude of colors since then. The original colors were Blue Opalescent, Cranberry, French Opalescent, and Green Opalescent. Several colors of this basket were produced during multiple eras. The basket was made in Amber (AR) for the first six months of 1959. Later, in 1967 it reappeared in amber as Colonial Amber (CA) and this color remained in the line until the end of 1980. Blue Opalescent was initially discontinued at the end of 1954. This color basket was also made during two later periods — from July 1959 through December 1964, and from July 1978 through December 1981. The initial production of Green Opalescent was replaced with Topaz Opalescent around mid-1941. Later, in mid-1959, the basket came back into the line for two years in Green Opalescent. The original issue of this basket in milk was discontinued at the end of 1989. It was also made for one more year during 1991. Topaz Opalescent was first produced from 1941 through 1944. Later this color basket was again in the line from the beginning of 1959 through the end of 1960. In the 1980s, this basket was made in Topaz Opalescent and Ruby Satin for The Levay Distributing Company. The basket was also made for QVC in Black Rose (RZ) during 1992. This basket bears the signature of Frank M. Fenton.

No. 3837 Basket	Color Code	Introduced	Discontinued	Value
Amber	AR	1959	July 1959*	$25.00 – 30.00
Black Rose	RZ	1992	1992	$120.00 – 140.00
Blue Opalescent	BO	1940	1955**	$65.00 – 85.00
Blue Pastel	BP	1954	1955	$50.00 – 60.00
Cameo Opalescent	CO	1979	1982	$60.00 – 65.00
Carnival	CN	1980	1981	$40.00 – 50.00
Colonial Blue	CB	1967	1980	$35.00 – 40.00
Colonial Green	CG	1967	1977	$25.00 – 30.00
Cranberry	CR	1940	1978	$100.00 – 125.00
Crystal	CY	1968	1969	$12.00 – 15.00
Decorated Holly	DH	July 1973	1975	$55.00 – 65.00
Decorated Roses	RW	1974	1976	$55.00 – 70.00
French Opalescent	FO	1940	1956	$40.00 – 50.00
Green Opalescent		1940	1941***	$145.00 – 175.00
Green Pastel	GP	1954	1956	$55.00 – 60.00
Jonquil Yellow	JO	1968	1969	$75.00 – 95.00
Lime Opalescent	LO	1952	1955	$150.00 – 180.00
Milk	MI	1951	1990†	$30.00 – 35.00
Orange	OR	1967	1978	$27.00 – 37.00
Peach Blow	PB	July 1952	1957	$90.00 – 110.00

No. 3837 Basket	Color Code	Introduced	Discontinued	Value
Plum Opalescent	PO	July 1959	1964	$160.00 – 180.00
Rose Overlay		1943	1945	$100.00 – 125.00
Rose Pastel	RP	1954	1958	$45.00 – 55.00
Ruby	RU	1972	1986	$25.00 – 35.00
Ruby Overlay	RO	1968	1969	$85.00 – 95.00
Ruby Satin	RA	1982	1983	$100.00 – 125.00
Silver Crest (Milk Glass Royal)	SC	1993	1995	$40.00 – 45.00
Springtime Green	GT	1977	1979	$35.00 – 45.00
Topaz Opalescent	TO	1941	1944††	$125.00 – 140.00
Turquoise	TU	1955	1959	$40.00 – 50.00
Violet Opalescent		1942	1945	$100.00 – 145.00

*Also made from 1967 to 1981.

**Reissued in 1959 and 1978.

***Also made from July 1959 to July 1961. This color is more blue-green, $90.00 – 125.00.

†Also made in 1991.

††Also made from 1959 to 1961 and for Levay in 1980.

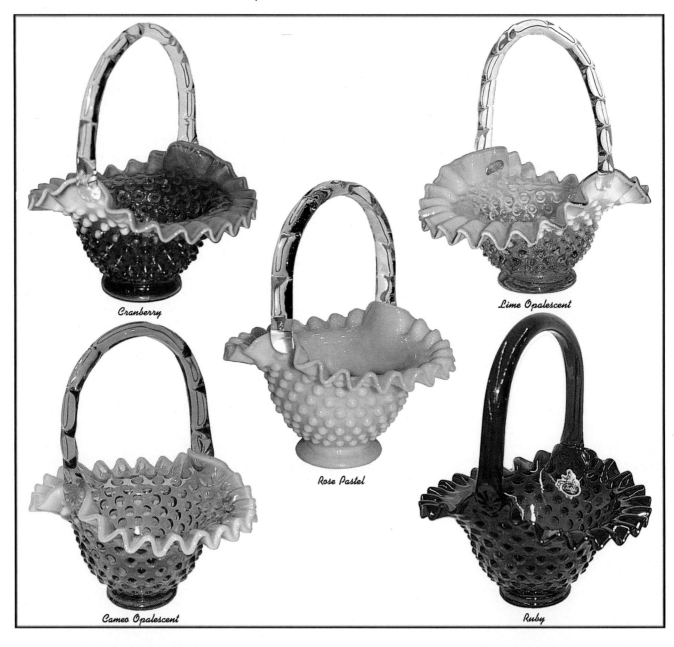

Cranberry

Lime Opalescent

Rose Pastel

Cameo Opalescent

Ruby

NO. 3337-7" BASKET

Fenton's No. 3337-7" basket was made for The Levay Distributing Company during 1983 in Topaz Opalescent (TO). Later, from January through June 1993, the basket was made in Rose Magnolia (RV) as a part of the Historical Collection.

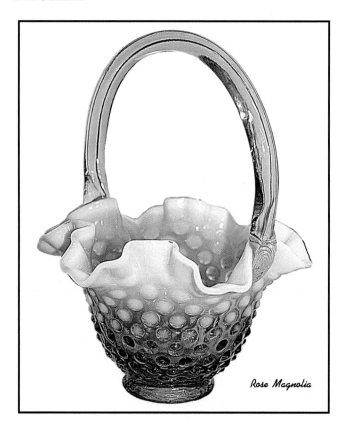

Rose Magnolia

No. 3337 Basket	Introduced	Discontinued	Value
Rose Magnolia	1933	July 1993	$85.00 – 95.00
Topaz Opalescent	1983	1983	$110.00 – 130.00

NO. 3637-7" DEEP BASKET

Cranberry

This basket has a pie crust edge crimp. It is 7" high and 7" in diameter and was introduced into the line in Cranberry and milk in 1963. Cranberry examples of this basket have become elusive.

No. 3637 Basket	Introduced	Discontinued	Value
Cranberry	1963	1965	$300.00 – 350.00
Milk	1963	1969	$50.00 – 60.00

NO. 3346-7" BASKET

Fenton's No. 3346-7" basket is a contemporary item that entered the line in 1995. The basket is 7" in diameter and stands 8½" high. The original Cranberry basket had a French Opalescent twisted rib handle. This basket was made in 2002 with a ribbed French Opalescent handle. A milk version of this basket was made for QVC in 1996.

Cranberry

No. 3346 Basket	Introduced	Discontinued	Value
Cranberry	1995	2005	$45.00 – 55.00
Milk (QVC)	December 1996		$30.00 – 35.00

NO. 1158-7" BASKET

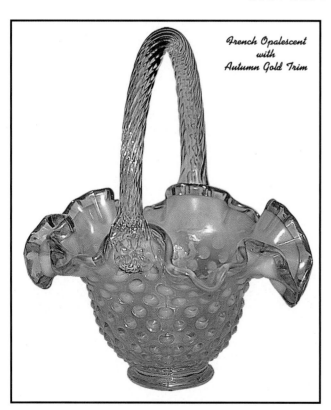
French Opalescent with Autumn Gold Trim

This style basket was introduced into the regular Fenton line in 1994. This basket was in the regular line for one year in French Opalescent with a colored edge and handle. Colors produced were French Opalescent with Autumn Gold trim (FT), French Opalescent with Dusty Rose trim (FD), and French Opalescent with Sea Mist Green trim (FR). This shape basket was also made in an iridized topaz opalescent color as part of the Historical Collection in 1997.

No. 1158 Basket	Produced	Value
French Opalescent w/Autumn Gold trim	1994	$40.00 – 50.00
French Opalescent w/Dusty Rose trim	1994	$45.00 – 55.00
French Opalescent w/Sea Mist Green trim	1994	$45.00 – 55.00
Topaz Opalescent	1997	$45.00 – 55.00

NO. GSOO7-7" BASKET

This Burmese Spiral Optic 7" basket was sold through the Fenton Gift Shop in 1996. Baskets sold through the Fenton Gift Shop during the February sale had Bill Fenton's signature.

No. GS007 Basket	**Produced**	**Value**
Burmese	1996	$100.00 – 125.00

NO. C1169 BASKET

This 7" diameter Cranberry Opalescent Hobnail Spiral Optic basket was made for QVC in 1993. The basket is 7½" high and has an opal twisted rib handle.

No. C1169 Basket	**Produced**	**Value**
Cranberry	1993	$100.00 – 125.00

NO. 3032-7¾" BASKET

This basket was made from 1987 through 1988 in milk. It has a waved design between the Hobnail pattern. The basket measures 7½" in diameter and is 9" tall.

An Ice Blue Iridized basket was made for QVC in June 2000. This basket has a Violet double crimped crest and a rib twisted handle.

Ice Blue
Iridescent

No. 3032	Introduced	Discontinued	Value
Basket			
Milk	1987	1989	$45.00 – 55.00
Ice Blue Iridescent	2000	2000	$65.00 – 75.00

NO. 389-8" FOOTED BASKET

Blue Opalescent

Fenton's slender 8" footed basket was made in Blue Opalescent, French Opalescent, and Topaz Opalescent. This basket was made for the regular line during the mid-1940s. The basket measures about 13" in height and is about 7¾" in diameter. This style footed basket may also be found in the 6¼" size in these same colors.

No. 389-8"	Introduced	Discontinued	Value
Basket			
Blue Opalescent	1943	1947	$125.00 – 145.00
French Opalescent	1943	1947	$70.00 – 80.00
Topaz Opalescent	1943	1944	$150.00 – 180.00

NO. 3333-8" BASKET

This 8" tall Cranberry basket was made for The Levay Distributing Company in 1982. It has a ribbed French Opalescent handle.

No. 3333 Basket	Produced	Value
Cranberry	1982	$180.00 – 210.00

NO. 3347-8" BASKET

Fenton made this tall, slender six-point crimped basket in Cranberry for The Levay Distributing Company in 1982. It is 8" tall and about 4¾" in diameter. This basket has a looped, ribbed, French Opalescent handle.

No. 3347 Basket	Produced	Value
Cranberry	1982	$225.00 – 250.00

NO. 3638-8½" BASKET

This Hobnail basket was introduced into the Fenton line in 1967. The basket measures approximately 8½" high and the body is adorned with vertical ribs. This basket was made in Plum Opalescent for The Levay Distributing Company in 1984. Baskets in Ruby were also offered to Gracious Touch customers in the June 1987 catalog supplement. This shape basket was revived in 1994 with a colored edge and handle. Colors produced for the regular line were French Opalescent w/Autumn Gold trim (FT), French Opalescent w/Dusty Rose trim (FD), and French Opalescent w/Sea Mist Green trim (FR). In 1996, this basket was made in milk with a rib twisted handle for QVC.

Orange

No. 3638 Basket	Introduced	Discontinued	Value
Colonial Amber	1967	1971	$30.00 – 40.00
Colonial Blue	1967	July 1970	$40.00 – 45.00
Colonial Green	1967	July 1971	$25.00 – 35.00
Decorated Holly	July 1972	July 1973	$90.00 – 110.00
French Opal w/Autumn Gold trim	1994	1995	$50.00 – 60.00
French Opal w/Dusty Rose trim	1994	1995	$55.00 – 65.00
French Opal w/Sea Mist Green trim	1994	1995	$55.00 – 65.00
Milk	1967	1990*	$30.00 – 38.00
Orange	1967	July 1971	$35.00 – 45.00
Pink Chiffon Opal	2001	2002	$60.00 – 75.00
Plum Opalescent	1984	1984	$260.00 – 280.00
Ruby	July 1987	July 1989	$45.00 – 55.00

*Also made in 1991 in the regular line and for QVC in March 1996.

Milk

Colonial Amber

Colonial Blue

NO. 1160-8½" BASKET

This basket was made in French Opalescent with decorated trim for Easter 1995. The colors produced were French Opalescent with Dusty Rose trim (IH), French Opalescent with Sea Mist Green trim (IM), and French Opalescent with Cobalt trim (IQ).

No. 1160 Basket	Produced	Value
French Opalescent w/Dusty Rose trim	1995	$45.00 – 55.00
French Opalescent w/Sea Mist Green trim	1995	$45.00 – 55.00
French Opalescent w/Cobalt trim	1995	$50.00 – 60.00

French Opalescent with Sea Mist Green Trim

NO. 3678-9" BASKET

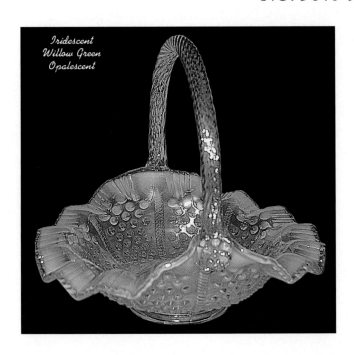

Iridescent Willow Green Opalescent

Two iridized colors of 9" zipper crimped baskets were made for the 2003 Easter season. The baskets have hobs on a body that is divided into panels with roped accents. This basket is a little over 9" long and about 8½" tall. The baskets have twisted rope handles.

No. 3678 Basket	Produced	Value
French Opalescent with Violet Iridescent trim	2003	$65.00 – 75.00
Iridescent Willow Green Opalescent	2003	$65.00 – 75.00

NO. 1156 -9" BASKET

This 9" tall basket was part of Fenton's 1993 Easter Collection. These baskets had a lightly iridized body and were made with a colored edge and handle. Two different colors were produced — French Opalescent with Dusty Rose trim (FD) and French Opalescent with Twilight Blue trim (F3).

No. 1156 Basket	Produced	Value
French Opalescent w/Dusty Rose trim	1993	$80.00 – 90.00
French Opalescent w/Twilight Blue trim	1993	$85.00 – 95.00

French Opalescent with Dusty Rose Trim

NO. 3357-9½" BASKET

This contemporary 9" tall footed basket was introduced into the Fenton line in 2000. It has appeared in the regular line in several opalescent colors during the last few years. The basket measures about 5½" across and has a rope twisted applied handle.

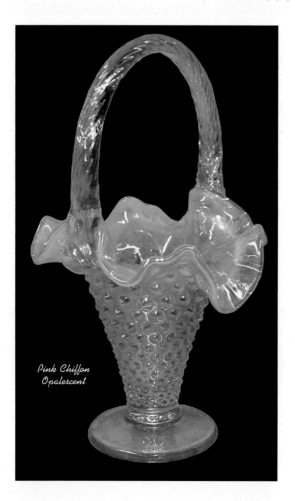

Pink Chiffon Opalescent

No. 3357 Basket	Introduced	Discontinued	Value
Champagne	2000	2001	$45.00 – 55.00
Pink Chiffon Opalescent	2001	2003	$40.00 – 50.00
Willow Green Opalescent	2001	2003	$40.00 – 50.00

NO. 3830-10" BASKET

This popular style basket entered the Fenton line in 1940 in the early Blue, French Green, and Cranberry Opalescent colors. Topaz Opalescent was added in 1941 and the basket was also made in Rose Overlay during the mid-1940s. Peach Blow was produced in the 1950s. Milk, the color produced for the longest time, was introduced in 1953. This color basket continued to be made until 1990. The basket was introduced to the Colonial colors of Amber, Blue, and Green during the late 1960s. These colors continued into the late 1970s. The Topaz Opalescent version of this basket was revived for The Levay Distributing Company in 1980 and Cranberry with a French Opalescent ribbed handle was made for Levay in 1982. Pink Opalescent baskets were made for the Collector's Extravaganza Collection in 1988. This basket was made in French Opalescent with decorated trim for Easter 1995. The colors produced were French Opalescent with Dusty Rose trim (IH), and French Opalescent with Sea Mist Green trim (IM). The milk version of this basket enjoyed a long run in the general line and was also in the Gracious Touch catalog in 1989.

French Opalescent with Sea Mist Green Trim

No. 3830 Basket	Introduced	Discontinued	Value
Blue Opalescent	1940	1955	$145.00 – 165.00
Colonial Amber	1968	1978	$40.00 – 50.00
Colonial Blue	1968	1978	$55.00 – 65.00
Colonial Green	1968	1977	$40.00 – 45.00
Cranberry	1940	1978*	$190.00 – 220.00
Crystal	1968	1969	$25.00 – 30.00
French Opalescent	1940	July 1954	$90.00 – 110.00
French Opalescent w/Dusty Rose trim	1995	1995	$95.00 – 115.00
French Opal w/Sea Mist Green trim	1995	1995	$95.00 – 115.00
Green Opalescent	1940	July 1941	$200.00 – 250.00
Milk	July 1953	1990	$45.00 – 55.00
Orange	1968	July 1970	$65.00 – 75.00
Peach Blow	July 1952	1957	$160.00 – 180.00
Pink Opalescent	1988	1989	$85.00 – 95.00
Rose Overlay	1943	1945	$275.00 – 375.00
Ruby Overlay	1968	1969	$150.00 – 175.00
Topaz Opalescent	1941	July 1944**	$200.00 – 225.00

*Also made for Levay in 1982.
**Also July through December 1959; for Levay in 1980.

Cranberry

Colonial Green

NO. 3348-10½" BASKET

This zipper crimped basket with a French Opalescent spiral ribbed handle was made in Cranberry Opalescent in 1995 and 1996. The basket is about 10" long, 8½" wide, and 10½" tall. It has the oval Fenton mark embossed in the base.

No. 3348 Basket	Introduced	Discontinued	Value
Cranberry	1995	1997	$55.00 – 65.00

NO. CV169-10½" BASKET

Willow Green Opalescent with Empress Rose Trim

This basket was first made for QVC in 1997 in French Opalescent Hobnail with a Dusty Rose edge and handle (IH). It measures 10½ "high and is also about 10½" in diameter. In 2000, Fenton produced a Willow Green Opalescent Iridized (GW) Hobnail basket for QVC. This basket had an Empress Rose edge and Willow Green handle. This color basket is shown to the left.

In 2003 this shape basket was again made for QVC. The color of the basket was Plum Opalescent and the accent color for the handle was French Opalescent.

No. CV169 Basket	Color Code	Produced	Value
French Opalescent w/Dusty Rose trim	IH	March 1997	$60.00 – 65.00
Willow Green Opal Iridescent with Empress Rose trim	GW	April 2000	$75.00 – 85.00
Plum Opalescent	PO	April 2003	$75.00 – 85.00

NO. 3734-12" BASKET

This large double crimped basket entered the Fenton line in milk in July 1959. The basket is 11½" in diameter, and 10½" high. It was also in the regular line in Ruby and Topaz Opalescent. Later, in 1984, this basket was made in Plum Opalescent for The Levay Distributing Company.

No. 3734 Basket	Introduced	Discontinued	Value
Milk	July 1959	1990*	$60.00 – 65.00
Plum Opalescent	1984	1984	$375.00 – 425.00
Ruby	1972	1981	$50.00 – 65.00
Topaz Opalescent	July 1959	July 1960	$200.00 – 225.00

*Reissued 1991 through 1994.

NO. 3839-12" OVAL BASKET

Fenton's large oval basket entered the regular line in 1960. This basket is about 13" long, 7" wide, and 3¼" high. It was first made in milk and Plum Opalescent. In the early 1970s some milk examples were decorated with Fenton's Blue Bell pattern. Later, in 1984, this basket was produced in Plum Opalescent for The Levay Distributing Company. This basket will be marked on the bottom with the Fenton logo.

No. 3839 Basket	Introduced	Discontinued	Value
Blue Bell decorated	1971	July 1972	$90.00 – 110.00
Milk	1960	1975	$55.00 – 65.00
Plum Opalescent	1960	1963	$350.00 – 375.00

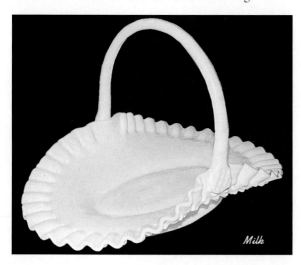

NO. 389-13½" BASKET

Fenton's large 13½" tall Hobnail basket entered the regular line in January 1941. These baskets are almost 11" long. The original colors were Cranberry, Blue Opalescent and French Opalescent. The basket was also made in Topaz Opalescent starting in July 1941. All colors of this basket were discontinued at the end of 1943.

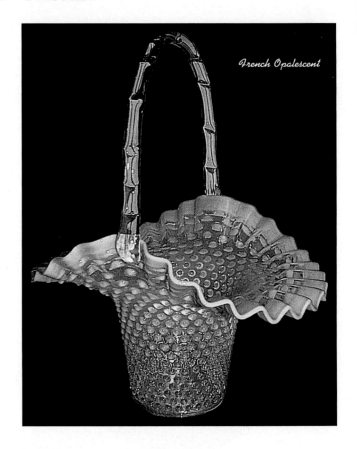

French Opalescent

No. 389-13½" Basket	Introduced	Discontinued	Value
Blue Opalescent	1941	1944	$350.00 – 450.00
Cranberry	1941	1944	$600.00 – 700.00
French Opalescent	1941	1944	$250.00 – 300.00
Topaz Opalescent	July 1941	1944	$400.00 – 500.00

9" FOOTED BASKET

This tall footed, smooth edge milk basket was not in the regular Fenton line. The basket is 9" high and measures about 8¼" long. It has a slightly twisted ribbed handle and a ribbed stem connecting the body of the basket to a plain foot.

Footed basket	Value
Milk	$100.00 – 125.00

LIME OPALESCENT LOOP HANDLE BASKET

Cupped, loop handle 4½" and 7" baskets are found infrequently. These shapes are known in Green Opalescent and Blue Opalescent, but were not in the Fenton general line.

Loop handle basket	Value
Blue Opalescent	$90.00 – 110.00
Green Opalescent	$120.00 – 140.00

6½" CRIMPED FLAT BASKET

This crimped edge basket has the Fenton logo with a "9" embossed in the bottom. It has a smooth applied handle and a tumbler-like 2¼" diameter base. The basket is 7¼" tall, 5½" long, and 4¾" wide.

Crimped flat basket	Value
Milk	$25.00 – 35.00

BELLS

NO. 3645-5½" BELL

Fenton's 5½" crimped bottom bell was made for The Levay Distributing Company in the 1980s. Colors for Levay included Blue Opalescent (BO) and Aqua Opalescent Carnival (IO) in 1982 and Plum Opalescent (PO) in 1984. This bell was also made in Milk for the regular line in 1991. The Historical Collection from 1993 included this bell in Rose Magnolia (RV).

No. 3645 Bell	Produced	Value
Aqua Opalescent		
Carnival	1982	$27.00 – 32.00
Blue Opalescent	1982	$30.00 – 35.00
Milk	1991	$18.00 – 22.00
Persian Blue		
Opalescent	1989	$27.00 – 32.00
Plum Opalescent	1984	$60.00 – 70.00
Rose Magnolia	1993	$30.00 – 35.00
Topaz Opalescent		$40.00 – 50.00

Rose Magnolia

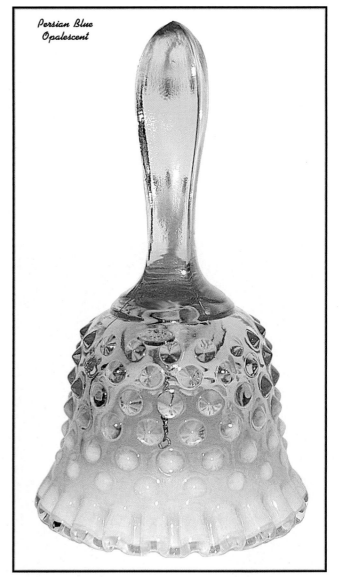

Persian Blue Opalescent

NO. 3368-5½" BELL

Fenton's new Hobnail bell shape for the regular line in 2001 is 5½" tall. This new No. 3368 crimped bell was made in Pink Chiffon Opalescent (YS) and Willow Green Opalescent (GY). Production of this bell in both colors continued until the end of 2002.

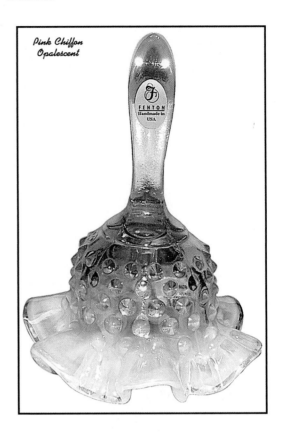

Pink Chiffon Opalescent

No. 3368 Bell	Introduced	Discontinued	Value
Pink Chiffon			
Opalescent	2001	2003	$18.00 – 22.00
Willow Green			
Opalescent	2001	2003	$18.00 – 22.00

NO. 3369-5½" BELL

Ruby

Fenton's 5½" crimped bottom Ruby bell was included in an assortment of ruby Hobnail that was offered for the Holiday season in 1987. This shape bell also was sold through Fenton's Gracious Touch division during the last half of 1987. Notice it differs in shape from the No. 3667 bell that was also made in Ruby.

No. 3369 Bell	Introduced	Discontinued	Value
Ruby	July 1987	1988	$22.00 – 27.00

NO. 3667-6" BELL

This 6" tall bell has a tapered 4-sided handle. There are two versions of the handle for this bell. Older bells have tiny beads on the edges of the handle. Later versions of this bell have smooth edges. Examples of both types of handles are illustrated. The Springtime Green bell has a plain handle and the Colonial Blue bell has a beaded handle. This shape bell was introduced in Fenton's Colonial colors and in Milk in 1967. Milk examples of this bell were decorated with Blue Bells, Holly, and Roses during the 1970s.

Purple Slag bells were made for The Levay Distributing Company in 1981. Ruby Satin bells were made for Levay in 1982.

No. 3667 Bell	Introduced	Discontinued	Value
Blue Opalescent	July 1978	1981	$40.00 – 45.00
Cameo Opalescent	July 1979	1981	$28.00 – 30.00
Carnival	1980	1981	$27.00 – 32.00
Colonial Amber	1967	1981	$14.00 – 18.00
Colonial Blue	1967	1980	$22.00 – 25.00
Colonial Green	1967	1977	$18.00 – 20.00
Decorated Blue Bell	1971	1973	$30.00 – 35.00
Decorated Holly	July 1971	1976	$35.00 – 40.00
Decorated Roses	1974	1976	$35.00 – 38.00
French Opalescent	1978	1981	$30.00 – 35.00
Milk	1967	1987	$20.00 – 22.00
Orange	1977	1978	$20.00 – 25.00
Purple Slag	1981	1981	$45.00 – 55.00
Springtime Green	1977	1979	$20.00 – 25.00
Ruby	1972	1985	$20.00 – 30.00
Ruby Satin	1982	1982	$30.00 – 40.00
Topaz Opal Iridescent	1975	1975	$50.00 – 55.00

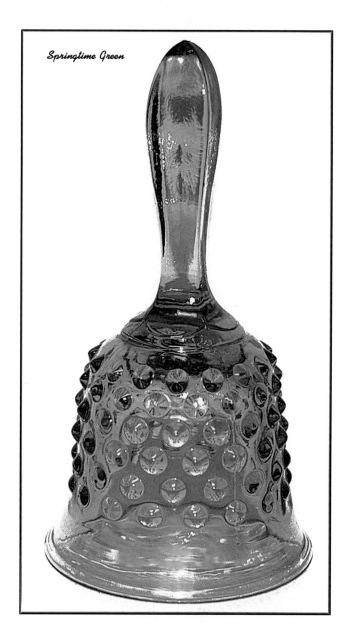

Springtime Green

Colonial Blue

NO. 3067-6¾" BELL

Fenton's waved design No. 3067 Hobnail bell is 6¾" high. This bell was introduced into the general line in milk in 1987. The bell has a waved design with large hobs on the body and a waved pattern on the handle. The bottom edge of the bell has 12 scallops. This bell was also in the regular line from 1987 until 1989 in Cobalt Marigold. In 1988, this carnival bell was offered as a gift to a Gracious Touch hostess who achieved a minimum gift show of $150.00 plus one party booking.

No. 3067 Bell	Introduced	Discontinued	Value
Cobalt Marigold	1987	1989	$55.00 – 65.00
Milk	1987	July 1989	$30.00 – 40.00

NO. CV326-P9 BELL

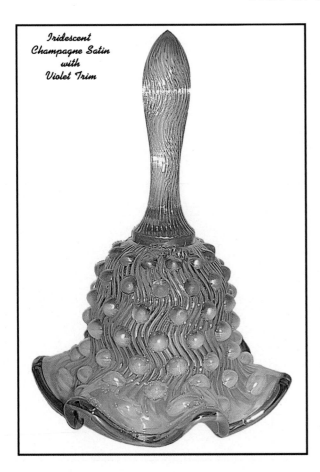

Fenton produced this waved design Hobnail bell for QVC in Iridescent Champagne Satin Opalescent with a Violet edge. The bell is 7" tall and 4¾" wide at the base.

No. CV326 Bell	Produced	Value
Iridescent Champagne Satin Opalescent w/Violet trim	2000	$30.00 – 35.00

BONBONS, BOWLS, AND NAPPIES

NO. 3928 BERRY DISH

This small square bowl has a crimped top edge and is 4" in diameter. It was introduced into the regular Fenton line in 1954 in milk and several pastel colors.

No. 3928 Berry	Introduced	Discontinued	Value
Blue Pastel	1954	1955	$15.00 – 18.00
Green Pastel	1954	1956	$17.00 – 20.00
Milk	July 1954	1968	$11.00 – 13.00
Rose Pastel	1954	1957	$16.00 – 18.00
Turquoise	1955	1957	$14.00 – 16.00

NO. 3630 BONBON

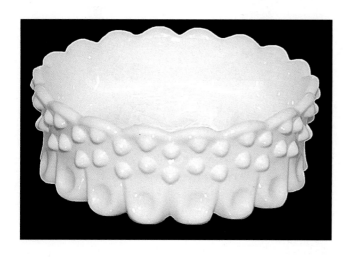

Fenton's No. 3630 round bonbon is 5" in diameter and 2" high with a concave shaped side. It has a scalloped top edge and thumbprints around the base. This small bonbon was introduced in milk in 1961. It remained in the regular line in this color through 1977. In the late 1980s this bonbon was made in Sapphire Blue Opalescent (BX).

No. 3630 Bonbon	Introduced	Discontinued	Value
Milk	1961	1978	$14.00 – 16.00
Sapphire Blue Opalescent	October 1987	July 1989	$20.00 – 25.00

NO. 389-4", 2-HANDLED BONBON

Fenton's 4", 2-handled bonbon is listed in Fenton catalogs from 1946 through 1950. This very shallow oval bonbon was made in Blue Opalescent and French Opalescent.

No. 389-H Bonbon	Introduced	Discontinued	Value
Blue Opalescent	1946	1951	$15.00 – 18.00
French Opalescent	1946	1951	$12.00 – 14.00

Blue Opalescent

NO. 3631 FOOTED NUT DISH

Fenton's No. 3631-4" diameter footed nut dish entered the general line in milk in 1962. This bowl is 2¾" high and has a plain foot. The body has five rows of hobs with 18 thumbprints around the bottom edge. The top of the bowl is scalloped.

No. 3631 Nut Dish	Introduced	Discontinued	Value
Milk	1962	1968	$15.00 – 18.00

NO. 3754 VIOLET BOWL

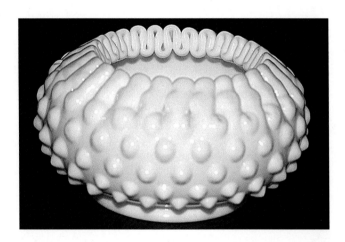

This small rose bowl was made in milk and Green Opalescent. It is 2¼" tall and 4" in diameter. This shape was introduced into the Fenton line in 1960.

No. 3754 Bowl	Introduced	Discontinued	Value
Green Opalescent	1960	July 1961	$30.00 – 40.00
Milk	1960	1969	$16.00 – 20.00

NO. 3828 SQUARE DESSERT BOWL

Fenton's 3½" square Hobnail dessert bowl was in the regular line in blue opalescent and French Opalescent. The bowls are about 2" high and have rounded corners. The shape entered the line in 1951 and was discontinued by the middle of the decade. Poor sales and a short production period have made this bowl elusive on the secondary market.

No. 3828 Bowl	Introduced	Discontinued	Value
Blue Opalescent	1951	1954	$35.00 – 45.00
French Opalescent	1951	1955	$25.00 – 28.00

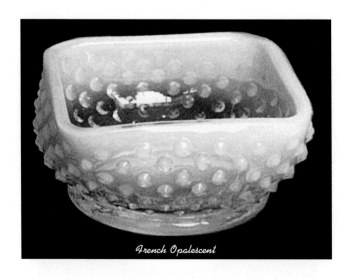

French Opalescent

NO. 3650 NUT OR ICE CREAM DISH

This small round bowl was in Fenton's general line in amber and milk. The bowl is 2½" high and 4¾" in diameter. It has 12 scallops around the top edge. There are rows of hobs on both the side and bottom.

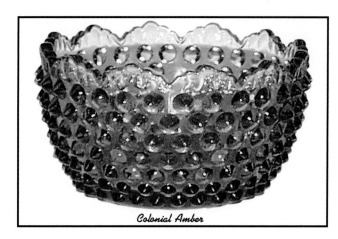

Colonial Amber

No. 3650 Nut dish	Introduced	Discontinued	Value
Colonial Amber	1967	July 1968	$10.00 – 12.00
Milk	1967	July 1969	$35.00 – 40.00

NO. 3729 NUT DISH

This round, small bowl was only in the general line in milk. The bowl has two plain open handles. It is 2½" high and 5" in diameter (not including the handles). The top edge of the bowl has a pie crust crimp.

No. 3729 Nut dish	Introduced	Discontinued	Value
Milk	July 1956	1965	$18.00 – 20.00

NO. 3732 OVAL 2-HANDLED NUT DISH

This oval 2-handled nut dish was in the general line in milk. The two solid handles are decorated with small hobs. The bowl is 2⅛" high and has five rows of hobs and a scalloped top edge. It is 5" long and 3¼" wide.

No. 3732 Nut dish	Introduced	Discontinued	Value
Milk	1958	1966	$16.00 – 18.00

NO. 3719 CEREAL BOWL

This small Hobnail bowl was in the regular Fenton line in milk from January 1960 until the end of 1963. This round ribbon crimped bowl is 5" in diameter and 2½" high.

No. 3719 Bowl	Introduced	Discontinued	Value
Milk	1960	1964	$40.00 – 45.00

NO. 3935-5" SQUARE 2-HANDLED BONBON

This small footed bonbon was introduced into the line in 1941. It has four sides pulled up and two plain handles. This bonbon was also made in an oval crimp shape during the 1940s.

Topaz Opalescent

No. 3935 Bonbon	Introduced	Discontinued	Value
Blue Opalescent	1941	1955	$22.00 – 25.00
French Opalescent	1941	1956	$14.00 – 18.00
Milk	1950	July 1956	$14.00 – 16.00
Topaz Opalescent	1941	1944	$30.00 – 35.00

NO. 389-5" OVAL 2-HANDLED BONBON

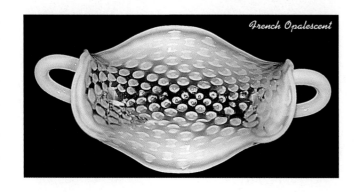

French Opalescent

This small bonbon was introduced into the line in 1941. It is the same mold as the bonbon above with a different style crimping. It has two sides pulled up with two plain handles and the other two sides are flared out. This shape bonbon was discontinued before Fenton began using ware numbers, therefore, it only has the generic Hobnail No. 389 identity.

No. 389-5" Bonbon	Introduced	Discontinued	Value
Blue Opalescent	1941	1952	$22.00 – 25.00
French Opalescent	1941	1952	$14.00 – 18.00
Topaz Opalescent	1941	1944	$30.00 – 35.00

NO. 3921-5" STAR BONBON

This small bonbon is 2¾" high. It has a six-point star shape crimp and was introduced into the regular line in 1953. Notice the Blue Opalescent color was only made for two years; therefore, acquiring this color will be more difficult.

Cranberry

No. 3921 Bonbon	Introduced	Discontinued	Value
Blue Opalescent	1953	1955	$30.00 – 35.00
Cranberry	1953	1957	$75.00 – 90.00
French Opalescent	1953	1957	$30.00 – 35.00
Milk	1953	1970	$18.00 – 20.00
Peach Blow	1953	1957	$45.00 – 55.00

NO. 3730 RIBBON CANDY BOWL

Fenton's footed No. 3730 ribbon candy bowl was made in milk and Topaz Opalescent. Both colors were only made for a very short time and are not often found today. The bowl is 6¾" high and 5½" in diameter and the stem of the foot has vertical ribbing.

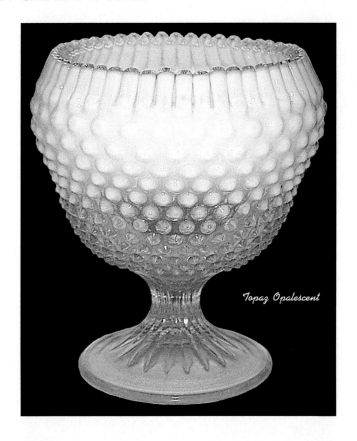

Topaz Opalescent

No. 3730 Bowl	Introduced	Discontinued	Value
Milk	July 1959	1960	$50.00 – 60.00
Topaz Opalescent	1959	1960	$175.00 – 225.00

NO. 389-6" BONBON

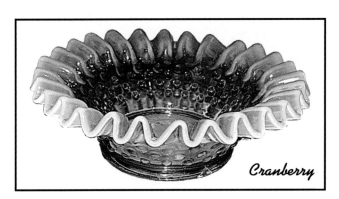

Cranberry

Beginning in 1940, Fenton's No. 389-6" bonbon was made in double crimped, flared, oval, plate, square, and triangle shapes. All shapes except the double crimped style were discontinued by July 1952, when the ware number system was initiated. The various shapes of crimping from an early 1940s catalog are illustrated below. Sizes of the bowls will vary with crimping style. Most bowls will range from 5" to 6" in diameter.

No. 389 Bonbon	Introduced	Discontinued	Value
Blue Opalescent	1940	1952	$25.00 – 30.00
Cranberry	1940	1952	$25.00 – 32.00
French Opalescent	1940	1952	$10.00 – 15.00
Green Opalescent	1940	1941	$22.00 – 27.00
Rose Overlay	1943	1945	$27.00 – 30.00
Topaz Opalescent	1941	1944	$27.00 – 30.00
Violet Opalescent	1942	1945	$22.00 – 27.00
Wisteria Opalescent	1943	1945	$22.00 – 27.00

6" Oval Bonbon   6" Flared Bonbon   6" Triangle Bonbon

6" Double Crimp Bonbon   6" Square Bonbon   6" Plate Bonbon

7" Bonbon May Be Had In Above Six Shapes

NO. 3926-6" DC BONBON

Fenton introduced this 6" bonbon into the regular line in 1940. Until July 1952 this bonbon was produced in numerous shapes as a No. 389-6" bonbon. After Fenton adopted the ware number system, the double crimped shape of this bonbon was assigned the No. 3926. Other shapes of bonbons produced from this mold are illustrated on page 56.

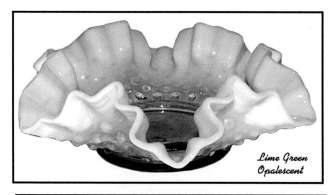

Lime Green Opalescent

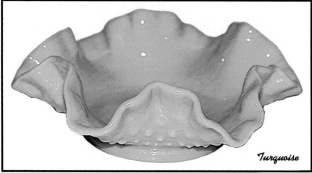

Turquoise

No. 3926 Bonbon	Introduced	Discontinued	Value
Blue Opalescent	1940	1955	$18.00 – 20.00
Blue Pastel	1954	1955	$16.00 – 18.00
Cranberry	1940	1957	$22.00 – 25.00
Decorated Blue Bell	1971	1973	$18.00 – 25.00
French Opalescent	1940	1956	$10.00 – 12.00
Green Opalescent	1940	1941	$25.00 – 27.00
Green Pastel	1955	1956	$14.00 – 16.00
Lime Green Opalescent	1952	1955	$20.00 – 25.00
Milk	1950	1990	$7.00 – 9.00
Peach Blow	July 1952	1957	$20.00 – 25.00
Plum	1984	1984	$20.00 – 25.00
Rose Overlay	1943	1945	$27.00 – 30.00
Rose Pastel	1955	1957	$12.00 – 14.00
Topaz Opalescent	1941	1944	$20.00 – 25.00
Turquoise	1955	1958	$10.00 – 12.00

NO. 389-6½" 2-HANDLED BONBON

Blue Opalescent

Fenton made a 6½" diameter, solid handled bonbon in oval and square shapes during the early 1940s. This size 2-handled bonbon then disappeared from the line for several years. In 1951, a 7" open two-handled oval shaped bonbon returned to the Fenton line.

No. 389-6½" Bonbon	Introduced	Discontinued	Value
Blue Opalescent	July 1941	1944	$25.00 – 30.00
French Opalescent	July 1941	1944	$18.00 – 22.00
Topaz Opalescent	July 1941	1944	$40.00 – 45.00

NO. 3033 HEART-SHAPED HANDLELESS BOWL OR CANDY

Fenton's No. 3033-6½" heart-shaped handleless candy was only in the line in milk. This candy was made from the same mold as the handled No. 3733 relish. The candy was only made for 2½ years and is elusive.

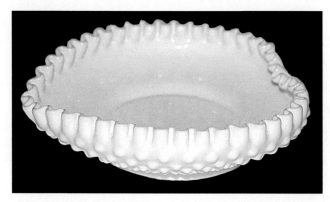

No. 3033 Candy	Introduced	Discontinued	Value
Milk	1987	July 1989	$55.00 – 65.00

NO. 3937-7" 2-HANDLED BONBON

Fenton's large size oval-shaped, open handled bonbon returned to the regular line in 1951. Blue opalescent and French Opalescent bonbons were discontinued by the mid-1950s. Pink Opalescent pieces were made for Collector's Extravaganza in 1988. Both Pink Opalescent and Sapphire Blue Opalescent bonbons were available as gifts for customers who purchased at least $75.00 worth of dinnerware through the Gracious Touch division in 1989.

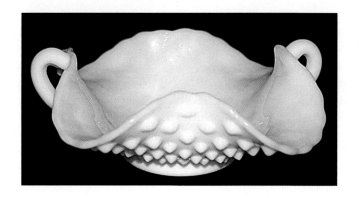

No. 3937-7" Bonbon	Introduced	Discontinued	Value
Blue Opalescent	1951	1955	$32.00 – 38.00
French Opalescent	1951	1956	$18.00 – 22.00
Milk	1951	July 1976*	$14.00 – 16.00
Pink Opalescent	1988	1990	$20.00 – 25.00
Sapphire Blue Opalescent	1988	1990	$20.00 – 25.00

*Also made in 1987 and 1988.

NO. 3633 OVAL 2-HANDLED NUT DISH

Black

This oval nut dish has two open handles with beading on the outside edge. It is 2½" high, 7" long, and 3½" wide. There are five rows of hobs on the body and 10 scallops around the top edge.

No. 3633 Nut dish	Introduced	Discontinued	Value
Black	1970	1971	$18.00 – 20.00
Colonial Amber	1964	1969	$10.00 – 12.00
Colonial Blue	1963	July 1968	$12.00 – 14.00
Decorated Roses	1974	July 1976	$28.00 – 32.00
Colonial Green	1964	July 1969	$10.00 – 12.00
Milk	1964	1990	$15.00 – 18.00

NO. 389-7" BONBON

Fenton offered 7" bonbons in double crimped, flared, oval, plate, square, and triangle shapes during the early 1940s. These bonbon shapes are the same as those shown in the reprint for the No. 389-6" bonbons on page 56.

No. 389-7" Bonbon	Introduced	Discontinued	Value
Blue Opalescent	1940	1941	$30.00 – 32.00
Green Opalescent	1940	1941	$35.00 – 45.00
French Opalescent	1940	1941	$18.00 – 22.00

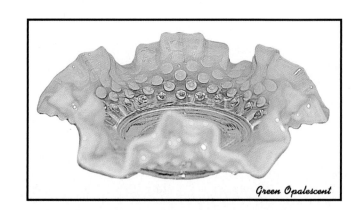

Green Opalescent

NO. 3822, 3-PART RELISH

Fenton introduced a cloverleaf-shaped relish into the general line in 1954. This relish measures about 7" in diameter and is 1½" high. The sides and the bottom have hobs and the outside edge is scalloped. The relish may be found with and without the center divisions. The same ware number was used for both styles of bowl. Examples without the divisions are elusive.

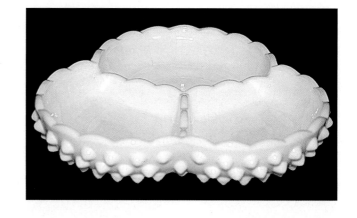

No. 3822 3-part relish	Introduced	Discontinued	Value
Amber	1959	1960	$45.00 – 55.00
Crystal	1968	1969	$8.00 – 10.00
French Opalescent	1954	1957	$95.00 – 120.00
Milk	1956	1973	$18.00 – 20.00*

*Without divisions, $95.00 – 110.00.

NO. 3607 CHROME HANDLED RELISH

This chrome handled, 3-part, clover-shaped relish is 7" in diameter and 1½" high. The relish tray was created by adding a raised center core to the No. 3822 relish through which the chrome handle could be inserted. This elevated barrier prevented the contents from any of the three sections from leaking through the center hole.

No. 3607 Chrome handled relish	Introduced	Discontinued	Value
Milk	1970	1985	$22.00 – 25.00

NO. 3927-7" DC BOWL

This double crimped, 4" high, 7" diameter bowl was introduced in 1940. The original colors were Blue Opalescent, Cranberry, and French Opalescent. These colors and Milk were made for many years, therefore, the supply on the resale market should be plentiful. Other colors such as Topaz Opalescent and Lime Opalescent are scarce. During the 1940s this bowl was also crimped into flared, oval, and triangle shapes. See page 60 for information about these additional shapes.

No. 3927 Bowl	Introduced	Discontinued	Value
Ruby Overlay	1968	1969	$40.00 – 50.00
Topaz Opalescent	1959	1960	$45.00 – 55.00

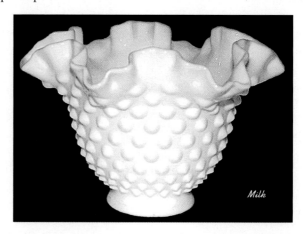

Milk

No. 3927 Bowl	Introduced	Discontinued	Value
Blue Opalescent	1940	1955	$35.00 – 45.00
Cranberry	1940	1979	$50.00 – 60.00
French Opalescent	1940	July 1956	$20.00 – 25.00
Lime Opalescent	1952	1955	$50.00 – 60.00
Milk	1950	1981	$22.00 – 27.00
Peach Blow	July 1952	1958	$35.00 – 45.00

NO. 389-7" FLARED, OVAL, OR TRIANGLE BOWL

This 7" bowl entered the Fenton line in 1940 in opalescent colors. Shapes made include double crimped, flared, oval, and triangular. Rose Overlay Hobnail was made in 1943. A triangle shape bowl in this color is shown in the photo to the right. After the conversion to ware numbers in 1952, the double crimp shape became No. 3927 and the other shapes were discontinued. Wisteria Opalescent was made for Sherwin-Williams in the mid-1940s.

No. 389-7" Bowl	Introduced	Discontinued	Value
Blue Opalescent	1940	1944	$35.00 – 45.00
Cranberry	1940	1944	$60.00 – 70.00
French Opalescent	1940	1944	$22.00 – 27.00
Green Opalescent	1940	1941	$45.00 – 55.00
Rose Overlay	1943	1944	$50.00 – 60.00
Topaz Opalescent	1941	1944	$45.00 – 55.00
Violet Opalescent	1942	1945	$40.00 – 45.00
Wisteria Opalescent	1943	1945	$40.00 – 45.00

Oval Shape — Green Opalescent

Triangle Shape — Rose Overlay

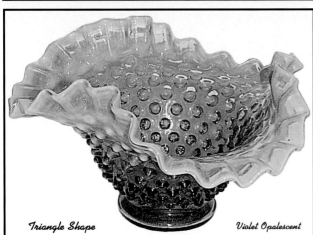

Triangle Shape — Violet Opalescent

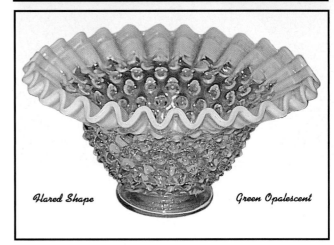

Flared Shape — Green Opalescent

NO. 389-7" SPECIAL BOWL

Fenton's No. 389-7" special rose bowl is a low flared and cupped-in bowl with a small opening in the top. These bowls will often be found drilled for lamp parts.

No. 389-7" Bowl	Introduced	Discontinued	Value
Blue Opalescent	1940	1944	$35.00 – 45.00
Cranberry	1940	1944	$55.00 – 65.00
French Opalescent	1940	1944	$25.00 – 32.00
Green Opalescent	1940	1941	$50.00 – 60.00
Lime Opalescent			$65.00 – 75.00
Topaz Opalescent	1941	1944	$55.00 – 65.00

Blue Opalescent

NO. 389-7½" FLARED BOWL

This elusive 7½" flared, scalloped Hobnail bowl was first listed in a 1942 Fenton catalog. By 1943 the bowl was listed as discontinued. The bowl is 3¼" high and has eight scallops around the top edge.

No. 389-7½" Flared bowl	Introduced	Discontinued	Value
Blue Opalescent	1942	1943	$35.00 – 45.00
French Opalescent	1942	1943	$22.00 – 27.00
Topaz Opalescent	1942	1943	$50.00 – 60.00

NO. 389-8" OVAL HANDLED BONBON

This oval 8½" long by 7½" wide closed handle oval bonbon was produced in Blue Opalescent and French Opalescent for one year in the early 1950s. As a result of this short production, this bonbon is not easily found today.

No. 389-8" Bonbon	Introduced	Discontinued	Value
Blue Opalescent	1951	1952	$325.00 – 350.00
French Opalescent	1951	1952	$100.00 – 125.00

NO. 3635 3-TOED BOWL

This 3-toed bowl is 3¾" high and 8" in diameter. It was introduced into the regular Fenton line in Milk in 1963. A blue opalescent example has been found. This bowl was also made in Sapphire Blue Opalescent in 1989 for Fenton's Gracious Touch division.

No. 3635 Bowl	Introduced	Discontinued	Value
Blue Opalescent			$250.00 – 300.00
Milk	1963	1990	$22.00 – 27.00
Sapphire Blue Opalescent	1989		$27.00 – 32.00

NO. 3706-8" CHROME HANDLED BONBON

This double crimped bonbon is 8" in diameter and has a hole drilled through the center to fit a chrome handle. The shape was introduced into the line in Milk in 1969. Although Ruby was discontinued from the regular line at the end of 1985, Fenton offered this color from June through December from 1986 until 1990.

No. 3706 Bonbon	Introduced	Discontinued	Value
Colonial Amber	1979	1981	$10.00 – 12.00
Blue Marble	1970	1974	$30.00 – 35.00
Colonial Blue	1979	1981	$18.00 – 22.00
Decorated Blue Bell	1971	1972	$30.00 – 40.00
Milk	1969	1990	$20.00 – 22.00
Ruby	1972	1986*	$22.00 – 25.00

*Also in the line from July 1987 until 1990.

NO. 3716-8" BONBON

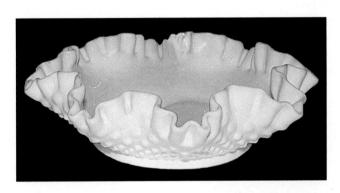

Fenton's No. 3716-8" double crimped shallow bonbon first appeared in the regular line in July 1960. This bonbon was offered to customers in Milk and Ruby.

No. 3716-8" Bonbon	Introduced	Discontinued	Value
Milk	July 1960	July 1981	$18.00 – 20.00
Ruby	1972	1973	$18.00 – 22.00

NO. 3640-8" OVAL PICKLE DISH

Fenton's No. 3640 oval pickle dish was introduced into the regular line in January 1964. This piece was produced in Milk for 20 years. This shallow, 4-footed bowl is 8" long and 4" wide. The top edge is scalloped.

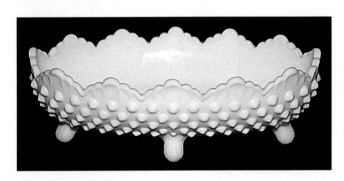

No. 3640 Oval Pickle Dish	Introduced	Discontinued	Value
Milk	1964	1984	$18.00 – 22.00

NO. 3625-8" OVAL BOWL

Fenton introduced a Milk Hobnail oval bowl into the regular line in 1961. This bowl is 8" long, 6" wide, and 3" high. It has a plain shallow curved foot and a top edge with 12 scallops. This bowl was sampled in Topaz Opalescent.

No. 3626 Bowl	Introduced	Discontinued	Value
Milk	1961	1969	$25.00 – 30.00
Topaz Opalescent			UND

NO. 3639-8" DC BOWL

This 8" diameter double crimped bowl has intervals of vertical ropes dividing the rows of hobs. It entered the Fenton line in milk and Colonial Amber in 1967. This bowl was also converted to a basket with the addition of an applied glass handle. Baskets were made in many colors and some have colored edges and handles.

Milk

No. 3639 Bowl	Introduced	Discontinued	Value
Colonial Amber	1967	1969	$35.00 – 40.00
Milk	1967	July 1978	$27.00 – 30.00

NO. 3626-8" BOWL

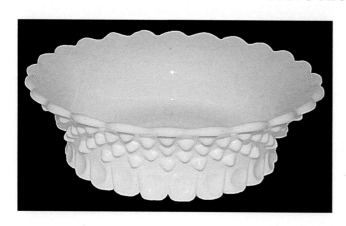

This bowl was only in the regular Fenton line in milk. It measures 8¾" in diameter and is 2¾" high. It has four rows of hobs and a row of thumbprints around the base.

No. 3626 Bowl	Introduced	Discontinued	Value
Milk	1961	1969	$35.00 – 42.00

NO. 3733 HANDLED RELISH

Fenton's No. 3733 handled heart-shaped relish or open candy is 8½" long, 6¼" wide, and about 2" high. The opalescent colors were only made for a short time and are becoming elusive. The top edge is ribbon crimped. The bottom is plain and the side has seven rows of hobs. Milk Glass Royal has a crystal edge and handle. In the early 1990s, several hand-painted decorations on satin Burmese were produced for the Fenton Gift Shop and a special order customer. The Plum Opalescent relish was made for The Levay Distributing Company in 1984.

No. 3733 Relish	Introduced	Discontinued	Value
Blue Marble	1970	1973	$30.00 – 35.00
Blue Opalescent	1960	1962	$70.00 – 85.00
Burmese	1991	1992	$100.00 – 125.00
Burmese, HP	1991	1991	$150.00 – 175.00
Green Opalescent	1960	July 1961	$90.00 – 125.00
Milk	1958	1988	$18.00 – 20.00
Milk Glass Royal	1993	1996	$25.00 – 35.00
Plum Opalescent	1984	1984	$150.00 – 175.00
Topaz Opalescent	1959	July 1960	$85.00 – 95.00

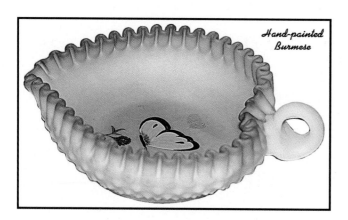
Hand-painted Burmese

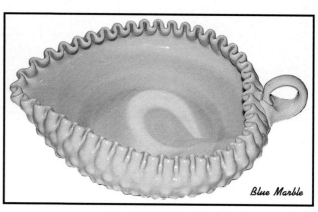
Blue Marble

NO. 3724-8½" BOWL

Fenton's No. 3724 round 3-footed bowl was introduced into the regular Fenton line in 1959 in Amber, Milk, and Topaz Opalescent. Amber and Topaz Opalescent were made only for six months, but the milk bowl remained in the line until the end of 1977. The bowl is 8½" in diameter and 3¾" high. There are five rows of hobs on the side and four rows on the bottom.

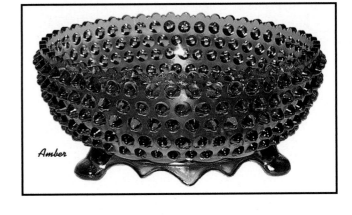

No. 3724 Bowl	Introduced	Discontinued	Value
Amber	1959	July 1959	$40.00 – 45.00
Milk	1959	1978	$35.00 – 45.00
Topaz Opalescent	1959	July 1959	$225.00 – 250.00

NO. 3735-9" CUPPED BOWL

This 9" diameter cupped bowl was made initially in Topaz Opalescent starting in January 1959. It was made in milk from July 1959 through 1964. The bowl is 4" high and has a ribbon crimped top. This ware number was later used for a 5½" basket that was made from 1971 through 1984.

No. 3735 Bowl	Introduced	Discontinued	Value
Milk	July 1959	1965	$85.00 – 100.00
Topaz Opalescent	1959	July 1960	$200.00 – 250.00

NO. 3924-9" DC BOWL

This 9" diameter round bowl entered the Fenton line in 1940. In the early years the bowl was made in double crimped and flared shapes. After the implementation of ware numbers, the double crimped shape of this bowl continued with the 3924-DC designation. The Topaz Opalescent bowls made for The Levay Distributing Company in 1980 are marked with the oval Fenton logo. A small number of Ruby Satin (RA) bowls were made for Levay in 1982. Bowls have also been found with the Abels, Wasserberg & Company Charleton Pink Mist and Roses decoration.

No. 3924	Introduced	Discontinued	Value
Bowl			
Blue Opalescent	1940	1955*	$40.00 – 50.00
Blue Pastel	1954	1955	$35.00 – 45.00
Coral			$40.00 – 45.00
Cranberry	1940	1978**	$70.00 – 90.00
Crystal	1968	1969	$10.00 – 12.00
French Opalescent	1940	1956	$35.00 – 40.00
Green Opalescent	July 1959	July 1961	$65.00 – 75.00
Green Pastel	1954	1956	$35.00 – 45.00
Milk	1951	1989	$30.00 – 35.00
Orange Opalescent			$140.00 – 160.00
Peach Blow	July 1952	1957	$65.00 – 75.00
Plum Opalescent	July 1959	July 1961	$95.00 – 120.00
Rose Pastel	1954	1957	$35.00 – 40.00
Ruby	1981	1986	$35.00 – 40.00
Ruby Satin	1982	1982	$70.00 – 80.00
Topaz Opalescent	1959	1961***	$85.00 – 95.00
Turquoise	1955	1959	$35.00 – 45.00
Violet Opalescent	1942	1945	$65.00 – 75.00

*Reissued from 1959 – 1964.

** Available from QVC.com with Frank. M. Fenton, Thomas K. Fenton, and Scott Fenton signatures.

***Also made for Levay in 1980.

Coral

Rose Pastel

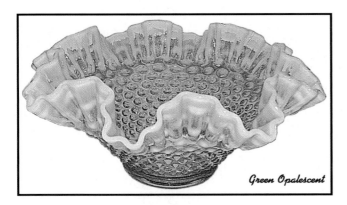

Green Opalescent

Plum Opalescent

NO. 389-9" FLARED BOWL

Fenton's 9" Hobnail round bowl was introduced in 1940. Shapes produced were double crimped and flared. For more information about the double crimped shape of this bowl see the listing on page 65.

Green Opalescent

No. 389-9" Bowl	Introduced	Discontinued	Value
Blue Opalescent	1940	1944	$40.00 – 50.00
Cranberry	1940	1944	$85.00 – 95.00
French Opalescent	1940	1944	$35.00 – 45.00
Green Opalescent	1940	1941	$90.00 – 110.00
Topaz Opalescent	1941	1944	$85.00 – 95.00

NO. 3929-9" SQUARE BOWL

Fenton's 9" square Hobnail bowl was introduced into the regular line in 1954 in Blue Pastel (BP), Green Pastel (GP), and Rose Pastel (RP). The bowl is 3" high and has hobs on the bottom in addition to the hobs on the sides.

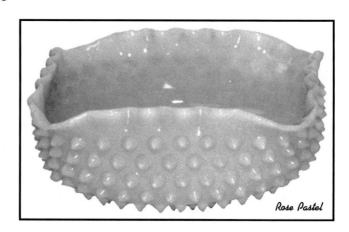

Rose Pastel

No. 3929 Bowl	Introduced	Discontinued	Value
Blue Pastel	1954	1955	$65.00 – 75.00
Green Pastel	1954	1956	$65.00 – 75.00
Milk	July 1954	July 1961	$50.00 – 60.00
Rose Pastel	1954	1957	$55.00 – 65.00
Turquoise	1955	1957	$55.00 – 65.00

NO. 3621-9" FOOTED OVAL BOWL

This large, footed oval bowl was introduced in milk in 1965. The bowl is 9" long, 5½" wide, and 7" high. The ribbed pedestal foot is separated from the bowl by a large collar.

No. 3621 Bowl	Introduced	Discontinued	Value
Milk	1965	1977	$45.00 – 55.00

NO. 3622-9½" SHALLOW BOWL

Fenton introduced this large shallow bowl in Milk in 1961. Although it was listed as a 9½" bowl, it actually measures slightly over 10" in diameter. The bowl is 3½" high and has a pie crust crimped top edge.

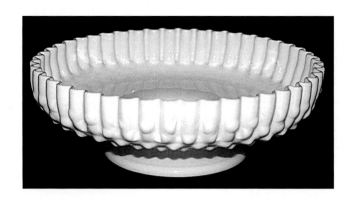

No. 3622 Bowl	Introduced	Discontinued	Value
Milk	1961	1969	$50.00 – 55.00

NO. 3322-10" CRIMPED BOWL

Fenton introduced a new 10" diameter crimped Hobnail bowl into the general line in 2002. The bowl was removed from the line in 2005, after three years of production.

No. 3322 Bowl	Introduced	Discontinued	Value
Cranberry	2002	2005	$35.00 – 45.00

NO. 3731-10" FOOTED BOWL

This 10" diameter double crimped bowl has a ribbed stem. The bowl is 7" high and was made in numerous colors beginning in July 1959. Jonquil Yellow was made in the 1960s and was not in the regular line.

No. 3731 Bowl	Introduced	Discontinued	Value
Blue Marble	1970	1974	$55.00 – 65.00
Blue Opalescent	July 1959	1962	$125.00 – 145.00
Green Opalescent	July 1959	July 1961	$125.00 – 150.00
Jonquil Yellow	1968	1969	$110.00 – 125.00
Milk	July 1959	1980	$30.00 – 35.00
Plum Opalescent	July 1959	1964	$185.00 – 210.00
Topaz Opalescent	July 1959	July 1960	$125.00 – 150.00

Blue Opalescent

Blue Marble

NO. 3623-10½" BOWL

This low footed 10½" diameter bowl has sides that flare out at about a 45 degree angle. The bowl was made in milk beginning in 1961. It is 4½" high and has a pie crust crimped top edge.

No. 3623 Bowl	Introduced	Discontinued	Value
Milk	1961	1965	$80.00 – 90.00

NO. 3723-10½" FOOTED BOWL

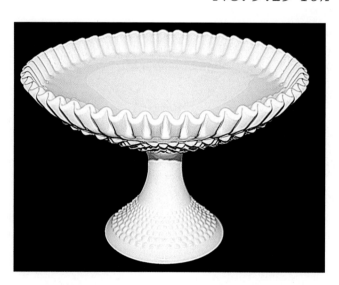

Fenton's No. 3723 large 10½" footed bowl has a cupped pie crust crimped edge. This bowl is 7" high. It has hobs on the bowl and on the foot. The stem is plain. This bowl is similar to the earlier No. 389-11" bowl made in blue opalescent and French opalescent. See page 70.

No. 3723 Bowl	Introduced	Discontinued	Value
Milk	1957	1978	$35.00 – 45.00
Topaz Opalescent	1959	1960	$150.00 – 185.00

NO. 3624-10½" FOOTED DC BOWL

Starting in 1961, Fenton made a 10½" footed bowl with a double crimped top edge. This bowl is 5" high and has a plain foot. This bowl was also made in milk with a holly decoration in 1971.

No. 3624 Bowl	Introduced	Discontinued	Value
Milk	1957	1978	$30.00 – 32.00
Decorated Holly	1971	1972	$55.00 – 65.00

NO. 3705 11" HANGING BOWL

This hanging bowl came packaged with brass chains, hooks, and a mounting assembly so it could be attached to a ceiling or wall. It was introduced into the regular Fenton line in milk and Topaz Opalescent in mid-1959. Notice this bowl was only produced in Topaz Opalescent for six months.

No. 3705 Bowl	Introduced	Discontinued	Value
Milk	July 1959	1968	$140.00 – 160.00
Topaz Opalescent	July 1959	1960	$300.00 – 325.00

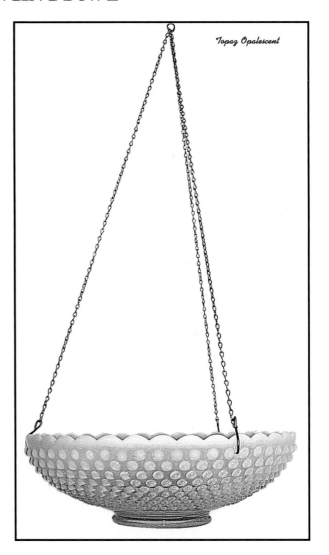

Topaz Opalescent

NO. 3824-11" DC BOWL

Ruby Overlay

This large double crimped bowl entered the Fenton line in 1940 and was made in three colors until the mid-1950s. This bowl was used as the centerpiece for the No. 3804 console set. The 3-piece console set was produced by combining two No. 3974 candleholders with this bowl. Console sets were only offered in Blue Opalescent and French Opalescent since the candlestick was not made in Cranberry. This bowl was made as part of an assortment in Ruby Overlay. In the early years of Hobnail production, the double crimped Hobnail bowl that became the No. 3824-11" bowl was also made with other styles of crimping. Other shapes for this size bowl include flared, oval, and triangular.

No. 3824 Bowl	Introduced	Discontinued	Value
Blue Opalescent	1940	1954	$60.00 – 65.00
Cranberry	1940	1955	$80.00 – 90.00
French Opalescent	1940	1955	$45.00 – 50.00
Ruby Overlay	1943		$65.00 – 75.00
Topaz Opalescent	July 1941	1944	$95.00 – 120.00
Violet Opalescent	1942	1945	$90.00 – 110.00

NO. 389-11" SHALLOW FOOTED BOWL

This early version of an 11" footed bowl that was made from the cake stand mold is less flared than the later version. This style just has the cake stand sides cupped upward with a pie crust crimped rim to form a shallow bowl. This shape bowl was produced until the end of 1943. When production from this mold resumed in 1948, the bowl was deeper (see below) and this version of the bowl evolved into the No. 3923 style.

Blue Opalescent

No. 389-11" Bowl	Introduced	Discontinued	Value
Blue Opalescent	July 1941	1943	$125.00 – 145.00
French Opalescent	July 1941	1943	$80.00 – 95.00
Topaz Opalescent	July 1941	1944	$100.00 – 145.00

NO. 3923-11" FOOTED DC BOWL

Blue Opalescent

This large footed bowl was made from the same mold as the large 13" footed cake plate. The bowl flares upward and is double crimped. There are hobs on both the top of the foot and the outside of the bowl.

No. 3923 Bowl	Introduced	Discontinued	Value
Blue Opalescent	1948	1955	$125.00 – 145.00
French Opalescent	1948	1955	$80.00 – 95.00

NO. 3938-12" DC BOWL

Fenton's No. 3938-12" double crimped bowl first appeared in the regular line in milk during July 1960. It was discontinued at the end of 1989, but was made again for another two years beginning in 1991. The Blue Slag "Almost Heaven" bowl shown below was made for the Fenton Gift Shop. In the 1980s, it was made in Blue Opalescent with mother-of-pearl iridescence (IQ) and Plum Opalescent (PO) for The Levay Distributing Company. This bowl was used with the C3000 pitcher and bowl sets made for QVC in Dusty Rose Iridescent with Teal trim (DO) and in Shell Pink Iridescent with Salem Blue trim (YK). A Persian Pearl (XV) bowl was made in the last half of 1992 as part of Fenton's Historic Collection.

No. 3938 Bowl	Introduced	Discontinued	Value
Dusty Rose Iridescent			
w/Teal trim	1988	1989	$55.00 – 65.00
Milk	July 1960	1990*	$35.00 – 40.00
Persian Pearl	July 1992	1993	$50.00 – 60.00
Plum Opalescent	1984	1984	$225.00 – 250.00
Shell Pink Iridescent			
w/Salem Blue trim	1990	1990	$55.00 – 65.00

*Also in the line in 1991 and 1992.

No. 3938 Bowl	Introduced	Discontinued	Value
Blue Slag	1988	1988	$85.00 – 95.00
Blue Opalescent with MOP Iridescence	1980	1980	$75.00 – 85.00

Blue Slag "Almost Heaven"

NO. 3739-12" CELERY

Fenton introduced this 12" handled celery into the regular line in July 1959. The celery is 2" high and 6¼" wide, and has no inside division. This same shape bowl may also be found with divisions as a 3-part relish.

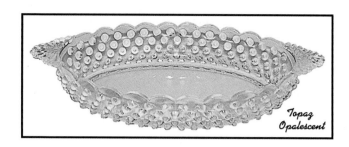

Topaz Opalescent

No. 3739 Celery	Introduced	Discontinued	Value
Milk	July 1959	1963	$60.00 – 70.00
Topaz Opalescent	July 1959	1960	$200.00 – 225.00

NO. 3740-12" DIVIDED RELISH

Milk

This 12" long bowl is a 3-part divided relish. It is 6¼" wide and 2" high. There are hobs on the tab handles and the top edge of the bowl is scalloped. There is one long section convenient for celery on one side. The other half of the bowl is split into two equal partitions.

No. 3740-12" Divided relish	Introduced	Discontinued	Value
French Opalescent			$100.00 – 150.00
Glossy Custard			$25.00 – 30.00
Milk	July 1959	July 1982	$25.00 – 30.00
Topaz Opalescent	July 1959	1960	$225.00 – 250.00

NO. 3922 CHIP 'N DIP

Fenton produced only this large 2-handled, 1-piece chip 'n dip bowl in 1970. The bowl is 12¼" in diameter and 3¼" high. The body of the bowl has 12 paneled sections and the top edge is scalloped. The inside of the bowl has a division that separates the chips from the dip. This curved division has been found with both a smooth and a scalloped top edge. Fenton had production problems with this large piece. As a result few bowls were made and the piece was discontinued after one year.

No. 3922 Chip 'n dip	Introduced	Discontinued	Value
Milk	1970	1971	$600.00 – 700.00

NO. 3720 FOOTED BANANA BOWL

Fenton's footed banana bowl was in the regular line in milk and Topaz Opalescent. It was also made in a pink opalescent color for the Fenton Collector's Extravaganza. The bowl was also made in a number of colors for The Levay Distributing Company during the 1980s. This later issue has the oval Fenton logo on the bottom. Therefore, collectors are able to easily distinguish between the two issues of topaz opalescent. The bowl is 12½" long and 7" high and has a pie crust crimped edge. Many of these banana stands will be found with a slightly twisted stem. However, there is a variation with a sharply defined twist in the stem. See the photo below.

Footed banana bowl	Introduced	Discontinued	Value
Milk	July 1959	1984	$25.00 – 35.00
Topaz Opalescent	1959	July 1960	$150.00 – 185.00
Pink Opalescent	1988	1989	$65.00 – 75.00

Colors for Levay	Produced	Value
Aqua Opalescent Carnival	1982	$100.00 – 125.00
Blue Opalescent	1982	$125.00 – 150.00
Plum Opalescent	1984	$295.00 – 310.00
Topaz Opalescent	1980	$225.00 – 250.00

Milk with Twist Stem

Plum Opalescent

NO. 3620 LOW BANANA BOWL

The low banana bowl is 12" long and 5" high. This bowl has a pie crust crimped edge and a low foot. This bowl was only in the line in milk. The Topaz Opalescent piece shown below is a sample piece, courtesy of the Fenton Art Glass Museum.

Low banana bowl	Introduced	Discontinued	Value
Milk	1961	1979	$25.00 – 35.00
Topaz Opalescent			UND

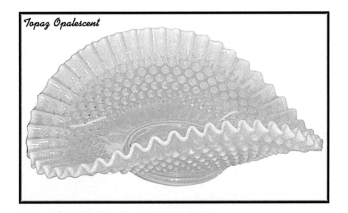

Topaz Opalescent

Milk

BOOTS AND SLIPPERS

NO. 3992 BOOT

Fenton's No. 3992 boot was introduced into the general line in Milk in 1971. Since that time boots have been produced in numerous colors and some have been hand-painted. The boots are 4¼" high and 3¾" long. The underside of the boot has indented areas on both the heel and sole. The boot shown to the right is hand-painted with roses and forget-me-nots on burmese satin and was produced in 2000 as part of a collection designed for QVC. This Victorian Glass Shoe Signature Collection consisted of a combination of 12 decorated boots, shoes, and slippers, each with the signature of a family member. This boot was signed by George Fenton. Another boot was a decorated iridescent aquamarine color with the signature of Frank M. Fenton.

No. 3992 Boot	Introduced	Discontinued	Value
Amber			$18.00 – 20.00
Aquamarine Iridescent			
HP (QVC)	February 2000	2000	$70.00 – 80.00
Black			$25.00 – 30.00
Blue Burmese	1983	1983	$40.00 – 45.00
Burmese (Glossy)	2000	2000	$35.00 – 45.00
Burmese Satin			
HP (QVC)	February 2000	2000	$60.00 – 70.00
Emerald Green	July 2001	2002	$12.00 – 15.00
French Opal			$22.00 – 27.00
Jade			$25.00 – 30.00

No. 3992 Boot	Introduced	Discontinued	Value
Milk Glass	1971	1985	$16.00 – 18.00
Periwinkle Blue			$22.00 – 27.00
Pink Chiffon	2001	2003	$12.00 – 15.00
Rosalene			$40.00 – 45.00

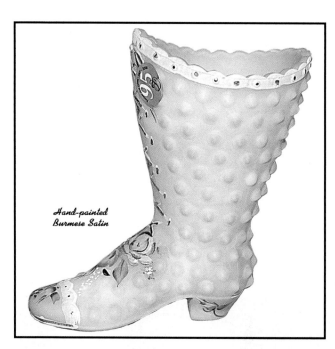

Hand-painted Burmese Satin

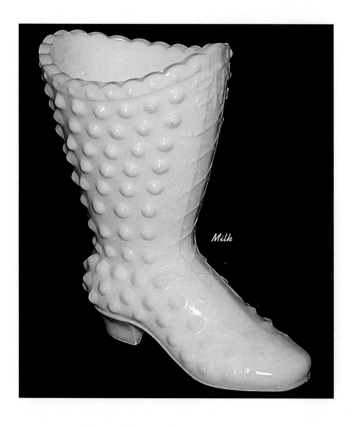

Milk

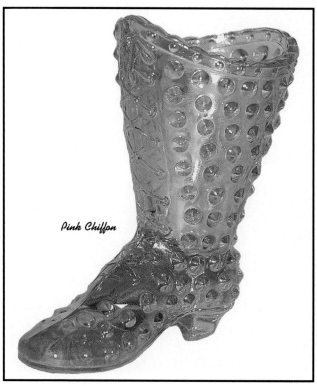

Pink Chiffon

NO. 3995 SLIPPER

Fenton's "kitten head" slipper was introduced in 1941. Since that time it has been made in just about every color imaginable. It has been in the general line, produced for the Fenton Gift Shop, made as a special order item, and made for QVC. The slipper is about 5½" long. It has a solid heel and toe. Purple Slag (PS) and Chocolate (CK) slippers were made in the 1980s for The Levay Distributing Company. Production for QVC included a number of hand-painted slippers. A pink and purple rose hand-painted slipper in Twilight Blue Iridescent was made for the June 1992 QVC program. Later that year, in October, a Green Carnival slipper was decorated with burgundy and white roses. A Rosalene Satin slipper was hand painted with pink roses for the October 1993 show. In October 1997, an Iridized Topaz Opalescent slipper with a hand painted green, blue, and mauve floral decoration was offered to QVC customers. Black slippers with hand-painted daisies were made for the October 2003 program.

No. 3995 Slipper	Introduced	Discontinued	Value
Amber	1962	1980	$11.00 – 13.00
Black HP	2003	2003	$25.00 – 30.00
Blue Marble	1970	1974	$20.00 – 22.00

No. 3995 Slipper	Introduced	Discontinued	Value
Blue Opalescent	1941	1955*	$18.00 – 24.00
Blue Pastel	1954	1955	$25.00 – 35.00
Blue Satin Opal			$20.00 – 25.00
Blue Slag	1988	1988	$30.00 – 40.00
Champagne	2000	2001	$20.00 – 25.00
Chocolate	1982	1982	$50.00 – 60.00
Colonial Blue	1964	July 1979	$18.00 – 20.00
Colonial Green	1964	July 1977	$10.00 – 14.00
Colonial Pink	1967	July 1969	$18.00 – 22.00
Crystal	1968	1969	$6.00 – 8.00
French Opalescent	1941	1956	$14.00 – 18.00
Green Carnival HP	1992	1992	$35.00 – 45.00
Green Opalescent	1969	July 1961	$30.00 – 35.00
Green Pastel	1954	1956	$25.00 – 35.00
Milk	1950	1990**	$15.00 – 18.00
Orange	1964	July 1978	$18.00 – 20.00
Plum	1984	1984	$30.00 – 40.00
Purple Slag	1981	1981	$50.00 – 60.00
Rosalene Satin with HP Roses	1993	1993	$45.00 – 55.00
Rose Pastel	1954	1957	$20.00 – 25.00
Ruby	1966	1980***	$15.00 – 17.00
Springtime Green	1977	1979	$18.00 – 22.00
Topaz Opalescent	1960	1962†	$30.00 – 35.00
Topaz Opalescent Iridescent HP	1997	1997	$30.00 – 35.00
Topaz Satin Opal			$20.00 – 25.00
Turquoise	1955	1957	$20.00 – 25.00
Twilight Blue Carnival HP	1992	1992	$30.00 – 35.00

*Reissued from July 1959 through 1964.
**Reintroduced from 1991 through 1995.
***Also produced from July 1987 through 1989.
†Also made for Levay in 1980.

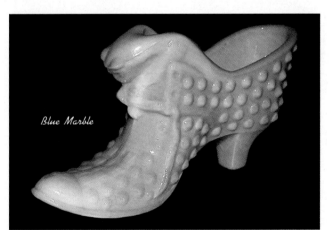
Blue Marble

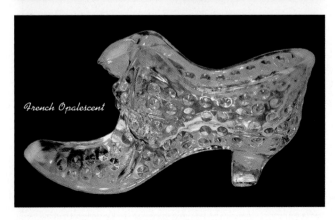
French Opalescent

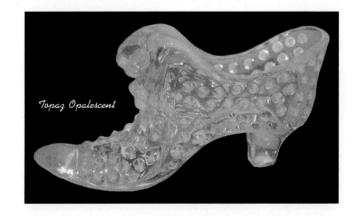
Topaz Opalescent

BUTTER DISHES

NO. 3977 QUARTER-POUND BUTTER

Fenton's first Hobnail covered quarter-pound butter was introduced in mid-year 1954. This rectangular butter is 7½" long, 3¾" wide, and 2¾" high. Only the bottom has scallops around the outside edge, and the corners are rounded. The lid has an all-over pattern of hobs. The original colors were blue opalescent, French Opalescent, and Milk. Blue Opalescent was only made for six months. At the end of the decade the butter was made in Colonial Amber for one year.

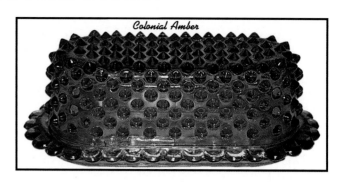

Colonial Amber

Blue Opalescent

No. 3977 Butter	Introduced	Discontinued	Value
Colonial Amber	1959	1960	$25.00 – 35.00
Blue Opalescent	July 1954	1955	$300.00 – 350.00
French Opalescent	July 1954	1956	$140.00 – 160.00
Milk	July 1954	1978	$25.00 – 30.00

NO. 3777 OVAL QUARTER-POUND BUTTER

Milk

An oval covered quarter-pound butter was introduced in milk in 1963. This butter is 7½" long and 3½" high to the top of the tab-like hob covered knob. The butter was discontinued in milk at the end of 1989. However, it reentered the line for another two years starting in 1991.

No. 3777 Butter	Introduced	Discontinued	Value
Crystal	1968	1969	$10.00 – 12.00
Milk	1963	1990*	$20.00 – 28.00

*Also 1991 and 1992.

NO. 3677 COVERED BUTTER AND CHEESE

Fenton's round covered butter was only in the regular line in milk. This butter is 8" in diameter and 5" high. The bottom plate is scalloped and curves slightly upward. There are hobs on the bottom of the plate. The dome-shaped lid has rows of hobs on the outside and is topped with a beaded knob. During the early 1980s, this butter was made in Blue Opalescent and Topaz Opalescent for The Levay Distributing Company.

Blue Opalescent

No. 3977 Butter	Introduced	Discontinued	Value
Blue Opalescent	1982	1982	$220.00 – 240.00
Milk	1961	1968	$150.00 – 175.00
Topaz Opalescent	1980	1980	$250.00 – 300.00

CANDLE BOWLS AND CANDLEHOLDERS

NO. 3873-4" MINIATURE CANDLE BOWL

Fenton's 4" diameter miniature candle bowl was introduced into the line in 1969. It can accommodate 1", 2", or 3" candles. The bowl is 3½" high and has a scalloped top edge. This candle bowl was made in Colonial Amber, Colonial Blue, Colonial Green, and Milk. The same ware number was used for Fenton's oval ashtray during the early 1950s.

Colonial Blue

No. 3873-4" Candle bowl	Introduced	Discontinued	Value
Colonial Amber	1969	July 1972	$12.00 – 15.00
Colonial Blue	1969	July 1972	$18.00 – 22.00
Colonial Green	1969	July 1972	$12.00 – 14.00
Milk	1969	1977	$20.00 – 25.00

NO. 3872-6" CANDLE BOWL

This candle bowl shares its ware number with a fan-shaped ashtray that was discontinued in the mid-1950s. It is 8-paneled, measures 6½" in diameter and 4" high, and has 16 scallops on the top edge. The candle bowl will accept ½", 1", 2", and 3" candles. This candle bowl was also used extensively with flower arrangements during the 1970s. Scented candles and floral rings were included with the candle bowl. These were marketed in an attractive gift box and the colors were coordinated with the seasons. This candle bowl also appeared in the 1988 and 1989 Gracious Touch catalogs in Sapphire Blue Opalescent with a candle and flower ring (No. Q3309 BX).

No. 3872 Candle bowl	Introduced	Discontinued	Value
Black	July 1968	1975	$18.00 – 20.00
Blue	1975	1977	$15.00 – 18.00
Blue Marble	1970	1974	$22.00 – 27.00
Colonial Amber	July 1968	1979	$10.00 – 15.00
Colonial Blue	1969	1980	$14.00 – 18.00
Colonial Green	July 1968	1977	$10.00 – 15.00
Custard (Glossy)	July 1973	1977	$15.00 – 18.00
Lime (Glossy)	1975	1977	$18.00 – 20.00
Milk	July 1968	1988	$14.00 – 18.00
Ruby			$20.00 – 22.00
Sapphire Blue Opalescent	1988	1990	$16.00 – 18.00

Blue Marble

Ruby

NO. 3971 FOOTED CANDLE BOWL

This candle bowl was designed to take either taper or pillar candles. It measures approximately 4¾" high and is 7" in diameter. Fenton also used this same ware number for the Hobnail miniature cornucopia candleholder that was made through the mid-1950s. The Willow Green Opalescent Iridized Hobnail candle bowl was made for QVC in 2000 and the Violet Iridized color candle bowl was made for QVC in 2002.

Blue Opalescent

No. 3971 Candle bowl	Introduced	Discontinued	Value
Blue Opalescent	1978	1979	$45.00 – 50.00
Milk	1978	1980	$20.00 – 25.00
Violet Iridescent	2002	2002	$35.00 – 40.00
Willow Green Opalescent Iridized	2000	2000	$30.00 – 35.00

NO. 3771 CANDLE BOWL

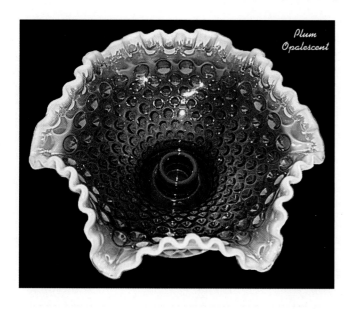

Plum Opalescent

Fenton's No. 3771 candle bowl flares out much like a comport. It is 3¾" high, 8" in diameter, and features a double crimped top edge. The candle bowl was introduced into the regular line in July 1959.

No. 3771 Candle bowl	Introduced	Discontinued	Value
Blue Opalescent	July 1959	1961	$45.00 – 50.00
Green Opalescent	July 1959	1960	$55.00 – 65.00
Milk	July 1959	1969	$20.00 – 25.00
Plum Opalescent	July 1959	July 1961	$110.00 – 125.00
Topaz Opalescent	July 1959	July 1960	$75.00 – 90.00

NO. 3748 CHIP 'N DIP CANDLE BOWL

Fenton's large No. 3748-9½" chip 'n dip candle bowl entered the regular line in milk in January 1973. The bowl has 15 panels and 15 scallops around the top edge. This piece doubles as the bottom to the 3-piece No. 3742 centerpiece set.

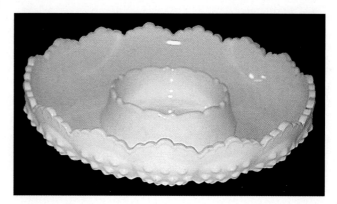

No. 3748 Chip 'n dip candle bowl	Introduced	Discontinued	Value
Milk	1973	1976	$22.00 – 27.00

NO. 3670 LOW CANDLEHOLDER

This round flat candleholder was made in milk during the 1960s. It is 2" high and 5" in diameter. It has a scalloped top edge and thumbprints around the base. It is the same as the No. 3630 bonbon except for the addition of the candle receptacle.

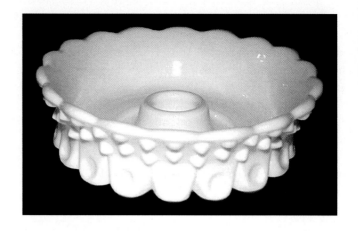

No. 3670 Candleholder	Introduced	Discontinued	Value
Milk	1961	1969	$15.00 – 18.00

NO. 3770 CANDLEHOLDER

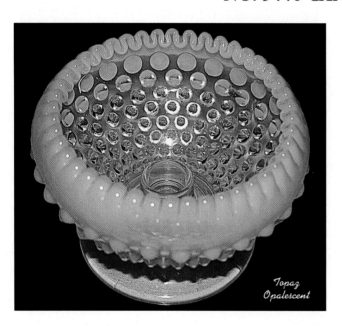

Topaz Opalescent

This footed candleholder is shaped like a cupped comport. It has a ribbon crimped top edge and is 3½" high and 6" in diameter. The Topaz Opalescent color was only made for one year and is not easily found.

No. 3770 Candleholder	Introduced	Discontinued	Value
Milk	July 1959	1965	$40.00 – 50.00
Topaz Opalescent	July 1959	July 1960	$65.00 – 75.00

NO. 3870 HANDLED CANDLEHOLDER

Fenton's No. 3870 handled candleholder was introduced into the line in 1953. The colors produced were Cranberry and milk. The candleholder is 3" high and 4" in diameter without the handle.

No. 3870 Candleholder	Introduced	Discontinued	Value
Cranberry	1953	1978	$55.00 – 65.00
Milk	1953	1974	$22.00 – 25.00
Ruby Overlay	1968	1969	$45.00 – 55.00

Cranberry

NO. 3974 CANDLEHOLDER

Two styles of this short footed candleholder may be found. The early version that was made until the end of 1954 is 3" high and has a flat base. Candleholders produced after the beginning of 1955 are 3½" high and have a dome-shaped base. Both styles are illustrated in the photos below. The Ruby candle was made later and has the dome-style base. The Green Opalescent and Topaz Opalescent candles have a flat base. Jonquil Yellow and Pekin Blue II were made in the 1960s. Most of these examples were sold through the Fenton Gift Shop.

No. 3974 Candleholder	Introduced	Discontinued	Value
Amber	1959	July 1959	$9.00 – 12.00
Blue Marble	1970	July 1972	$14.00 – 16.00
Blue Opalescent	1941	1955*	$25.00 – 27.00
Blue Pastel	July 1954	1955	$20.00 – 25.00
Cranberry	1953	1978	$55.00 – 65.00
Decorated Holly	July 1971	1972	$15.00 – 20.00
French Opalescent	1941	1955	$18.00 – 20.00
Green Opalescent	July 1959	July 1961	$30.00 – 40.00
Green Pastel	1955	1956	$20.00 – 25.00
Jonquil Yellow	1968	1969	$20.00 – 25.00
Milk	1951	1990**	$10.00 – 12.00
Pekin Blue II	1968	1969	$20.00 – 25.00
Plum Opalescent	July 1959	1963	$45.00 – 55.00
Rose Pastel	1955	1957	$20.00 – 22.00
Ruby	1972	July 1985	$14.00 – 16.00
Ruby Satin	1982	1982	$32.00 – 37.00
Topaz Opalescent	1959	1961***	$35.00 – 45.00
Turquoise	1955	1955	$20.00 – 22.00

*Reissued in both 1955 and 1978.

**Also made from January 1991 through December 1993.

***Also made for Levay in 1980.

Green Opalescent

Topaz Opalescent

Ruby

NO. 3874 CORNUCOPIA CANDLEHOLDER

Fenton's No. 3874 large cornucopia candleholder entered the regular line in 1943 in Blue Opalescent and French Opalescent. It is 6½" high and 4¼" long. The candleholder has a plain oval base and a pie crust crimped top edge. This candleholder was also made in Topaz Opalescent for Levay in 1983. Other colors that have been found include Green Opalescent and Green Transparent.

No. 3874 Candleholder	Introduced	Discontinued	Value
Blue Opalescent	1943	1954	$45.00 – 65.00
French Opalescent	1943	1954	$40.00 – 45.00
Green Opalescent			$55.00 – 65.00
Green Transparent			$30.00 – 40.00
Milk	July 1953	1965	$25.00 – 30.00
Topaz Opalescent	1983	1983	$50.00 – 60.00

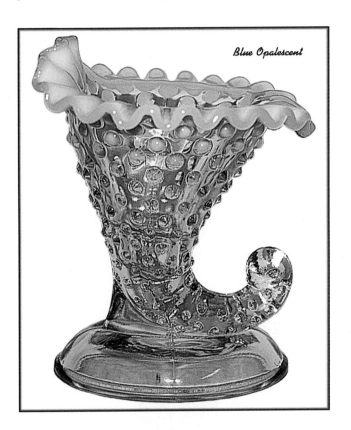

Blue Opalescent

Green Opalescent

NO. 3672-2-LITE CANDLEHOLDER

This milk glass 2-lite candleholder is 8½" wide and 5½" high. Fenton introduced this candleholder into the regular line in 1961. It was discontinued at the end of 1970.

No. 3672 Candleholder	Introduced	Discontinued	Value
Milk	1961	1971	$25.00 – 38.00

NO. 3774-10" CANDLEHOLDER

Fenton's No. 3774 candleholder is 10" tall and has a 4¾" diameter base. The candleholder was introduced in Milk in 1958. It was made in amber during the first half of 1959.

No. 3774 Candleholder	Introduced	Discontinued	Value
Amber	1959	July 1959	$40.00 – 50.00
Milk	1958	1971	$22.00 – 27.00

COMPORT CANDLEHOLDER

Fenton's No. 3728 footed double crimped comport was used to produce this candlestick. The candlestick is 5½" tall and 6½" in diameter. Examples of this candlestick have been found in Blue Opalescent and Milk. This shape candlestick was not part of the general line. It has been labeled as A-018 in the book *Pictorial Review of Fenton's White Hobnail Milk Glass* by Shirley Griffith.

Comport Candleholder	Value
Blue Opalescent	$125.00 – 150.00
Milk	$40.00 – 45.00

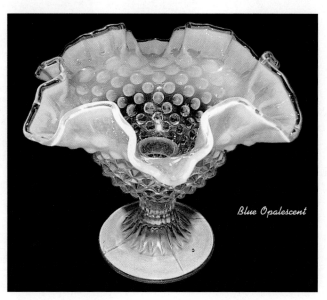

81

NO. 3775-4" CANDLEHOLDER

Fenton's No. 3775-4" high candleholder was made in milk glass. It has four panels around the top and eight panels around the dome-shaped base. Both the top and base have scalloped edges. This ware number was also used for the vanity tray produced during the 1960s.

No. 3775 Candleholder	Introduced	Discontinued	Value
Milk	1972	1977	$20.00 – 28.00

NO. 3674-6" CANDLEHOLDER

The Blue Slag candle shown in the photo was produced for the Fenton Gift Shop. This color was named "Almost Heaven" by Bill Fenton. Persian Pearl candleholders were made as a part of the Historical Collection in 1992. Sapphire Blue Opalescent candleholders were made for QVC in June 1990.

No. 3674 Candleholder	Introduced	Discontinued	Value
Blue Slag	1988	1988	$60.00 – 75.00
Crystal	1968	1969	$6.00 – 8.00
Decorated Holly	July 1971	1972	$30.00 – 35.00
Milk	1961	1990	$18.00 – 22.00
Persian Pearl	July 1992	1993	$22.00 – 27.00
Sapphire Blue Opalescent	1990	1990	$22.00 – 27.00

Blue Slag "Almost Heaven"

Crystal

Milk

NO. 3745-7" CANDLEHOLDER

This Milk candleholder is 7¼" tall. It has a round, dome-shaped 5" diameter base with eight panels. The stem and outside of the candle cup are covered with hobs. This candleholder was also used for the middle part of the No. 3742-3-piece centerpiece set.

No. 3745 Candleholder	Introduced	Discontinued	Value
Milk	1973	1976	$28.00 – 32.00

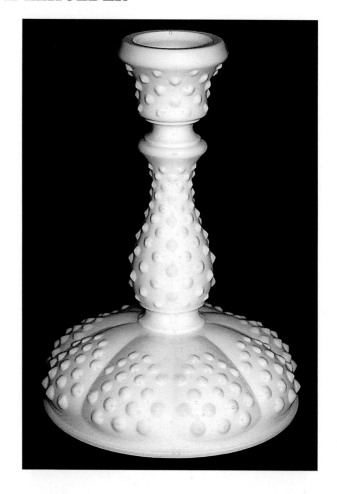

NO. 3746 CANDLE EPERGNE

This candle epergne was designed as the top part of the 3-piece centerpiece set with ware No. 3742. The 6" diameter epergne is paneled and has 12 scallops at the top. There are six ¾" divisions surrounding the central candle hole. The bottom of the candle epergne has a peg that fits into the top of the No. 3745-7" candleholder.

No. 3746 Candle epergne	Introduced	Discontinued	Value
Milk	1973	1976	$25.00 – 30.00

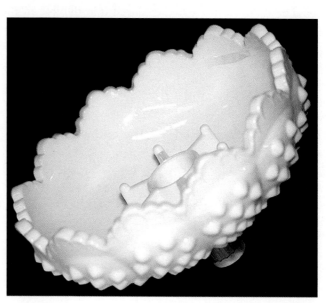

NO. 3678 CRESCENT CANDLEHOLDER

This 8" canoe-shaped candleholder is 2¾" high and 2½" wide. It has five rows of hobs on each side and a finely scalloped top edge. There are four small feet on the bottom. This candleholder is the same as the No. 3798 planter except for the addition of a candle receptacle to the inside center of the base.

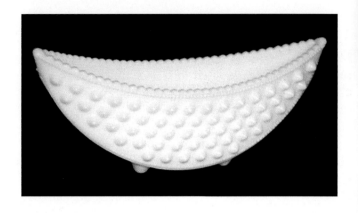

No. 3678 Candleholder	Introduced	Discontinued	Value
Milk	1962	1963	$65.00 – 75.00

NO. 3673 FOOTED CANDLEHOLDER

Fenton's No. 3673 footed candleholder was introduced in Milk in 1962. It is a round candleholder that is 2¾" high and 4¼" in diameter. It has a scalloped top edge and thumbprints around the bottom of the candle bowl.

No. 3673 Candleholder	Introduced	Discontinued	Value
Milk	1962	1976	$18.00 – 22.00

NO. 3971 MINIATURE CORNUCOPIA CANDLEHOLDER

This miniature cornucopia-shaped candleholder is 3½" high and 2¾" long. It has a plain oval base and a smooth top edge. The candleholder was introduced into the line in Blue Opalescent and French Opalescent in July 1941. It was produced in milk during the 1950s. Later, the same ware number was used for a footed 7½" diameter candle bowl that was made in the 1970s.

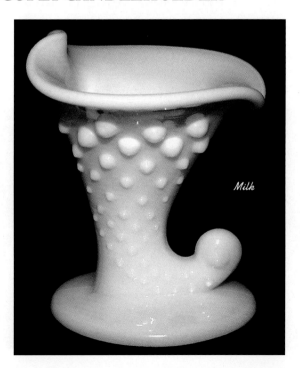

Milk

No. 3971 Candleholder	Introduced	Discontinued	Value
Blue Opalescent	July 1941	1955	$40.00 – 45.00
French Opalescent	July 1941	1956	$15.00 – 20.00
Milk	1950	1957	$35.00 – 45.00

COMPORTS

NO. 3825 SHERBET

This 4" tall footed sherbet entered the Fenton line in 1940. The sherbet is 3¾" in diameter. It has a plain foot and a shallow bowl that has nine rows of hobs. The stem is spiral and covered with hobs. Crystal sherbets were only listed in the catalog for the first year. Turquoise sherbets were not in the regular line. They were probably sampled in the mid-1950s. French Opalescent sherbets with a pie crust crimped top edge (T3824) were made for the Bismark Hotel of Chicago, Illinois, in mid-1953. Blue Opalescent and Aqua Opalescent Carnival sherbets were made for The Levay Distributing Company in 1982. These were produced to complement the No. 3611 champagne punch set.

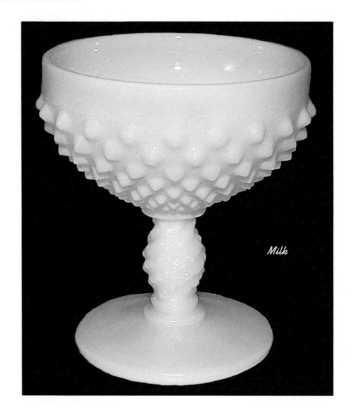

Milk

No. 3825 Sherbet	Introduced	Discontinued	Value
Aqua Opalescent Carnival	1982	1982	$20.00 – 25.00
Blue Opalescent	1940	1955*	$20.00 – 25.00
Crystal	1940	1941	$4.00 – 5.00
French Opalescent	1940	1965	$10.00 – 12.00**
Milk	1954	1968	$7.00 – 9.00
Topaz Opalescent	1941	1944	$25.00 – 35.00
Turquoise			$22.00 – 25.00

*Also made for Levay in 1982.
**with crimped top, $20.00 – 25.00

NO. 3826 SQUARE SHERBET

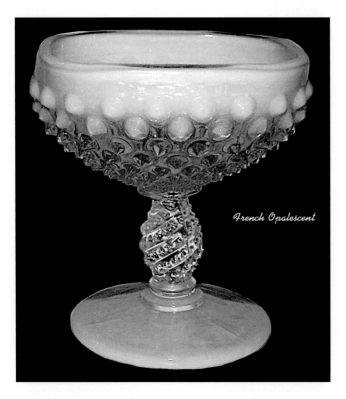

French Opalescent

Fenton introduced a square dinnerware service in the early 1950s in Blue Opalescent and French Opalescent colors. The sherbet has a plain round foot and a spiral stem with hobs. The sherbet bowl is square with rounded corners. The side of the bowl has seven rows of hobs.

No. 3826 Sherbet	Introduced	Discontinued	Value
Blue Opalescent	1951	1954	$40.00 – 45.00
French Opalescent	1951	1955	$25.00 – 30.00

NO. 3725 JELLY DISH

The No. 3725-5½" tall footed jelly dish was made in Milk from 1958 through 1957. The foot is plain, but the stem and bowl are covered with hobs. The diameter of the bowl is 4¾" and the top edge has six deep crimps.

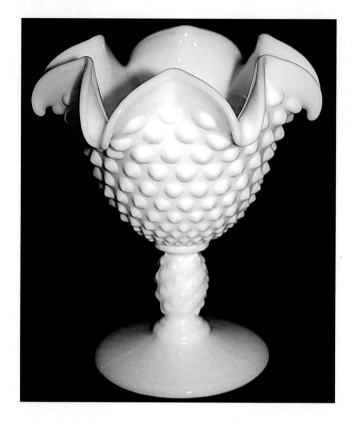

No. 3725 Jelly dish	Introduced	Discontinued	Value
Milk	1958	1968	$32.00 – 42.00

NO. 3629 FOOTED NUT DISH

Fenton's small Milk footed nut dish debuted in the regular line in 1961. This double crimped comport is 5" tall and 5½" in diameter. The foot is round and plain. The sides of the comport and the stem are covered with hobs.

No. 3629 Nut dish	Introduced	Discontinued	Value
Milk	1962	1978	$14.00 – 16.00

NO. 3627 FOOTED PEANUT DISH

This small footed peanut dish was in the general line in Milk. The comport measures 6" in diameter and is 5½" tall. It has a pie crust crimped top edge and a plain octagonal-shaped stem.

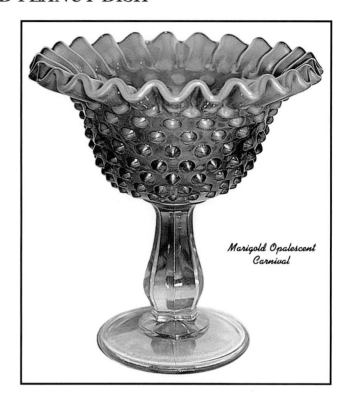

Marigold Opalescent Carnival

No. 3627 Peanut dish	Introduced	Discontinued	Value
Marigold Opalescent Carnival			$30.00 – 35.00
Milk	1962	1978	$15.00 – 18.00

NO. 3628-6" FOOTED COMPORT

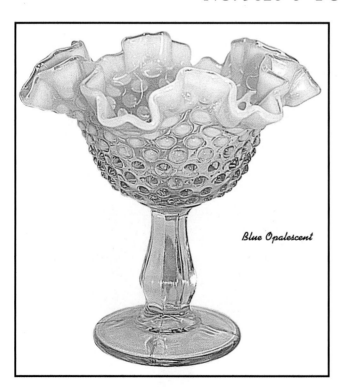

Blue Opalescent

Fenton's 6" tall, double crimped No. 3628 comport was introduced into the regular line in January 1962. This comport is 5½" in diameter and has an octagonal-shaped stem that connects to a plain round foot. Milk versions of this comport were hand painted with the Decorated Holly (DH) and Decorated Roses (RW) patterns during the mid-1970s.

No. 3628 Comport	Introduced	Discontinued	Value
Blue Marble	1970	1974	$27.00 – 30.00
Blue Opalescent	July 1978	1983	$40.00 – 45.00
Cameo Opalescent	July 1979	1982	$20.00 – 25.00
Carnival	1980	1981	$30.00 – 35.00
Colonial Amber	1969	1981	$9.00 – 12.00
Colonial Blue	1975	1981	$16.00 – 18.00
Colonial Green	1969	1977	$10.00 – 12.00
Decorated Holly	July 1973	1974	$35.00 – 38.00
Decorated Roses	1974	July 1975	$35.00 – 38.00
Milk	1962	1990	$14.00 – 16.00
Orange	1969	1978	$12.00 – 14.00
Ruby	1972	1980*	$20.00 – 25.00
Ruby Satin	1982		$30.00 – 35.00
Springtime Green	1977	1979	$22.00 – 27.00

*Also sold as Q3628-RU as a hostess gift for Gracious Touch in 1989.

NO. 389-6" COMPORT

Fenton's footed 6" low Hobnail comport was in the line in opalescent colors during the early 1940s. This comport has a flared body with a smooth top edge. It has a plain round foot that is attached to the body via a short stem. Crimped shapes were flared and triangular. The 8" footed plate comport is the flat version of this shape.

French Opalescent

No. 389 Comport	Introduced	Discontinued	Value
Blue Opalescent	July 1941	1943	$40.00 – 50.00*
French Opalescent	July 1941	1943	$25.00 – 30.00*
Topaz Opalescent	July 1941	1943	$55.00 – 75.00*

*Double price for plate shape.

NO. 3728 COMPORT

Blue Opalescent

The No. 3728 comport was made in Milk and several opalescent colors. This comport is 6½" wide and 5½" tall. It has a double crimped top and is footed with a ribbed stem.

No. 3728 Comport	Introduced	Discontinued	Value
Blue Opalescent	July 1959	1965	$40.00 – 45.00
Green Opalescent	July 1959	July 1961	$38.00 – 42.00
Milk	1956	1983	$18.00 – 20.00
Plum Opalescent	July 1959	1964	$65.00 – 85.00
Topaz Opalescent	1959	1961	$65.00 – 75.00

Green Opalescent

Plum Opalescent

NO. 3920 FOOTED COMPORT

This 8" diameter footed comport with large hobs entered the regular Fenton line in 1954 in Milk and pastel opaque colors. In the 1970s the Decorated Blue Bell pattern was hand painted on Milk comports. The comport is 5½" tall. It is double crimped around the top edge and has a plain stem connecting the foot. The foot has four rows of hobs on the top surface. This comport has also been found in several opaque pastel colors decorated with the Abels, Wasserberg & Co. Charleton Roses design.

No. 3920 Comport	Introduced	Discontinued	Value
Amber	1959	July 1959	$30.00 – 35.00
Blue Pastel	1954	1955	$40.00 – 45.00
Decorated Blue Bell	1971	July 1972	$45.00 – 55.00
Green Pastel	1954	1956	$40.00 – 45.00
Milk	1954	1980*	$18.00 – 22.00
Rose Pastel	1954	1958	$35.00 – 40.00
Topaz Opalescent	July 1959	1961	$75.00 – 90.00
Turquoise	1955	1959	$25.00 – 30.00

*Also made in 1987.

Blue Pastel

Topaz Opalescent

NO. 3727-8" COMPORT

Fenton introduced the No. 3727-8" comport into the regular line in 1958. This footed, flared double crimped comport is 3¾" high.

No. 3727 Comport	Introduced	Discontinued	Value
Amber	1959	July 1959	$18.00 – 20.00
Blue Opalescent	1960	1965	$40.00 – 45.00
Green Opalescent	1960	July 1961	$40.00 – 45.00
Milk	1958	1980	$14.00 – 18.00
Plum Opalescent	1960	1964	$100.00 – 125.00
Topaz Opalescent	1959	July 1960	$65.00 – 75.00

Topaz Opalescent

CONDIMENT ITEMS AND SNACK SETS

NO. 3809 CONDIMENT SET

Fenton introduced the No. 3809, 7-piece condiment set into the regular line in the fall of 1950. The set consisted of a No. 3879-7¾" round tray with a chrome center handle that held the following condiment jars: a No. 3869 oil, a No. 3900 individual sugar and creamer, a No. 3806 flat salt and pepper, and a No. 3889 mustard with a flat spoon.

No. 3809 Condiment set	Introduced	Discontinued	Value
Blue Opalescent	Sept. 1950	1954	$170.00 – 205.00
French Opalescent	Sept. 1950	1954	$140.00 – 160.00
Milk	Sept. 1950	1974	$88.00 – 108.00

Blue Opalescent

Milk

NO. 389, 5-PIECE CONDIMENT SET

French Opalescent

Fenton's early 1940s 5-piece condiment set consisted of a 10½" fan tray, a footed salt and pepper, an oil bottle with a stopper, and a covered mustard with a flat spoon.

No. 389 Condiment set	Introduced	Discontinued	Value
Blue Opalescent	1942	1944	$205.00 – 250.00
French Opalescent	1942	1944	$98.00 – 122.00
Topaz Opalescent	1942	1944	$260.00 – 330.00

NO. 3990 KETTLE

Fenton's No. 3990, 3-footed open kettle is 2½" high and 3" in diameter. The side of the kettle has six rows of hobs with small burrs around the base of each hob. Near the top are two small indents where the ends of a small wire handle are placed. The top edge of the kettle has a narrow ribbed collar that flares outward.

No. 3990 Kettle	Introduced	Discontinued	Value
Blue Pastel	1954	1955	$20.00 – 25.00
Green Pastel	1954	1956	$20.00 – 25.00
Milk	1950	1969	$12.00 – 14.00
Rose Pastel	1954	1957	$18.00 – 20.00

NO. 3979 MUSTARD KETTLE

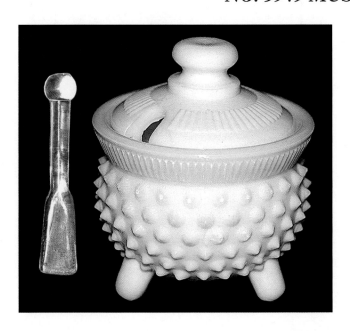

This covered mustard kettle entered the Fenton line in Milk in 1954. The kettle is 3¼" high with the lid. The base of the kettle is the same as that of the No. 3990 kettle. A slotted lid with a knob and a 3" long crystal paddle were included with this kettle. The paddle is the same as the one included with the No. 3889 mustard (see page 92).

No. 3979 Mustard kettle	Introduced	Discontinued	Value
Milk	1954	1967	$14.00 – 16.00

NO. 3803 MAYONNAISE SET

Fenton's No. 3803 mayonnaise set entered the line in opalescent colors in 1948. The set is comprised of three pieces — a 6" crimped underplate, a 4" deep bowl, and a 5" long crystal spoon.

Cranberry

No. 3803 Mayonnaise set	Introduced	Discontinued	Value
Blue Opalescent	1948	1955	$45.00 – 55.00
Cranberry	1948	1957	$90.00 – 110.00
French Opalescent	1948	1957	$25.00 – 28.00
Milk	1950	1984	$20.00 – 25.00

NO. 3605 MUSTARD AND SPOON

This small covered mustard was in the regular Fenton line in Milk during the 1970s. The mustard is 3½" in diameter and has a 5" long crystal spoon that fits through a slot in the lid. The bowl has nine scallops around the top edge. The narrow foot is plain with scallops.

No. 3605	Introduced	Discontinued	Value
Mustard & spoon			
Milk	1970	July 1976	$25.00 – 30.00

NO. 3889 MUSTARD AND SPOON

This cylindrical-shaped mustard jar is 3½" tall and 2¾" in diameter. Most examples will be found with six rows of hobs on the body, but some have only five rows of hobs. The round slotted lid only has hobs on the top of the knob. A crystal 3" long paddle-shaped spoon fits through the slot in the lid. This mustard was used with the No. 3809, 7-piece condiment set pictured on page 90.

Topaz
Opalescent

No. 3889	Introduced	Discontinued	Value
Mustard & spoon			
Blue Opalescent	1942	1955	$30.00 – 38.00
French Opalescent	1942	1957	$25.00 – 28.00
Milk	1950	1969	$14.00 – 18.00
Topaz Opalescent	1942	1944	$60.00 – 85.00

NO. 3715 OIL, MUSTARD, AND TRAY

Fenton sold a 3-piece condiment set comprised of the No. 3889 mustard, No. 3869 oil, and a 7½" oval handled tray. This set was in the general line in Milk.

No. 3715 Oil,	Introduced	Discontinued	Value
mustard & tray			
Milk	1956	July 1961	$30.00 – 46.00

NO. 3601 JAM JAR

Fenton's No. 3601 covered jam jar was made in Milk beginning in 1970. The jar is 5" high and 4" in diameter. It has a scalloped top edge and a scalloped foot. There are six panels with hobs on the side. A 5" long crystal ladle designed to fit through the slotted lid was supplied with the jam jar.

No. 3601 Jam jar	Introduced	Discontinued	Value
Milk	1970	1982	$25.00 – 35.00

NO. 3903 JAM SET

Fenton's jam set consists of a covered jar with a saucer underplate and a 5" long crystal ladle. The pie crust edge saucer is 6" in diameter. The covered jar has a slotted lid and is 4¾" tall. The crystal ladle is 5" long. Cranberry jam jars have a French Opalescent lid.

No. 3903 Jam set	Introduced	Discontinued	Value
Blue Opalescent	1948	1955	$100.00 – 125.00
Cranberry	1948	1957	$165.00 – 180.00
French Opalescent	1948	1956	$65.00 – 85.00
Milk	1950	1974	$25.00 – 30.00

NO. 3915 JAM AND JELLY WITH TRAY

This jam and jelly set consists of a chrome handled tray, two covered jars, and two crystal ladles. The scalloped edge tray measures 7½" long and 3¾" wide. The covered jars have slotted lids and are 4¾" tall. The crystal ladles are 5" long.

No. 3915 Jam, jelly & tray	Introduced	Discontinued	Value
Crystal	1968	1969	$18.00 – 20.00
French Opalescent	1955	1956	$100.00 – 115.00
Milk	1955	1975	$50.00 – 55.00

NO. 3916 OIL, VINEGAR, AND TRAY

Fenton's No. 3916 condiment set consists of a chrome handled tray and two oil bottles with stoppers. The scalloped edge tray measures 7½" long and 3¾" wide. The oil bottles are the same as the No. 3869 oil bottle shown on page 111. Although French Opalescent oil bottles are seen frequently, trays in this color are elusive.

No. 3916 Oil, vinegar & tray	Introduced	Discontinued	Value
French Opalescent	1955	1956	$90.00 – 110.00
Milk	1955	1978	$45.00 – 55.00

NO. 3703 CHIP 'N DIP SET

This set consists of two bowls — a large one for chips and a small footed bowl for dip. The large bowl is 2½" high and 12" in diameter. It has an upward curved edge with 36 scallops. The dip bowl is shaped like a small footed comport. It is 5" high and 4" in diameter. There are 16 scallops around the top edge and it has a ribbed stem.

No. 3703 Chip 'n dip set	Introduced	Discontinued	Value
Milk	1958	1980	$55.00 – 65.00

CONSOLE SETS

NO. 3704 CONSOLE SET

The No. 3704 console set consists of a No. 3724-8½" bowl and two No. 3774-10" tall candlesticks. This ware number was also used for a 2-piece Milk Hobnail epergne set produced during the 1970s that was also made for QVC in 2000.

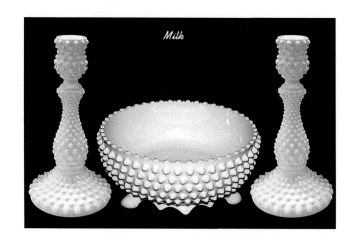

No. 3704 Console set	Introduced	Discontinued	Value
Amber	1959	July 1959	$120.00 – 145.00
Milk	1958	July 1961	$85.00 – 95.00

NO. 3802 CONSOLE SET

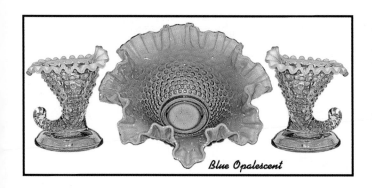

Blue Opalescent

Fenton's No. 3802 console set was introduced in 1943. The set consisted of a No. 3924-9" double crimped bowl and two No. 3874 large cornucopia candlesticks. This ware number was also used for the Hobnail candy jar/butter bowl introduced into the Fenton line in the late 1970s.

No. 3802 Console set	Introduced	Discontinued	Value
Blue Opalescent	1943	1954	$135.00 – 175.00
French Opalescent	1943	1954	$115.00 – 140.00
Milk	1954	July 1958	$80.00 – 95.00

NO. 3904 CONSOLE SET

Fenton combined its No. 3924-9" double crimped console bowl with two No. 3974 candleholders to produce the 3-piece No. 3904 console set. This set was first offered in opalescent colors in 1946. This ware number was also used for the 4-piece milk Hobnail napkin ring set produced during the late 1970s.

No. 3904 Console set	Introduced	Discontinued	Value
Plum Opalescent	1959	1961	$185.00 – 230.00
Rose Pastel	1954	1957	$70.00 – 80.00
Turquoise	1955	1959	$75.00 – 90.00

No. 3904 Console set	Introduced	Discontinued	Value
Blue Opalescent	1946	1955	$90.00 – 100.00
Blue Pastel	July 1954	1955	$70.00 – 85.00
French Opalescent	1946	1956	$70.00 – 80.00
Green Pastel	July 1954	1956	$70.00 – 85.00
Milk	1951	1959	$50.00 – 60.00

Plum Opalescent

COVERED BOXES, CANDIES, AND JARS

NO. 3969 TRINKET BOX

Fenton resurrected an old mustard jar mold with a restyled lid for an introduction as a trinket box. The new lid does not have the hole for the spoon. The trinket box is 3½" high and 3½" in diameter. The first color produced was Willow Green Opalescent (GY) in 2001. The following year boxes were made in Blue Topaz (SY) and Pink Chiffon Opalescent (YS).

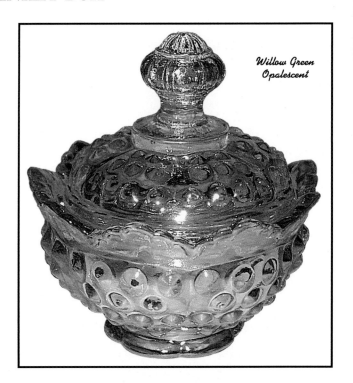

Willow Green Opalescent

No. 3969 Trinket box	Introduced	Discontinued	Value
Blue Topaz	2002	2003	$20.00 – 22.00
Iridescent French Opalescent	2004	2005	$18.00 – 20.00
Pink Chiffon Opalescent	2002	2003	$18.00 – 20.00
Sunset Iridescent	2004		$20.00 – 22.00
Willow Green Opalescent	2001	2002	$20.00 – 22.00

NO. 3600 CANDY JAR OR JAM BOX

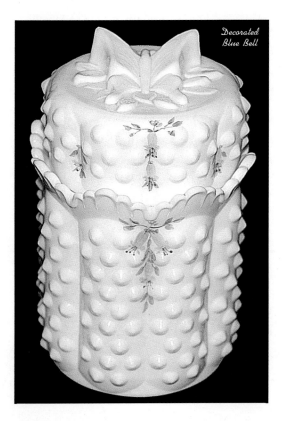

Decorated Blue Bell

This tall narrow candy is 6" high and 4" in diameter. The base has eight panels with eight scallops around the top edge. The lid has eight panels and an embossed butterfly finial in the center of the top side. A Dusty Rose Carnival (DN) candy was made for QVC in June 1995. The Emerald Green Iridized (EY) candy was produced for the April 2002 QVC show.

No. 3600 Candy jar	Introduced	Discontinued	Value
Decorated Blue Bell	1972	1973	$75.00 – 85.00
Dusty Rose Carnival	1995	1995	$55.00 – 65.00
Emerald Green Iridized	2002	2002	$50.00 – 60.00
Milk	1971	1990*	$45.00 – 50.00

*Also made in 1992.

NO. 389-5" COVERED JAR

Fenton introduced this 5" diameter covered jar in 1940 in four opalescent colors. Topaz Opalescent replaced Green Opalescent by mid-1941. This jar utilized the puff box lid as its cover. Two different styles of this jar were produced — elongated and squat. These jars were only produced for a few years and are not easily found today.

No. 389-5" Covered jar	Introduced	Discontinued	Value
Blue Opalescent	1940	1942	$275.00 – 325.00
Cranberry	1940	1943	$400.00 – 450.00
French Opalescent	1940	1942	$185.00 – 225.00
Green Opalescent	1940	1941	$400.00 – 500.00
Topaz Opalescent	1941	1943	$500.00 – 600.00

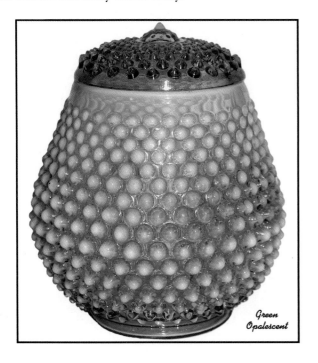

Green Opalescent

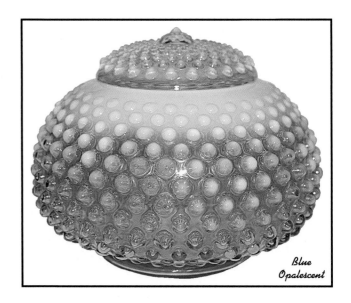

Blue Opalescent

NO. 3886 HONEY JAR

This No. 3886 milk Hobnail round covered honey jar is 7¼" tall and 4¾" in diameter. This jar was only made in Milk for seven years and these are somewhat difficult to find on the secondary market. The honey jar has the same ware number as a covered candy box introduced in the early 1970s.

No. 3886 Honey jar	Introduced	Discontinued	Value
Milk	1953	1960	$95.00 – 120.00

NO. 3689 APOTHECARY JAR

Fenton introduced this narrow, 11" tall Hobnail covered apothecary jar in four colors in January 1964. The jar is 5" in diameter. The base is footed and has a scalloped top. The cover has a beaded knob. Colonial Blue was made for the shortest time and Milk enjoyed the longest production.

No. 3689 Apothecary jar	Introduced	Discontinued	Value
Colonial Amber	1964	1970	$45.00 – 50.00
Colonial Blue	1964	July 1968	$110.00 – 135.00
Colonial Green	1964	1970	$55.00 – 65.00
Milk	1964	1973	$85.00 – 100.00

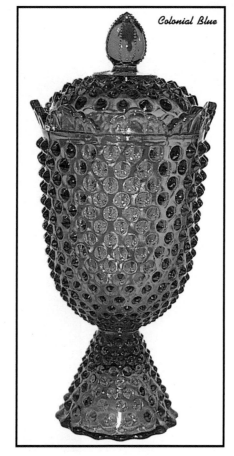

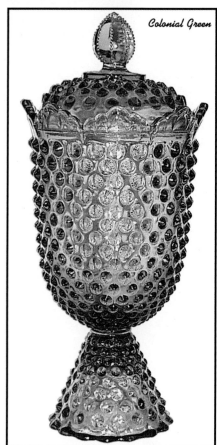

NO. 3780 WEDDING JAR

Fenton introduced a 5" square footed wedding jar into the Hobnail line in 1957. There are five rows of hobs on the body and three rows of hobs on the foot. The stem is plain. The square lid has four rows of hobs and a plain 4-sided finial.

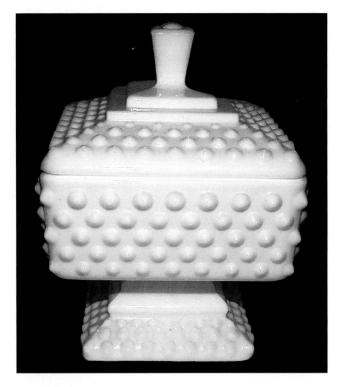

No. 3780 Wedding jar	Introduced	Discontinued	Value
Milk	1957	1977	$28.00 – 32.00

NO. 3802 CANDY JAR OR BUTTER BOWL

Fenton's No. 3802 small round candy also doubled as a butter tub. It is 4¾" high and 5¼" in diameter. The bottom has eight panels with 12 scallops around the top edge. The lid has eight panels and a plain round edge. This candy was made in Spruce Green Iridized (SI) for the August 1999 QVC show. This ware number was also used for the 3-piece Hobnail console set composed of one No. 3924-9" DC bowl and two No. 3874 large cornucopia candleholders.

No. 3802 Candy	Introduced	Discontinued	Value
Blue Opalescent	July 1978	1980	$65.00 – 75.00
Cameo Opalescent	July 1979	1981	$35.00 – 40.00
Colonial Amber	1979	1981	$35.00 – 40.00
Colonial Blue	1979	1981	$40.00 – 45.00
Milk	1974	1990*	$25.00 – 35.00
Spruce Green Carnival	1999	1999	$30.00 – 35.00

*Also made from 1991 through 1993.

Spruce Green Carnival

Cameo Opalescent

NO. 3688 CANDY JAR

Fenton's tall round footed candy jar is 7¼" high and 5¼" in diameter. The base is covered with hobs, and has a narrow foot and a scalloped top edge. The cover has a plain round edge, four rows of hobs, and an oval beaded knob. The candy was originally made in milk. In 2001, it reentered the Fenton line in two opalescent colors. Both Pink Chiffon Opalescent and Willow Green Opalescent remained in production for two years.

Pink Chiffon Opalescent

No. 3688 Candy jar	Introduced	Discontinued	Value
Milk	1963	1977	$70.00 – 85.00
Pink Chiffon Opalescent	2001	2003	$25.00 – 30.00
Willow Green Opalescent	2001	2003	$25.00 – 30.00

NO. 3883 CANDY JAR

Topaz Opalescent

Fenton's No. 3883 candy is 5" high and 5¼" in diameter. The base has three rows of large hobs and one row of small hobs on the side. There are three rows of large hobs on the bottom of the base and the top edge is crimped. The lid has three rows of large hobs and a scalloped edge. The knob has eight hobs. A similar Cranberry butter was made by Northwood. The Hobbs Cranberry butter has the same color lid. The Fenton Cranberry candy has a French Opalescent lid. Jars in crystal satin and those with gold decoration were made by Northwood. Other colors of Fenton jars will have matching color lids. A slightly smaller version of this style jar was also made by Imperial.

No. 3883 Candy jar	Introduced	Discontinued	Value
Blue Opalescent	1953	1955	$100.00 – 125.00
Blue Pastel	1954	1955	$60.00 – 70.00
Cranberry	July 1954	1959	$180.00 – 200.00
French Opalescent	1953	1955	$55.00 – 60.00
Green Pastel	1954	1956	$55.00 – 60.00
Milk	1953	1969	$27.00 – 32.00
Rose Pastel	1954	1955	$50.00 – 60.00
Topaz Opalescent	1959	July 1960	$125.00 – 150.00
Turquoise	1955	1959	$50.00 – 60.00

NO. 3887 FOOTED COVERED COMPORT

Fenton's No. 3887 Hobnail footed covered comport was made in numerous colors during the 1950s and early 1960s. The candy jar is 8½" tall and 5¼" in diameter. The base has a bowl with three rows of large hobs and one row of small hobs. The stem is plain and the foot has four rows of hobs. The lid has three rows of large hobs and a scalloped edge. The knob on the lid is rounded and has eight hobs. This covered comport is similar in shape to the No. 3885 tall footed candy shown on page 102. Note differences in the shape of the knob and the lack of large hobs on the other candy.

Topaz Opalescent

No. 3887	Introduced	Discontinued	Value
Footed comport			
Amber	1959	July 1959	$35.00 – 40.00
Blue Opalescent	July 1953	July 1954*	$100.00 – 125.00
Blue Pastel	1954	1955	$80.00 – 90.00
French Opalescent	July 1953	1954	$65.00 – 80.00
Green Opalescent	July 1959	July 1961	$125.00 – 145.00
Green Pastel	1954	1956	$65.00 – 70.00
Milk	July 1953	1969	$40.00 – 50.00
Plum Opalescent	July 1959	July 1961	$185.00 – 200.00
Rose Pastel	1954	1955	$55.00 – 65.00
Topaz Opalescent	1959	1961	$150.00 – 185.00
Turquoise	1955	1959	$55.00 – 65.00

*Also made from 1959 until 1964.

NO. 3980 FOOTED CANDY JAR

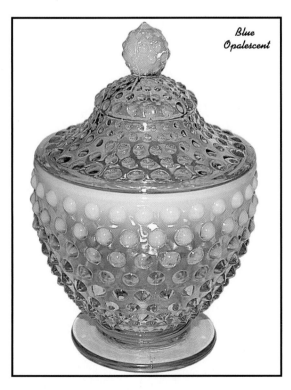

Blue Opalescent

This early Hobnail footed candy jar entered the Fenton line in opalescent colors in 1941. Ten years later production was also begun in Milk. The candy is 6½" tall and 4½" in diameter. It has hobs on both the body of the jar and the lid. The foot is round and lacks hobs. The lid is the same as the lid for the No. 3886 honey jar. Early versions of this candy have a foot that is connected to the body with a stem about ½" in height. This stem has a single row of hobs. The later version of this jar, which is shown in the photo, appeared in Fenton catalogs about 1948.

No. 3980	Introduced	Discontinued	Value
Footed candy			
Blue Opalescent	1941	1955	$65.00 – 75.00
French Opalescent	1941	1954	$55.00 – 60.00
Milk	1951	1976	$25.00 – 30.00
Topaz Opalescent	1941	1944	$150.00 – 185.00

NO. 3885 FOOTED CANDY JAR

This tall footed candy jar was in the general line in Milk. The jar is 8½" tall and the bowl is 5¼" in diameter. The lid is scalloped and has four rows of hobs. The knob is pointed and has a single row of eight hobs around the center. The foot has four rows of hobs and is connected to the body with a plain stem. Note the differences between this candy and the No. 3887 tall footed comport shown on page 101.

No. 3885 Footed Candy jar	Introduced	Discontinued	Value
Milk	1968	1978	$50.00 – 60.00

NO. 3700 COVERED SLIPPER CANDY BOX

Blue Marble

Fenton's covered slipper candy box was introduced into the regular line in 1971. The candy is 5¼" tall and 5¼" long. The base has seven scalloped panels and the lid has eight scalloped panels. The sole of the shoe has a slightly depressed area. Collectors will find a similar foreign-made, look-alike covered candy in black, pink, amber, and possibly other transparent and opaque colors.

No. 3700 Candy box	Introduced	Discontinued	Value
Blue Marble	1971	1974	$40.00 – 50.00
Milk	1971	1985*	$35.00 – 40.00

* Also made in 1993.

NO. 3784 FOOTED CANDY BOX

Fenton's No. 3784 footed candy box is 8¾" tall and 6" in diameter. The footed base has a scalloped top edge. The bowl and the foot are covered with hobs, but the short stem has plain wide vertical panels. The knobbed lid has four rows of hobs and a plain round edge. Persian Pearl (XV) was made for the Historical Collection in 1992. Rose Magnolia (RV) was made for the Historical Collection in 1993. Violet Iridescent (OQ) was produced for the September 2002 QVC show.

Orange

No. 3784 Candy box	Introduced	Discontinued	Value
Colonial Amber	1966	1971	$35.00 – 40.00
Colonial Blue	1966	1970	$35.00 – 45.00
Colonial Green	1966	1971	$30.00 – 35.00
Milk	1966	1982*	$35.00 – 40.00
Orange	1966	1970	$30.00 – 35.00
Persian Pearl	July 1992	1993	$35.00 – 45.00
Rose Magnolia	1993	July 1993	$30.00 – 40.00
Violet Iridescent	2002	2002	$30.00 – 40.00

*Also made in 1993.

NO. 3786 OVAL CANDY BOX

Crystal

No. 3786 Candy box	Introduced	Discontinued	Value
Carnival	1980	1981	$30.00 – 35.00
Colonial Amber	1968	July 1970	$20.00 – 30.00
Colonial Blue	1968	1970	$30.00 – 35.00
Colonial Green	1968	July 1970	$18.00 – 20.00
Crystal	1968	1969	$12.00 – 15.00
Milk	1960	1987	$22.00 – 25.00
Orange	1968	1970	$22.00 – 25.00

This oval-shaped candy box is 5" high, 6½" long, and 5" wide. The candy bottom is 4-footed and has 12 scallops around the top edge. The knobbed cover has four rows of hobs and a smooth oval edge.

Colonial Amber

NO. 3668 CANDY BOX

Fenton's footed No. 3668 candy box was produced during the last half of the 1970s. This candy is 6½" tall and 6½" in diameter. The base has nine panels, a scalloped top edge, and a plain foot. The lid is covered with hobs that are separated into nine paneled sections. A hand-painted Aquamarine Satin (J4) candy was made for the April 2000 QVC program.

Colonial Green

No. 3668 Candy box	Introduced	Discontinued	Value
Aquamarine Satin, hand-painted	2000	2004	$35.00 – 45.00
Colonial Amber	1975	1980	$35.00 – 40.00
Colonial Blue	1975	1978	$40.00 – 45.00
Colonial Green	1975	1977	$25.00 – 30.00
Milk	1975	1980	$45.00 – 55.00
Springtime Green	1977	1979	$45.00 – 55.00

NO. 3984 CANDY BOX

The No. 3984 covered candy is 6" high and 6" in diameter, and has large hobs. The base is 3-footed with three scallops draping the space between the feet. The knobbed lid is covered with six rows of large hobs.

No. 3984 Candy box	Introduced	Discontinued	Value
Blue Satin	1974	1976	$60.00 – 80.00
Custard	1974	1976	$35.00 – 40.00
Lime Sherbet	1974	1976	$40.00 – 50.00
Milk	1974	1978	$55.00 – 58.00

Blue Satin

Lime Sherbet

NO. 3886 FOOTED CANDY BOX

Fenton's No. 3886 footed candy box is 6¾" tall and 6½" in diameter. The base has eight panels with 15 scallops around the top edge. The foot is scalloped and is divided into eight panels. The lid is also separated into eight paneled sections. The entire candy is covered with hobs. Pekin Blue II and Jonquil Yellow candy jars were made in the 1960s. These colors were sold through the Fenton Gift Shop. This same ware number was used for Fenton's milk glass honey jar made during the 1950s.

No. 3886	Introduced	Discontinued	Value
Candy box			
Blue Marble	1970	1974	$40.00 – 55.00
Decorated			
Blue Bell	1971	1973	$60.00 – 80.00
Decorated Holly	July 1973	1974	$50.00 – 60.00
Decorated Roses	1974	1976	$60.00 – 75.00
Jonquil Yellow	1968	1969	$65.00 – 85.00
Milk	1969	1990*	$30.00 – 35.00
Pekin Blue II	1968	1969	$65.00 – 85.00
Ruby	1972	1980	$35.00 – 45.00

*Also produced in 1991 and 1992.

Pekin Blue II

NO. 389 FOOTED, SCALLOPED BODY CANDY JAR

This elusive candy jar was in the regular Fenton line during the early 1940s. It is 6½" in diameter and 7¼" tall. The base has a scalloped body and a narrow plain round foot. The lid is scalloped and has a pointed ribbed knob. Two different styles of knobs have been found as may be seen in the photos below.

No. 389	Introduced	Discontinued	Value
Candy jar			
Blue Opalescent	1942	1944	$145.00 – 165.00
French Opalescent	1942	1944	$95.00 – 125.00
Topaz Opalescent	1942	1944	$200.00 – 225.00

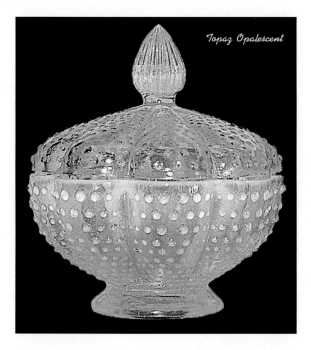

Topaz Opalescent

Blue Opalescent

NO. 3986 COVERED URN

Fenton introduced a large footed covered jar, called an urn, into the general line in 1968. This urn is 11" tall. It has a round foot with three rows of hobs and there are 12 scallops around the top edge of the base. The cover has a beaded finial. These jars were made only for a short time, and are relatively elusive.

Colonial Amber

No. 3986 Covered urn	Introduced	Discontinued	Value
Colonial Amber	1968	1970	$85.00 – 95.00
Colonial Green	1968	1969	$85.00 – 100.00
Crystal	1968	1969	$30.00 – 35.00
Milk	July 1968	1970	$200.00 – 225.00

NO. 3880 LOW CANDY JAR

Blue Opalescent

This low flat candy jar is 3½" high and 6½" in diameter. The bottom of the base is plain but the side is covered with five rows of hobs. The lid has eight rows of hobs, a plain round edge, and a plain bell-shaped knob.

No. 3880 Candy jar	Introduced	Discontinued	Value
Blue Opalescent	1951	1955	$90.00 – 110.00
French Opalescent	1951	1955	$55.00 – 60.00
Milk	1953	1976	$40.00 – 45.00

NO. 3680 COVERED COOKIE JAR

Fenton introduced a Milk covered cookie jar into the regular line in January 1962. This cookie jar is 11" tall and 7½" in diameter. The top of the base has a scalloped edge. The lid has seven rows of hobs and a beaded knob. The original issue of this cookie jar was discontinued at the end of 1973. It was reissued for another year during 1987.

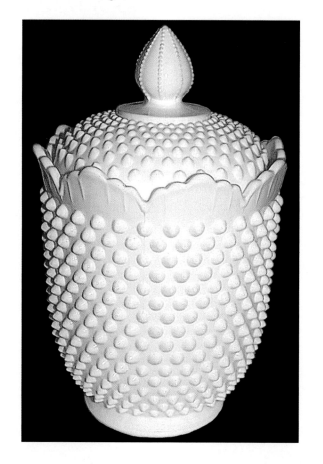

No. 3680 Cookie jar	Introduced	Discontinued	Value
Milk	1962	1974*	$100.00 – 125.00

*Reissued from January through December 1987.

NO. 389 HANDLED COOKIE JAR

Topaz Opalescent

Fenton's original Hobnail covered cookie jar entered the line in July 1941. This jar was produced in Blue Opalescent, French Opalescent, and Topaz Opalescent. It was only produced for a few years and is scarce on the secondary market. The base of this jar has two large knobs which anchor the end loops of a wicker handle. The covered jar is 7" wide and 7¼" tall.

No. 389 Cookie jar	Introduced	Discontinued	Value
Blue Opalescent	July 1941	1943	$500.00 – 600.00
French Opalescent	July 1941	1943	$250.00 – 300.00
Topaz Opalescent	July 1941	1943	$600.00 – 700.00

CREAMER AND SUGAR SETS

NO. 3665 MINIATURE CREAMER

Fenton's No. 3665 miniature creamer is 3⅛" tall and 2" in diameter (3" from the spout to the back of the handle). The creamer has hobs on the side and on the bottom. The outside edge of the handle and top edge of the creamer are beaded.

Colonial Blue

No. 3665	Introduced	Discontinued	Value
Mini creamer			
Colonial Amber	1965	1969	$7.00 – 9.00
Colonial Blue	1965	1969	$8.00 – 10.00
Colonial Green	1965	1969	$7.00 – 9.00
French Opalescent			$12.00 – 14.00
Milk	1965	1969	$8.00 – 10.00
Orange	1965	1969	$6.00 – 8.00

NO. 3900 INDIVIDUAL CREAMER AND SUGAR

Blue Opalescent

Both the creamer and sugar in this set are 2" tall. They each have plain handles, plain bottoms, and either five or six rows of hobs on the sides. In addition to being offered as a creamer and sugar set, pieces were used to complete the No. 3809 condiment set.

No. 3900	Introduced	Discontinued	Value
Creamer & sugar			
Blue Opalescent	1942	1955	$35.00 – 40.00
French Opalescent	1942	1956	$25.00 – 30.00
Milk	1950	1973	$15.00 – 18.00

NO. 3702 CREAMER AND SUGAR

This creamer and sugar set was made only in Milk for the general line. Both pieces are 3" tall and have angular beaded handles and a pie crust crimped top edge. The top of the crimped edge is usually beaded, but a variation without beads may sometimes be found.

No. 3702	Introduced	Discontinued	Value
Creamer & sugar			
Milk	1970	1974	$25.00 – 30.00

NO. 3901 CREAMER AND SUGAR

This 3½" tall handled creamer and sugar set was introduced in 1940 in opalescent colors. Topaz Opalescent replaced Green Opalescent about mid-1941. Cranberry and Topaz Opalescent were discontinued before the mid-1940s, but the other two colors were made into the mid-1950s. A Milk version of this set entered the line in 1950. The set was later made in Topaz Opalescent for The Levay Distributing Company. This issue has the Fenton logo impressed in the bottom.

No. 3901 Creamer & sugar	Introduced	Discontinued	Value
Blue Opalescent	1940	1955	$52.00 – 60.00
Cranberry	1940	1944	$80.00 – 90.00
French Opalescent	1940	1957	$35.00 – 45.00
Green Opalescent	1940	1941	$65.00 – 85.00
Milk	1950	1968	$18.00 – 22.00
Topaz Opalescent	1941	1944*	$70.00 – 80.00

*Also made for Levay in 1983.

Blue Opalescent

Green Opalescent

NO. 3708 CREAMER AND SUGAR

This oval-shaped set has a creamer and sugar that are both 3½" tall. The top edge of both is scalloped. Note the amber set was only made for six months and is elusive.

No. 3708 Creamer & sugar	Introduced	Discontinued	Value
Amber	1959	July 1959	$15.00 – 25.00
Milk	1956	1969	$25.00 – 30.00

Milk

NO. 3917 CREAMER, SUGAR, AND TRAY

The No. 3917 set consists of the No. 3906 star-shaped creamer and sugar and a chrome handled tray with a scalloped edge. The oval-shaped tray is 7½" long and 3¾" wide. French Opalescent trays are elusive.

French Opalescent

No. 3917 Creamer, sugar & tray	Introduced	Discontinued	Value
French Opalescent	1955	1956	$70.00 – 100.00
Milk	1955	1984	$40.00 – 45.00

NO. 3906 STAR-SHAPED CREAMER AND SUGAR

This set originally appeared in the Fenton line as the #3 creamer and sugar set during late 1949. Both pieces are 3" tall and have a star-shaped top edge. Cranberry sets are elusive since they were not produced after Fenton changed these from mold-blown to pressed production in 1950. Rosalene sets were made recently for the Fenton Art Glass Collectors of America. The creamer spout was changed to a more elongated style in the early 1960s. Examples of Milk creamers may be found in either style.

No. 3906 Creamer & sugar	Introduced	Discontinued	Value
Amber	1959	1960	$35.00 – 45.00
Blue Opalescent	October 1949	1955	$85.00 – 90.00
Blue Pastel	1954	1955	$35.00 – 40.00
Cranberry	October 1949	1951	$200.00 – 250.00
French Opalescent	October 1949	1956	$55.00 – 65.00
Green Pastel	1954	1956	$25.00 – 30.00
Milk	1951	1981	$20.00 – 25.00
Rosalene			$80.00 – 90.00
Rose Pastel	1954	1957	$35.00 – 45.00
Turquoise	1955	1957	$25.00 – 35.00

Blue Opalescent

Cranberry

NO. 3606 CREAMER, SUGAR, AND LID

This covered sugar and open creamer were introduced into the regular Fenton line in Milk in 1961. The sugar with lid is 5¾" tall and 3¾" in diameter. The creamer is 4" tall and 5" across from lip to handle. Topaz Opalescent was made for The Levay Distributing Company. Peaches 'n Cream Opalescent and Sapphire Blue Opalescent were made for Fenton's Gracious Touch division. Sapphire Blue Opalescent was also produced for the June 1990 QVC show. This ware number was used later for a Hobnail epergne made for QVC.

No. 3606 Creamer & sugar	Introduced	Discontinued	Value
Crystal	1968	1969	$8.00 – 12.00
Milk	1961	1990*	$20.00 – 25.00
Peaches 'n Cream Opalescent (Pink)	1989	1990	$45.00 – 55.00
Sapphire Blue Opalescent	1989	1990	$45.00 – 55.00
Topaz Opalescent	1980	1980	$85.00 – 95.00

*Also made from 1991 until 1993.

Topaz Opalescent

Milk

NO. 3902 CREAMER, SUGAR, AND LID

Both the creamer and sugar in this set have paneled sides and are footed. The two pieces also have scalloped top edges and scalloped feet. The lids also have paneled divisions. The Milk version of this set was sold with lids on both the creamer and sugar. The iridized sets made during 2002 were made for QVC and did not have a cover on the cream pitcher. This ware number was also used for the 2-piece Hobnail petite epergne set made during the 1950s.

Milk

No. 3902	Introduced	Discontinued	Value
Creamer & sugar			
Milk	1969	July 1983	$30.00 – 35.00
Opal Mist Iridized	2002	2002	$40.00 – 45.00
Rose Opalescent			
Iridized	2002	2002	$40.00 – 45.00

CRUETS AND BOTTLES

NO. 3869 OIL BOTTLE

This small oil bottle entered the Fenton line in 1942 in Blue Opalescent and French Opalescent. The bottle measures about 4¾" tall with its stopper. It has a ribbed neck, a plain or ribbed handle, and a plain bottom. There are seven rows of hobs on the side and the stopper is covered with hobs. Blue Opalescent and Topaz Opalescent were also made in the 1980s for The Levay Distributing Company. These later issues have the Fenton logo embossed on the bottom. Aqua Opalescent Carnival was also made for Levay. Cranberry Opalescent oil bottles reappeared in the general line during 1996. Early opalescent bottles were usually sold with a crystal stopper.

No. 3869	Introduced	Discontinued	Value
Oil bottle			
Amber	1959	1960	$27.00 – 30.00
Aqua Opalescent			
Carnival	1982	1982	$40.00 – 45.00
Blue Opalescent	1942	1955*	$20.00 – 25.00
Cranberry	October 1949	1965**	$90.00 – 110.00
French Opalescent	1942	1963	$25.00 – 30.00
Milk	1950	1973	$12.00 – 14.00
Topaz Opalescent	1942	1944*	$95.00 – 110.00
Turquoise	1955	1957	$30.00 – 40.00

*Also made in the 1980s for Levay.

**Also in 1996 in the general catalog.

Cranberry   *Turquoise*   *Topaz Opalescent*   *Milk*

NO. 3767 OIL BOTTLE

Fenton's No. 3767-7 oz. oil bottle was only in the line in Milk. The bottle is 8" tall. The narrow ribbed neck tapers to a 3¼" diameter flat bottom. The stopper is milk and has fine vertical ribbing.

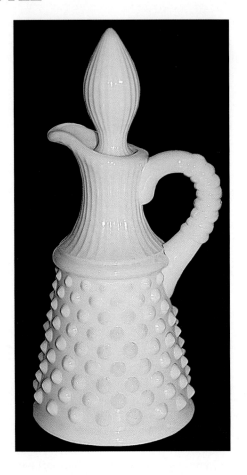

No. 3767 Oil bottle	Introduced	Discontinued	Value
Milk	1956	1965	$70.00 – 80.00

NO. CV140 CRUET AND STOPPER

The No. CV140 Cranberry Opalescent Spiral Optic Hobnail cruet was made for the June 1996 QVC show. The cruet has a French Opalescent ribbed handle and a French Opalescent stopper with hobs. It measures approximately 6½" high and 4¼" in diameter.

No. CV140 Cruet	Produced	Value
Cranberry	1996	$125.00 – 150.00

NO. 3863 CRUET AND STOPPER

This 6½" tall cruet entered the regular Fenton line in Blue Opalescent, Cranberry, French Opalescent, and Topaz Opalescent during mid-1941. Later, numerous other colors were made. Purple Carnival, Aqua Opalescent Carnival, Cranberry Opalescent, Blue Opalescent, and Topaz Opalescent Carnival were made for The Levay Distributing Company during the 1970s and early 1980s. Pink Opalescent was made in the last half of 1988 as part of Fenton's Collector's Extravaganza series. The Rose Magnolia cruet was in the Historical Collection sold during the first half of 1993. Several colors of cruets were made for QVC. These included a cruet in milk with a Spruce handle and an iridescent stopper made in 1999. An Iridescent Champagne Opalescent cruet made for the August 1997 show and a Spruce Green Iridized Overlay (milk glass covered with spruce green and iridized) cruet were sold on the August 1999 show. A Pink Chiffon Overlay cruet with a Violet stopper and handle was made for the Museum Collection in 2001.

Cranberry

No. 3863 Cruet	Introduced	Discontinued	Value
Aqua Opalescent Carnival	1982	1982	$85.00 – 95.00
Blue Opalescent	July 1941	1955*	$100.00 – 125.00
Champagne Opalescent Iridescent	1997	1997	$55.00 – 65.00
Cranberry	July 1941	1978**	$135.00 – 150.00
French Opalescent	July 1941	1957	$50.00 – 65.00
Gold Pearl	1992	July 1992	$75.00 – 85.00
Lime Green Opal	July 1952	1955	$250.00 – 300.00
Milk	1952	1975	$20.00 – 25.00
Milk Glass w/Spruce Handle & Iridescent Stopper	1999	1999	$60.00 – 70.00
Persian Blue Opal	July 1989	1990	$55.00 – 65.00
Pink Chiffon Overlay, Violet Stopper & Handle	2001	2001	$65.00 – 75.00
Pink Opalescent	1988	1989	$55.00 – 65.00
Purple Carnival			$125.00 – 150.00
Rose Magnolia	1993	July 1993	$65.00 – 75.00
Ruby Overlay	1968	1969	$120.00 – 140.00
Silver Crest	1993	July 1994	$70.00 – 80.00
Spruce Green Iridized Overlay	1999	1999	$60.00 – 70.00
Topaz Opalescent	July 1941	1944	$200.00 – 225.00
Topaz Opalescent Iridescent	1975	1975	$125.00 – 150.00

*Also made for Levay in 1982.
**Also made for Levay in 1981.

Spruce Green Iridized Overlay

NO. 3761 HANDLED DECANTER

Fenton's handled decanter is approximately 12½" tall to the top of the stopper. The first Hobnail decanters entered the Fenton line in July 1941 in Blue Opalescent and French Opalescent. Topaz Opalescent and Plum Opalescent decanters were made in the early 1960s. The Plum Opalescent decanter has a crystal handle. A later post-2000 issue Plum Opalescent decanter made for a private party has a plum handle and is marked with the Fenton logo and a "0" in the oval. A currently available Topaz Opalescent special order issue has a cobalt handle and stopper. Most of the stoppers for the early opalescent decanters were crystal. However, some of these decanters have been found with matching colored stoppers. Milk, Ruby, and Red Carnival decanters have matching color stoppers. A Purple Carnival decanter and matching wine goblets were made for The Levay Distributing Company during the late 1970s.

No. 3761 Decanter	Introduced	Discontinued	Value
Blue Opalescent	July 1941	1950*	$390.00 – 425.00
French Opalescent	July 1941	1950	$200.00 – 225.00
Milk	1960	1968	$200.00 – 225.00
Plum Opalescent**	1960	1963	$500.00 – 550.00
Purple Carnival	1977	1977	$300.00 – 350.00
Ruby	1977	1979	$200.00 – 225.00
Red Carnival			$325.00 – 375.00
Topaz Opalescent	1960	1961	$600.00 – 650.00
Topaz Opalescent w/cobalt trim	2004	2004	$200.00 – 225.00

*Reissued from 1959 to 1964.

**With plum handle, $200.00 – 225.00.

Blue Opalescent

Milk

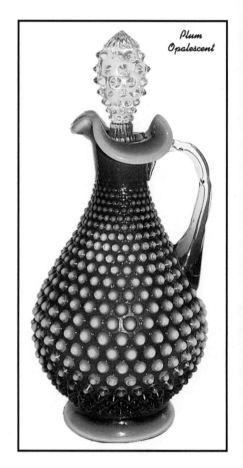

Plum Opalescent

EPERGNE SETS

NO. 3671 PETITE EPERGNE

This Milk 5" diameter candle epergne was produced from January 1961 through December 1965. This piece is 2½" high and 4½" in diameter. It has a single row of 18 thumbprints around its base and a peg on the underside that will fit into a candleholder. This candle epergne was pictured in Fenton catalogs with the No. 3674-6" candleholder, suggesting the two parts could be combined to produce an epergne set.

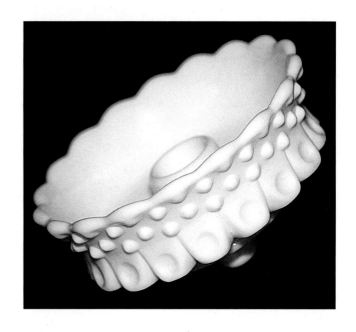

No. 3761	Introduced	Discontinued	Value
Petite epergne			
Milk	1961	1966	$20.00 – 25.00

NO. 3902, 2-PIECE PETITE EPERGNE SET

This 2-piece epergne set is composed of a No. 3926-6" diameter double crimped bonbon and a No. 3952-4" footed double crimped vase. The base for the epergne is distinguished from a regular bonbon by checking for the presence of an embossed ring into which the epergne foot rests. This ware number was also used with a creamer, sugar, and lid set that was introduced in 1969.

No. 3902	Introduced	Discontinued	Value
Epergne set			
Blue Opalescent	1950	1955	$100.00 – 125.00
French Opalescent	1950	1955	$65.00 – 85.00

Blue Opalescent Bonbon
with Embossed Ring

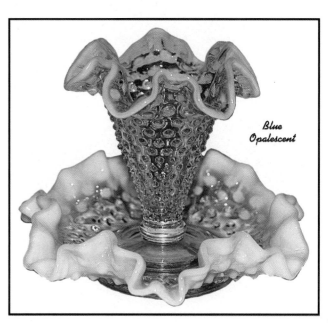

Blue Opalescent

NO. 389 EPERGNE AND BLOCK

Fenton's earliest Hobnail epergne set consisted of a single straight 7¼" tall epergne horn set in a crystal candle block that was placed in a 9" double crimped bowl. This set was marketed in Blue Opalescent, French Opalescent, and Topaz Opalescent during the early 1940s.

Blue Opalescent

No. 389 Epergne & block	Introduced	Discontinued	Value
Blue Opalescent	July 1941	1943	$350.00 – 450.00
French Opalescent	July 1941	1943	$165.00 – 195.00
Topaz Opalescent	July 1941	1943	$450.00 – 550.00

NO. 3704, 2-PIECE EPERGNE SET

This 2-piece epergne set is composed of a 6½" diameter bowl and a 7" long horn. The bowl is 2¾" high, and has a scalloped top edge and an 8-paneled side with five rows of hobs. The horn has six scallops around the top and hobs on a 6-paneled side. This ware number was also used with a 3-piece console set produced during the late 1950s.

No. 3704 Epergne Set	Introduced	Discontinued	Value
Empress Rose Iridescent	2000	2001	$60.00 – 65.00
Milk	1975	1978	$80.00 – 100.00
Sunset Iridescent	2003	2004	$50.00 – 60.00

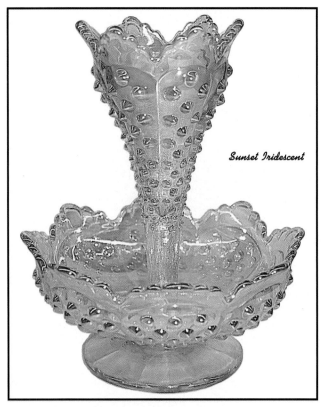

Sunset Iridescent

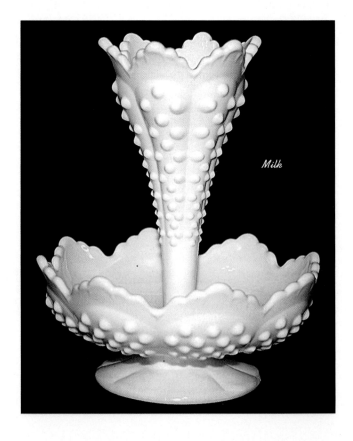

Milk

NO. 3801 MINIATURE EPERGNE SET

Fenton's No. 3801 miniature epergne set consists of a bowl and three horns. The double crimped bowl is 8" in diameter and has three holes in the bottom into which the horns fit. The curved horns are 6" long and have a pie crust crimped top edge. The epergne set entered the Fenton regular line in Blue Opalescent and French Opalescent in October 1949. Milk epergne sets appeared in 1950. Topaz Opalescent sets were made in 1959 and into the early 1960s. Later, in 1983 these Topaz Opalescent sets were made for The Levay Distributing Company. These later issues will have the Fenton logo on the base of the bowl. In 1980, this epergne set was also made for Levay in Blue Opalescent with mother-of-pearl iridescence. Pink Opalescent (UO) epergne sets were made for the 1988 Collector's Extravaganza. The Persian Pearl (XV) color was made for the Historic Collection in 1992 and 1993. Also, in the 1990s, numerous colors of this epergne set were made for QVC. The initial QVC color was Twilight Blue Carnival in 1992. Dusty Rose Carnival (DN) was offered in 1993. Ocean Blue Carnival (OZ) and Rosalene Iridescent (RJ) were marketed in 1994. Two carnival colors were promoted on QVC in 1995, Red Carnival (RN) and Spruce Green Carnival (SI). During 1997 the epergne was sold in Opaline Iridescent (TY), and in 1998 it appeared in Azure Blue Iridescent (MM). In 1999, the set was made for QVC in Iridized Misty Blue Opalescent (LK) and Iridized French Opalescent with an Empress Rose edge (IF). The horns to this set are iridescent Dusty Rose.

No. 3801 Epergne set	Introduced	Discontinued	Value
Azure Blue Iridescent	1998	1998	$60.00 – 70.00
*Blue Opalescent	Sept 1949	1955	$100.00 – 125.00
Blue Opalescent with MOP Iridescence	1980	1980	$120.00 – 140.00
Blue Pastel	1954	1955	$100.00 – 125.00
Dusty Rose Carnival	1993	1993	$60.00 – 70.00
French Opalescent	Sept 1949	1957	$80.00 – 85.00
Green Opalescent	July 1959	July 1961	$145.00 – 185.00
Green Pastel	1954	1956	$100.00 – 125.00
Iridized French Opal w/Empress Rose Edge	1999	1999	$75.00 – 85.00
Iridized Misty Blue Opalescent	1999	1999	$60.00 – 70.00
Milk	1950	1978	$35.00 – 45.00
Ocean Blue Carnival	1994	1994	$65.00 – 75.00
Opaline Iridescent	1997	1997	$60.00 – 70.00
Persian Pearl	1992	May 1993	$60.00 – 70.00
Pink Opalescent	1988	1988	$60.00 – 70.00
Plum Opalescent	July 1959	1963	$245.00 – 290.00
Red Carnival	1995	1995	$250.00 – 300.00
Rose Pastel	1954	1958	$80.00 – 90.00
Rosalene Iridescent	1994	1994	$200.00 – 250.00
Spruce Green Carnival	1995	1995	$65.00 – 75.00
Topaz Opalescent**	1959	July 1961	$200.00 – 225.00
Topaz Opalescent Carnival	1975	1975	$125.00 – 150.00
Turquoise	1955	1959	$95.00 – 110.00
Twilight Blue Carnival	1992	1992	$65.00 – 75.00

*Reissued from 1959 to 1965.
**Also made for Levay in 1983.

Iridized French Opalescent with Empress Rose Edge and Horns

Plum Opalescent

NO. 3800, 5-PIECE FOOTED EPERGNE SET

Fenton created this epergne set using the No. 3920-8" double crimped footed comport as the base. Three curved 5" long horns in a flower frog were placed in the center of the comport to produce the epergne set. This set was sold in Milk and pastel opaque colors during 1954.

Blue Pastel

No. 3800 Epergne set	Introduced	Discontinued	Value
Blue Pastel	1954	1955	$250.00 – 300.00
Green Pastel	1954	1955	$200.00 – 250.00
Milk	1954	1955	$185.00 – 200.00
Rose Pastel	1954	1955	$150.00 – 200.00

NO. 3742 CENTERPIECE SET

This 3-piece set was made in Milk during the 1970s. The No. 3748-9½" chip 'n dip candle bowl was used as the base. The center part was the No. 3745-7" candleholder and the No. 3746 candle epergne was used for the top.

No. 3742 Centerpiece set	Introduced	Discontinued	Value
Milk	1973	1976	$125.00 – 145.00

NO. 3701 EPERGNE SET

Fenton's No. 3701, 4-piece epergne set was introduced into the regular line in milk during July 1956. The 9½" diameter double crimped bowl has three holes to hold the epergne horns. The horns are about 8" long and have a pie crust crimped top edge. During the 1980s this epergne set was made for The Levay Distributing Company in Aqua Opalescent Carnival (IO), Blue Opalescent, Plum Opalescent, and Topaz Opalescent. Pink Opalescent (UO) sets were made for the Collector's Extravaganza promotion during the first half of 1988. Persian Pearl (XV) epergne sets were part of the 1992 and 1993 Historic Collection. Sales were limited to sets sold through May 1993. Rose Magnolia (RV) sets were produced for the Historic Collection during the first half of 1993. Dusty Rose Stretch (DL) sets were made for QVC in January 1989; Sapphire Blue Opalescent sets were produced for the June 1990 show. In 1997 epergne sets in Iridescent French Opalescent with Azure Blue trim (FC) were made for QVC.

No. 3701 Epergne set	Introduced	Discontinued	Value
Amber	1959	July 1959	$60.00 – 75.00
Aqua Opalescent Carnival	1982	1982	$110.00 – 130.00
Blue Opalescent	1982	1982	$100.00 – 125.00
Dusty Rose Stretch	1989	1989	$110.00 – 120.00

French Opalescent
  Iridescent w/Azure
  Blue trim
	1997	1997	$120.00 – 140.00

Milk	July 1956	1984	$45.00 – 50.00

No. 3701 Epergne set	Introduced	Discontinued	Value
Milk Glass Royal	1995	1996	$85.00 – 95.00
Persian Pearl	1992	May 1993	$75.00 – 85.00
Pink Opalescent	1988	July 1988	$75.00 – 85.00
Plum Opalescent	1984	1984	$350.00 – 400.00
Rose Magnolia	1993	July 1993	$90.00 – 110.00
Sapphire Blue Opalescent	1990	1990	$100.00 – 125.00
Topaz Opalescent	1980	1980	$325.00 – 350.00

Amber

Aqua Opalescent Carnival

Milk Glass Royal

FAIRY LIGHTS

NO. 3608, 2-PIECE FAIRY LIGHT

Fenton's No. 3608, 2-piece fairy light is 4½" tall. The fairy light entered the line in transparent Colonial colors and Opal in 1969. Later, this fairy light was made in numerous opaque and opalescent colors. Ruby Satin was made for The Levay Distributing Company in 1982. In addition to being in the general line, Dusty Rose Iridized fairy lights with hand-painted pink and white glass frit were made for the June 1997 QVC show. Ruby appeared in the June 1987 catalog supplement for Gracious Touch customers and was offered as a hostess gift to Gracious Touch participants in 1989.

No. 3608 Fairy light	Introduced	Discontinued	Value
Blue Opalescent	July 1978	1981	$40.00 – 50.00
Blue Satin	1974	1981	$30.00 – 35.00
Cameo Opalescent	1979	1981	$35.00 – 38.00
Colonial Amber	1969	1981	$18.00 – 20.00
Colonial Blue	1969	1981	$30.00 – 35.00
Colonial Green	1969	1977	$20.00 – 22.00
Custard	1972	1978	$25.00 – 35.00
Decorated Blue Bell	1971	1973	$45.00 – 55.00
Decorated Holly	July 1971	1976	$45.00 – 50.00
Decorated Roses	1974	1976	$45.00 – 50.00
Dusty Rose Iridized, hand-painted	1997	1997	$30.00 – 35.00
Lime Sherbet	1973	1980	$25.00 – 30.00
Milk	1970	1983	$20.00 – 25.00
Opal	1969	1970	$40.00 – 50.00
Orange	1969	1978	$28.00 – 30.00
Persian Blue Opalescent			$30.00 – 35.00
Ruby	1972	1984*	$25.00 – 35.00
Ruby Satin	1982		$60.00 – 70.00
Springtime Green	1977	1979	$30.00 – 32.00
Topaz Opalescent Iridescent	1975		$60.00 – 70.00

* Also made from July 1987 through December 1988 in the regular line and as a hostess gift for Gracious Touch in 1989.

Milk

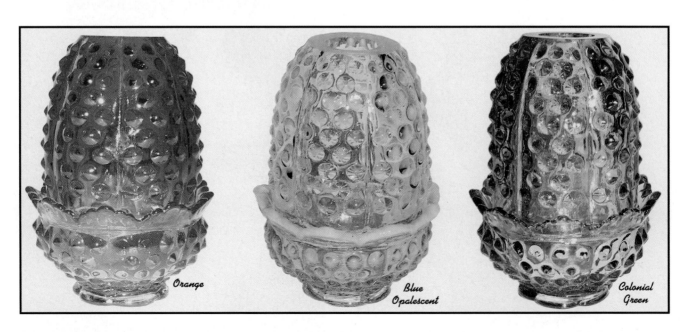

Orange   Blue Opalescent   Colonial Green

NO. CV290 FAIRY LIGHT

Fenton's Iridescent Willow Green Opalescent Hobnail with Spiral Optic 3-piece fairy light was made for the January 2000 QVC show. This fairy light is 6½" tall and 6" in diameter. The base is round with a downward flared pie crust crimped edge. The candle insert ring is Willow Green.

No. CV290 Fairy light	Produced	Value
Iridized Willow Green		
Opalescent w/Spiral Optic	2000	$80.00 – 90.00

NO. CV150 FAIRY LIGHT

This Cranberry Opalescent Spiral Optic 3-piece Hobnail fairy light was made for QVC in December 1996. It measures about 6½" high. It has a square crimped base and a crystal ring candleholder.

No. CV150 Fairy light	Produced	Value
Cranberry	1996	$120.00 – 140.00

NO. 3804, 3-PIECE FOOTED FAIRY LIGHT

This 3-piece tall footed fairy light was first made in 1975 in Milk and transparent Colonial colors. It is 8¾" tall and 6" in diameter. The base has a pie crust crimped, rolled down top edge and is footed with a long, 8-sided stem. The base of the violet light is trimmed with an opal ring. Plum opalescent (PO) was made for The Levay Distributing Company in 1984. The Opaline Iridescent (TY) color was made for a QVC show in November 1997.

No. 3804 Fairy light	Introduced	Discontinued	Value
Champagne	2000	2001	$50.00 – 60.00
Colonial Amber	1975	1981	$45.00 – 50.00
Colonial Blue	1975	1981	$50.00 – 60.00
Colonial Green	1975	1977	$45.00 – 50.00
Milk	1975	1983	$65.00 – 75.00
Opaline Iridescent	1997	1997	$50.00 – 60.00
Plum Opalescent	1984	1984	$200.00 – 250.00
Violet	2001	2001	$50.00 – 60.00

NO. 1167, 3-PIECE FAIRY LIGHT

This flat 3-piece fairy light is 7" tall and 6" in diameter. The Milk Glass Royal fairy light has a crystal ring insert and a silver edge around the top edge of the base. A Rose Magnolia light with a Sea Mist Green crest and insert was sold on the March 1994 QVC show. This light bears the signature of Shelley Fenton.

No. 1167 Fairy light	Introduced	Discontinued	Value
Milk Glass Royal	1995	1996	$60.00 – 70.00
Red Carnival	1994	1995	$150.00 – 175.00
Rose Magnolia with Sea Mist Green trim	1994	1994	$50.00 – 70.00

NO. 3380, 3-PIECE FAIRY LIGHT

This Cranberry Opalescent 3-piece fairy light was introduced into the regular Fenton line in 1995. It is 7¼" tall and 5½" in diameter. It has a crystal insert that holds the candle.

No. 3380 Fairy light	Introduced	Discontinued	Value
Cranberry Opalescent	1995	1998	$75.00 – 85.00

NO. CV327 FOOTED FAIRY LIGHT

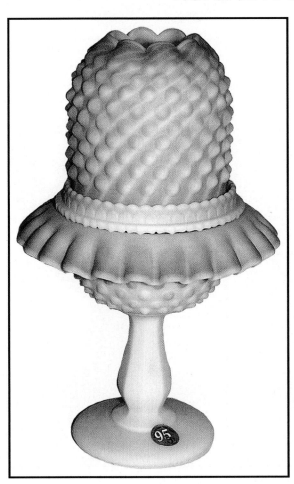

This Burmese Spiral Optic 3-piece Hobnail footed fairy light is about 8¾" tall. The base has a pie crust crimped, rolled down top edge and is footed with a long 8-paneled stem. The candle cup is also in Burmese. This fairy light was made for the October 2000 QVC show.

No. CV327 Fairy light	Produced	Value
Burmese Satin Spiral Optic	2000	$100.00 – 125.00

GOBLETS, MUGS, AND TUMBLERS

NO. 3843 WINE GOBLET

Production of Fenton's wine goblet began in 1940 in Blue Opalescent and French Opalescent colors. Later these goblets were made in Milk, Plum Opalescent, and Ruby. Blue Opalescent wine goblets were reissued from 1959 until 1964. Early goblets were made with a 3-ounce bowl. During the 1960s the mold was changed and the bowl was enlarged to hold four ounces. Both sizes of goblets have the same ware number. Three-ounce goblets are 3¾" tall and have 10 rows of hobs on the bowl. Four-ounce goblets are 4½" tall and 2½" in diameter, and have 12 rows of hobs on the bowl. Both styles have short stems with hobs. Wine goblets with the large size bowl were made for The Levay Distributing Company in Purple Carnival during the late 1970s.

Ruby

No. 3843 Wine goblet	Introduced	Discontinued	Value
Blue Opalescent	1940	1955*	$25.00 – 30.00
French Opalescent	1940	1957	$20.00 – 25.00
Milk	July 1960	1968	$15.00 – 18.00
Plum Opalescent	1961	1963	$90.00 – 120.00
Purple Carnival			$85.00 – 95.00
Red Carnival			$40.00 – 50.00
Ruby	1977	1979	$20.00 – 22.00

*Reissued from 1959 to 1964.

French Opalescent   Blue Opalescent   Plum Opalescent

NO. 3844 SQUARE WINE GOBLET

This wine goblet is 3¾" tall and 2" square at the top. It has nine rows of hobs on the bowl. There is a short twisted stem with hobs and a plain round foot. Square dinnerware entered the Hobnail line in 1951 in Blue Opalescent and French Opalescent. Square shapes were not popular with the consumers of the era. Therefore these shapes did not sell well and are not easily found on the secondary market.

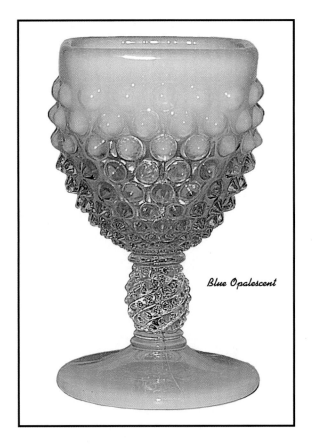

Blue Opalescent

No. 3844	Introduced	Discontinued	Value
Wine goblet			
Blue Opalescent	1951	1954	$60.00 – 70.00
French Opalescent	1951	1955	$35.00 – 45.00

NO. 3845 WATER GOBLET

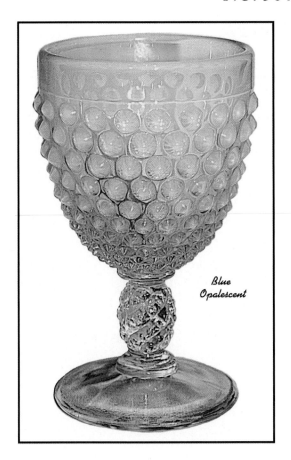

Blue Opalescent

Fenton's No. 3845-8 oz. water goblet is 5½" high and 3¼" in diameter. This goblet entered the regular line in Blue Opalescent and French Opalescent in 1940. It may also be found in Fenton's Opaque Turquoise color; it was not made in this color as a part of the regular line.

No. 3845	Introduced	Discontinued	Value
Water goblet			
Amber	1959	1960	$9.00 – 11.00
Blue Opalescent	1940	1955	$20.00 – 25.00
French Opalescent	1940	1965	$18.00 – 20.00
Milk	1954	1975	$18.00 – 20.00
Turquoise			$30.00 – 35.00

NO. 3846 SQUARE WATER GOBLET

This water goblet with a square bowl was part of a square dinnerware service that Fenton introduced into its regular line in 1951. The colors produced were Blue Opalescent and French Opalescent. This square dinnerware did not sell well and goblets are not easy to find on the secondary market today.

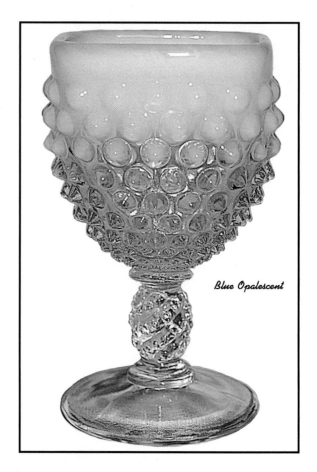

Blue Opalescent

No. 3846 Water goblet	Introduced	Discontinued	Value
Blue Opalescent	1951	1954	$60.00 – 75.00
French Opalescent	1951	1955	$30.00 – 35.00

NO. 3945-5 OZ. TUMBLER

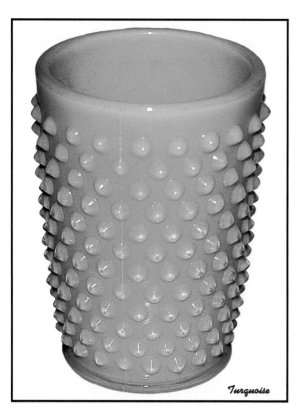

Turquoise

Fenton introduced the Hobnail juice tumbler in 1940. This tumbler is 3½" tall and 2½" in diameter. The side is covered with hobs and narrows slightly from the top to the base. Six of these 5 oz. juice tumblers were often combined with the No. 3965 squat jug to produce the No. 3905, 7-piece juice set.

No. 3645 5 oz. tumbler	Introduced	Discontinued	Value
Amber	1959	1960	$8.00 – 12.00
Blue Opalescent	1940	1955	$20.00 – 25.00
Crystal	1940	1941	$5.00 – 6.00
French Opalescent	1940	1965	$14.00 – 18.00
Milk	July 1952	1968	$7.00 – 9.00
Topaz Opalescent	1941	1944	$25.00 – 30.00
Topaz Opalescent Iridescent	1975	1975	$20.00 – 25.00
Turquoise	July 1955	1957	$14.00 – 16.00

NO. 3949-9 OZ. TUMBLER

Fenton's slightly tapered flat water tumbler is 4⅛" tall and 3" in diameter. This tumbler actually holds closer to eight ounces than the advertised nine ounces. Opalescent colors were among the first produced in 1940; Milk was added in 1953. Amber tumblers were made for one year — 1959. Topaz Opalescent and Plum Opalescent tumblers were produced to be combined with pitchers for sale as water sets during the early 1980s for The Levay Distributing Company. Pink Opalescent, called Peaches 'n Cream (UO), and Sapphire Blue Opalescent tumblers were made for the Gracious Touch division in 1989. Gold Pearl (GP) tumblers were part of the limited edition Hobnail assortment offered in the first half of 1992. The Historic Collection during the first half of 1993 included tumblers in Rose Magnolia (RV). Various colors of tumblers were also made for QVC. These tumblers were sold in sets of four using Fenton's CV015 ware number to indicate the set. Twilight Blue Carnival was made in August 1992 and Dusty Rose Carnival appeared on the March 1993 show. Matching color pitchers were also sold to go with these tumblers. In November 1998, Cobalt tumblers were made to go with a Cobalt Overlay water pitcher. Violet Iridescent tumblers were produced for the January 2002 show and Autumn Gold Iridescent tumblers were on the August 2003 program. Black Carnival tumblers were part of a 7-piece No. 3008 water set sold on QVC in 1990.

No. 3949 Tumbler	Introduced	Discontinued	Value
Amber	1959	1960	$15.00 – 18.00
Aqua Opal Carnival	1982	1982	$25.00 – 30.00
Autumn Gold Irid.	2003	2003	$20.00 – 25.00
Black Carnival	1990	1990	$30.00 – 35.00
Blue Opalescent	1940	1955*	$25.00 – 27.50
Blue Opalescent with MOP Iridescence	1980	1980	$35.00 – 40.00
Cobalt	1998	1998	$20.00 – 25.00
Crystal	1940	1941	$6.00 – 7.00
Dusty Rose Carnival	1993	1993	$22.00 – 25.00
French Opalescent	1940	1965	$18.00 – 20.00
Gold Pearl	1992	July 1992	$18.00 – 22.00
Green Opalescent	1940	1941	$4.00 – 45.00
Milk	July 1953	1968**	$10.00 – 14.00
Peaches 'n Cream	1989	1990	$18.00 – 20.00
Plum Opalescent	1984	1984	$35.00 – 40.00
Purple Carnival	1977	1977	$35.00 – 45.00
Rose Magnolia	1993	July 1993	$18.00 – 20.00
Sapphire Blue Opal	1988	1990	$20.00 – 22.00
Topaz Opalescent	1941	1944***	$35.00 – 40.00
Twilight Blue Carnival	1992	1992	$27.00 – 32.00
Violet Iridescent	2002	2002	$20.00 – 22.00

*Reissued for Levay in 1982.
**Reissued in 1991 and 1992.
*** Also made for Levay in 1981.

Green Opalescent

Plum Opalescent

NO. 3942-12 OZ. TUMBLER

Fenton's 5" tall, 12 oz. flat ice tea tumbler was introduced in 1954. The tumbler is 3" in diameter and there are 13 rows of hobs circling the outside. Blue Opalescent and French Opalescent were only made for a short time.

Milk

No. 3942 12 oz. tumbler	Introduced	Discontinued	Value
Blue Opalescent	1954	1955	$38.00 – 42.00
French Opalescent	1954	1957	$25.00 – 30.00
Milk	1954	1968	$12.00 – 14.00

NO. 3947-12 OZ. BARREL-SHAPED TUMBLER

Fenton introduced a barrel-shaped, 12 oz. flat tumbler in 1941. This popular tumbler is 5" tall. The opalescent tumblers have 14 rows of hobs and the Milk version has 16 rows. Notice the Milk tumbler was only made for six months. Fenton made a No. 3909, 7-piece Cranberry water set for The Levay Distributing Company in 1981. This set matched six of these tumblers with a No. 3360 Cranberry jug with a ribbed French Opalescent handle.

No. 3947 12 oz. tumbler	Introduced	Discontinued	Value
Blue Opalescent	1941	1955	$35.00 – 38.00
Cranberry	1941	1968*	$48.00 – 57.00
French Opalescent	1941	1954	$25.00 – 30.00
Milk	July 1953	1954	$18.00 – 25.00
Topaz Opalescent	1941	1944	$40.00 – 50.00

*Reissued for Levay in 1981.

Blue Opalescent

Cranberry

Topaz Opalescent

NO. 3842 FOOTED ICE TEA

This 5¾" tall footed tumbler entered the Fenton line in 1940. The tumbler is 3½" in diameter. It has rows of hobs on the side. It also has a short stem with hobs and a plain round foot. Peaches 'n Cream (UO) and Sapphire Blue Opalescent (BX) footed tumblers were also listed in the Gracious Touch catalog in 1988 and 1989.

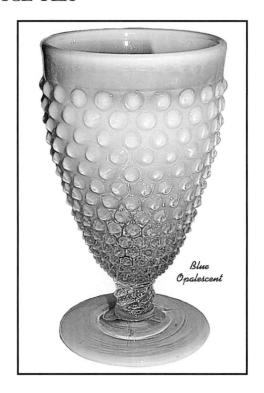

Blue Opalescent

No. 3842	Introduced	Discontinued	Value
12 oz. tumbler			
Blue Opalescent	1940	1955	$25.00 – 35.00
Crystal	1940	1941	$12.00 – 12.00
French Opalescent	1940	1955	$25.00 – 28.00
Milk	1954	1968	$14.00 – 16.00
Peaches 'n Cream Opalescent	1988	1990	$22.00 – 27.00
Sapphire Blue Opalescent	1988	1990	$25.00 – 30.00
Topaz Opalescent	1942	1944	$60.00 – 80.00

NO. 3946-16 OZ. TUMBLER

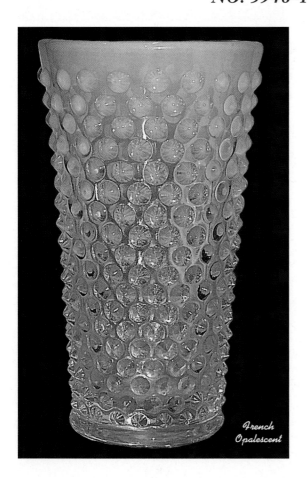

French Opalescent

Fenton's flat bottomed, 16 oz. tumbler entered the line in Blue Opalescent and French Opalescent in 1940. Later, this 6" tall tumbler was made in Milk. The tumbler is 3¼" in diameter and has 17 rows of hobs on its side.

No. 3946	Introduced	Discontinued	Value
16 oz. tumbler			
Blue Opalescent	1940	1955	$65.00 – 85.00
French Opalescent	1940	1955	$45.00 – 50.00
Milk	1954	1968	$25.00 – 30.00

NO. 3646-14 OZ. STEIN

Fenton's large 14 oz. tankard-style stein was in the general line in Milk. It measures 6¾" tall and 4¾" in diameter. There are hobs covering the side of the stein. Near the top and bottom edges is an embossed decorative scalloped border. Since this piece was only made for three years, it is somewhat elusive today.

No. 3646 Stein	Introduced	Discontinued	Value
Milk	1977	1980	$100.00 – 125.00

NO. A-016-6" GOBLET

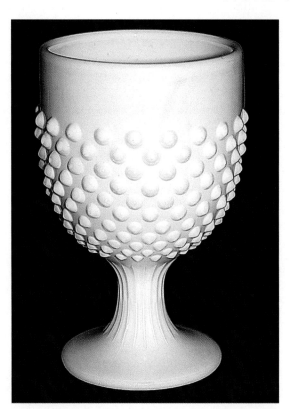

This 6" tall goblet, which was not in the regular Fenton line, may be found without too much difficulty. The goblet is 4" in diameter and has a vertical ribbed stem and a plain round foot. For identification purposes, Shirley Griffith gave this goblet the designation "A-016" in her book *Pictorial Review of Fenton's White Hobnail Milk Glass.*

No. A-016 Goblet	Value
Milk	$20.00 – 25.00

JARDINIERES AND PLANTERS

NO. 3994-4½" JARDINIERE

Fenton introduced two sizes of small pots in January 1952. This small jardiniere is 4½" in diameter and 4" high. It has a scalloped top edge. Colors made include light transparent green and Green Pastel.

Green Pastel

No. 3994 Jardiniere	Introduced	Discontinued	Value
Green Pastel	July 1955	1956	$30.00 – 35.00
Light Green	1955	1956	$20.00 – 25.00
Milk	1952	1969	$14.00 – 18.00

NO. 3898-5" JARDINIERE

This 5½" tall jardiniere was designed to hold either cut flowers or a 4" diameter red clay planter. The jardiniere is 6¼" in diameter. It has paneled sides and eight scallops around the top.

No. 3898 Jardiniere	Introduced	Discontinued	Value
Milk	1975	1979	$25.00 – 30.00

NO. 3996-6" JARDINIERE

Fenton's 6" diameter jardiniere is also 6" tall. The jardiniere was introduced into the Fenton line in January 1952 in Milk and Transparent Green. This jardiniere was designed for either cut flowers or to hold a 4½" red clay pot. The green color was no longer listed by July 1952, when Fenton converted to the new ware number system.

No. 3996 Jardiniere	Introduced	Discontinued	Value
Green, Transparent	1952	1953	$20.00 – 25.00
Milk	1952	1969	$18.00 – 25.00

NO. 3798-8" CRESCENT PLANTER

This small milk Hobnail canoe-shaped planter is 8" long and 2¾" wide. It has a scalloped top edge and is supported by four small feet. This mold was also used to produce a candleholder.

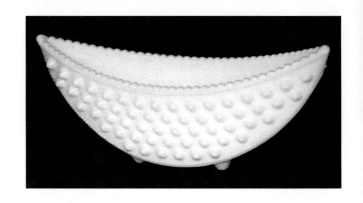

No. 3798	Introduced	Discontinued	Value
Crescent planter			
Milk	July 1960	1966	$30.00 – 35.00

NO. 3698-10" CRESCENT PLANTER

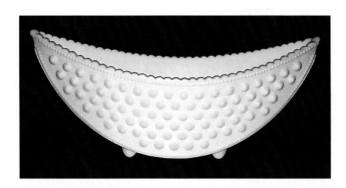

Fenton's 10" long canoe-shaped planter was made in milk during the 1960s. This planter is 3" wide. It has a scalloped top edge and four small feet on the bottom.

No. 3698	Introduced	Discontinued	Value
Crescent planter			
Milk	1961	1966	$45.00 – 55.00

NO. 3697 RECTANGULAR PLANTER

Fenton's No. 3697 planter is 8½" long and 4¼" wide. It has a scalloped top edge and rounded corners. Black, Glossy Opaque Blue, and Glossy Opaque Green planters may be found. These colors were not in the regular line. Some planters were sold through the Fenton Gift Shop and many were distributed to the florist trade through the A. L. Randall Company of Chicago.

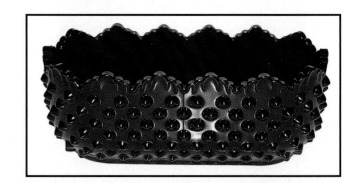

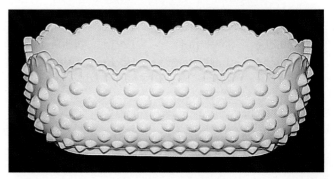

No. 3697	Introduced	Discontinued	Value
Planter			
Black	1970	1971	$35.00 – 45.00
Blue Opaque (Glossy)			$25.00 – 30.00
Green Opaque (Glossy)			$20.00 – 25.00
Milk	1966	1980	$18.00 – 22.00

NO. 3699 SQUARE PLANTER

This 4½" square planter has eight rows of hobs on its sides. It is 4" high and has a scalloped top edge. The base has a narrow plain foot. The Amber planter shown in the photo was not a regular line piece.

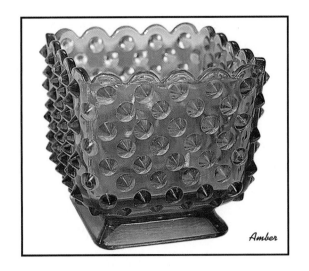

No. 3699 Square planter	Introduced	Discontinued	Value
Amber			$25.00 – 30.00
Milk	1961	1982	$14.00 – 16.00

NO. 3690-9½" PLANTER

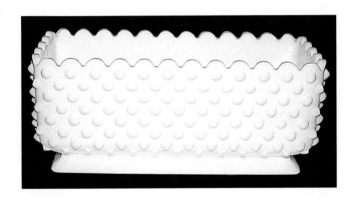

This rectangular planter is 9½" long and 4¼" wide. It has a scalloped top edge and a narrow footed base.

No. 3690 9½" planter	Introduced	Discontinued	Value
Milk	1962	1977	$25.00 – 28.00

NO. 3836-9" WALL PLANTER

Fenton sold the bottom part of the No. 3867 lavabo as a wall planter. This planter is 9" wide. It was listed in the general catalog in Milk and Turquoise during 1956.

No. 3836 Wall planter	Introduced	Discontinued	Value
Milk	1956	July 1956	$45.00 – 55.00
Turquoise	1956	July 1956	$65.00 – 85.00

NO. 3799-10" RECTANGULAR PLANTER

This rectangular planter is 10" long and 4¼" wide. It has a scalloped top edge. The sides of the planter have seven rows of hobs and the corners are rounded. The bottom is plain. This planter was only in the general line in Milk.

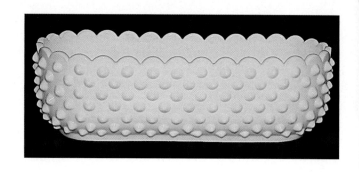

No. 3799 Rect. Planter	Introduced	Discontinued	Value
Milk	1961	1982	$35.00 – 45.00

NO. A-054-6" JARDINIERE

Green Transparent

This jardiniere is 6" high and 6" in diameter. It has a plain round edge and 12 rows of hobs around the side. It has been given the designation "A-054" by Shirley Griffith in her book *Pictorial Review of Fenton's White Hobnail Milk Glass.*

No. A-054 Planter	Value
Green Transparent	$18.00 – 20.00
Milk	$15.00 – 20.00

PLANTERS WITH WROUGHT IRON HANGERS

During the last half of 1964, Fenton marketed several planters, candle arrangements, and wall sconces that were bracketed by decorative wrought iron hangers. These attractive brackets were designed by Dave Ellies of Columbus, Ohio. Examples of the finished products are illustrated in a catalog reprint shown on the next page.

Wrought iron hangers	Introduced	Discontinued	Value
M698 Round Planter #1	July 1964	1965	$40.00 – 50.00
M694 Round Planter #2	July 1964	1965	$45.00 – 55.00
M672 Double Candle Sconce	July 1964	1965	$35.00 – 40.00
M677 Bull's Eye Candle Sconce	July 1964	1965	$15.00 – 20.00
M671 Round Candle Sconce	July 1964	1965	$18.00 – 22.00
M699 Rectangular Planter	July 1964	1965	$45.00 – 55.00

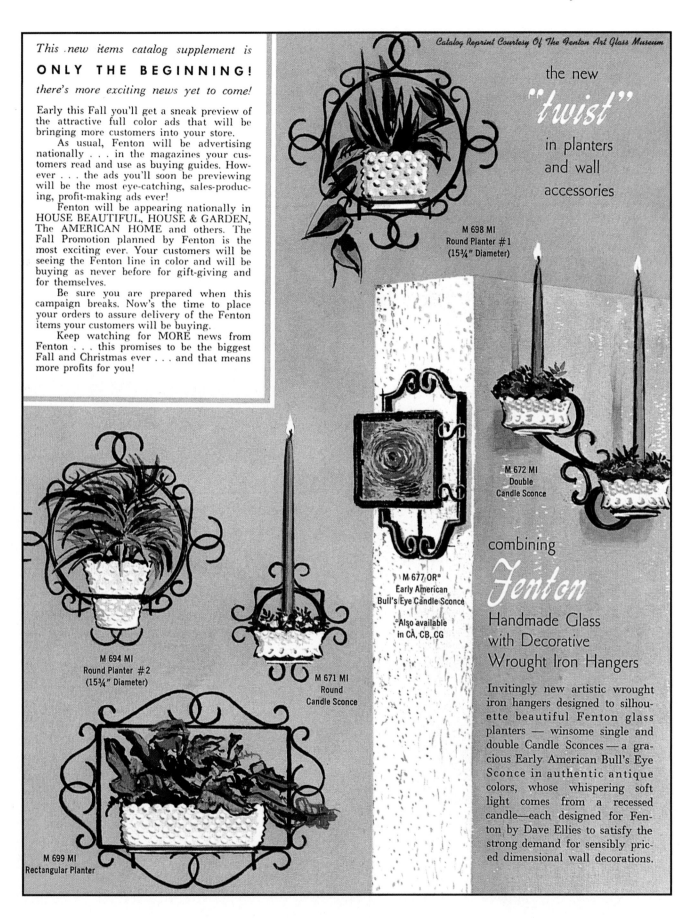

This new items catalog supplement is

ONLY THE BEGINNING!

there's more exciting news yet to come!

Early this Fall you'll get a sneak preview of the attractive full color ads that will be bringing more customers into your store.

As usual, Fenton will be advertising nationally . . . in the magazines your customers read and use as buying guides. However . . . the ads you'll soon be previewing will be the most eye-catching, sales-producing, profit-making ads ever!

Fenton will be appearing nationally in HOUSE BEAUTIFUL, HOUSE & GARDEN, The AMERICAN HOME and others. The Fall Promotion planned by Fenton is the most exciting ever. Your customers will be seeing the Fenton line in color and will be buying as never before for gift-giving and for themselves.

Be sure you are prepared when this campaign breaks. Now's the time to place your orders to assure delivery of the Fenton items your customers will be buying.

Keep watching for MORE news from Fenton . . . this promises to be the biggest Fall and Christmas ever . . . and that means more profits for you!

the new
"twist"
in planters
and wall
accessories

M 698 MI
Round Planter #1
(15¾" Diameter)

M 672 MI
Double
Candle Sconce

M 677 OR*
Early American
Bull's Eye Candle Sconce

*Also available
in CA, CB, CG

M 694 MI
Round Planter #2
(15¾" Diameter)

M 671 MI
Round
Candle Sconce

M 699 MI
Rectangular Planter

combining
Fenton
Handmade Glass
with Decorative
Wrought Iron Hangers

Invitingly new artistic wrought iron hangers designed to silhouette beautiful Fenton glass planters — winsome single and double Candle Sconces — a gracious Early American Bull's Eye Sconce in authentic antique colors, whose whispering soft light comes from a recessed candle—each designed for Fenton by Dave Ellies to satisfy the strong demand for sensibly priced dimensional wall decorations.

JUGS AND PITCHERS

NO. 3964-4½" JUG

Fenton's 4½" tall jug was produced in opalescent colors from 1941 until the mid-1950s. This jug will generally be found with a crystal ribbed applied handle. Rose Overlay Hobnail was made in the mid-1940s.

No. 3964 Jug	Introduced	Discontinued	Value
Blue Opalescent	1941	1954	$40.00 – 50.00
Cranberry	1941	1955	$50.00 – 60.00
French Opalescent	1941	1954	$20.00 – 25.00
Rose Overlay	1943		$70.00 – 80.00
Topaz Opalescent	1941	1944	$90.00 – 110.00

Cranberry

Topaz Opalescent

NO. 3366-5½" PITCHER

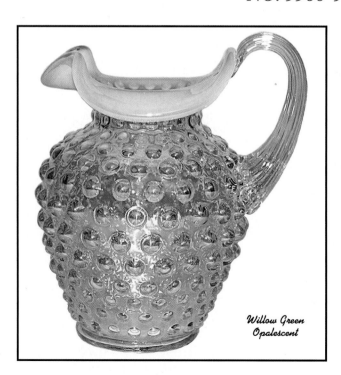

Willow Green
Opalescent

This 5½" tall jug with a saddle crimped top was first produced for the Fenton line in Cranberry during 1995. A few years later it was made in several other colors and also was reissued in Cranberry. In 2001, it was made in Cobalt Blue Overlay for QVC. These pitchers have an applied ribbed handle.

No. 3366 Pitcher	Introduced	Discontinued	Value
Champagne	2000	2001	$40.00 – 45.00
Cobalt Blue Overlay	2001	2001	$40.00 – 50.00
Cranberry	1995	1996*	$40.00 – 50.00
Pink Chiffon Opalescent	2001	2003	$40.00 – 45.00
Willow Green Opalescent	2001	2003	$40.00 – 45.00

*Also made in 2001 and 2002.

NO. 3660-12 OZ. SYRUP PITCHER

This 12 oz., No. 3660 syrup jug entered the Fenton regular line in Milk in 1987. The jug is 5¼" tall, and has a smooth handle and a pie crust crimped top edge.

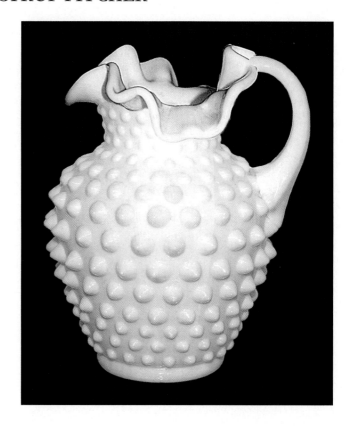

No. 3660 Pitcher	Introduced	Discontinued	Value
Milk	1987	1989	$40.00 – 45.00

NO. CV110 PITCHER

This Cranberry Opalescent Spiral Optic pitcher was made for the October 1995 QVC program. It has a saddle crimped top with a crimped edge. It is a 12 oz. pitcher with an applied ribbed French Opalescent handle. The jug measures approximately 5¼" high.

No. CV110 Pitcher	Produced	Value
Cranberry	1995	$65.00 – 75.00

NO. 389-5½" SYRUP PITCHER

Fenton's original style 12 oz., 5½" tall syrup jug entered the regular line in 1941. This syrup has a smooth top edge and a crystal applied handle. This syrup jug reappeared in the late 1950s with a pie crust crimped top edge. Blue Opalescent, Cranberry, and Topaz Opalescent syrups will be found in both styles.

Cranberry

No. 389 5½" Jug	Introduced	Discontinued	Value
Blue Opalescent	1941	1951	$45.00 – 55.00
Cranberry	1941	1950	$50.00 – 60.00
French Opalescent	1941	1951	$25.00 – 30.00
Rose Overlay	1943	1945	$85.00 – 95.00
Topaz Opalescent	1941	1944	$90.00 – 110.00
Violet Opalescent	1942	1942	$85.00 – 100.00

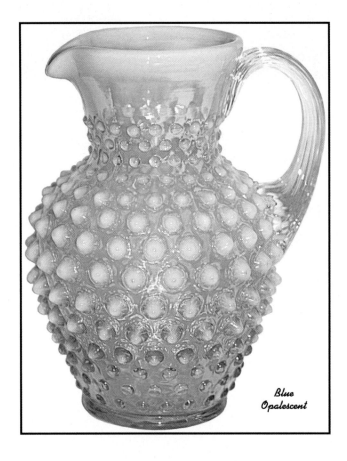

Blue Opalescent

Topaz Opalescent

NO. 3762-12 OZ. SYRUP PITCHER

This 12 oz. syrup jug is 5½" tall and has a pie crust crimped top edge. This style jug was introduced into the regular Fenton line in Milk in 1958. Later, it was made in numerous opalescent and overlay colors. Black Carnival was made for the August 1991 QVC show. The jug is similar to the earlier 5½" syrup jug with a smooth top edge that was made in primarily opalescent colors during the 1940s.

No. 3762 Pitcher	Introduced	Discontinued	Value
Amber	1959	1960	$20.00 – 25.00
Apple Green Overlay	1961	1962	$40.00 – 50.00
Black Carnival	1991	1991	$50.00 – 55.00
Blue Opalescent	1959	1964	$45.00 – 55.00
Coral	1961	1962	$35.00 – 45.00
Cranberry	1969	1978	$50.00 – 60.00
Green Opalescent	July 1959	1960	$65.00 – 85.00
Honey Amber	1961	1964	$30.00 – 35.00
Milk	1958	1979	$20.00 – 22.00
Opaque Blue Overlay	1962	1964	$40.00 – 50.00
Plum Opalescent	July 1959	1962	$100.00 – 110.00
Powder Blue Overlay	1961	1962	$35.00 – 45.00
Red Carnival	1994	1995	$55.00 – 65.00
Topaz Opalescent	1959	1961	$90.00 – 110.00
Wild Rose	1961	1963	$40.00 – 50.00

Green Opalescent

Coral

Red Carnival

NO. 3365-6" PITCHER

This medium-size jug was in the regular Fenton line in milk. It is 7" tall and about 6" in diameter. The jug has an applied ribbed handle. The top edge is crimped and the sides are pulled downward. The bottom has an embossed oval Fenton mark.

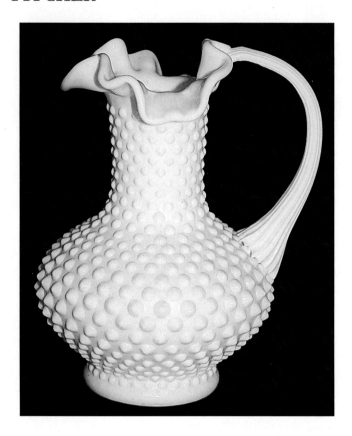

No. 3365 Pitcher	Introduced	Discontinued	Value
Milk	1992	1994	$25.00 – 30.00

NO. 3367-8" PITCHER

Cranberry

This Cranberry Opalescent jug measures about 7½" high. It has downward crimped side edges and a spout to the front. The pitcher has 27 rows of hobs and an applied ribbed French Opalescent handle. There is an oval Fenton mark embossed into the bottom.

No. 3367 Pitcher	Introduced	Discontinued	Value
Cranberry	2003	2005	$85.00 – 95.00
French Opalescent			$30.00 – 35.00

NO. 3965-32 OZ. SQUAT JUG

Fenton's 5½" high squat jug was introduced in 1940 in Blue Opalescent, Cranberry, Green Opalescent, and French Opalescent. Topaz Opalescent replaced Green Opalescent in mid-1941. Rose Overlay and Ruby Overlay colors were made in the mid-1940s. Iridized Topaz Opalescent juice sets were made fot The Levay Distributing Company during 1975. Violet Opalescent with an applied French Opalescent ribbed handle was made for the August 2002 QVC show.

No. 3965 Squat jug	Introduced	Discontinued	Value
Amber	1959	1960	$40.00 – 45.00

No. 3965 Squat jug	Introduced	Discontinued	Value
Blue Opalescent	1940	1955	$80.00 – 100.00
Cranberry	1940	1950	$125.00 – 150.00
French Opalescent	1940	July 1962	$55.00 – 65.00
Green Opalescent	1940	1941	$190.00 – 225.00
Milk	July 1952	1968	$32.00 – 42.00
Rose Overlay	1943		$120.00 – 140.00
Ruby Overlay	1968	1969	$100.00 – 125.00
Topaz Opalescent	July 1941	July 1944	$150.00 – 185.00
Topaz Opalescent Iridescent	1975	1975	$160.00 – 195.00
Turquoise	1955	1957	$75.00 – 85.00
Violet Opalescent	2002	2002	$55.00 – 65.00

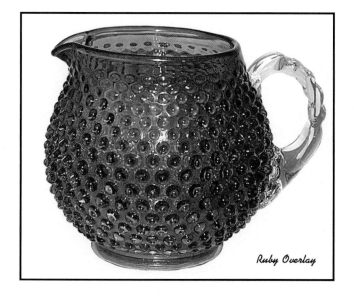

Ruby Overlay

Turquoise

NO. 3905, 7-PIECE JUICE SET

Fenton's No. 3905, 7-piece juice set consists of a No. 3965 squat jug and six No. 3945-5 oz. juice tumblers.

No. 3905 Juice set	Introduced	Discontinued	Value
Amber	1959	1960	$90.00 – 100.00
Blue Opalescent	1941	1955	$200.00 – 250.00
French Opalescent	1941	1961	$125.00 – 185.00
Milk	1950	1968	$75.00 – 95.00
Topaz Opalescent	1941	1944	$300.00 – 365.00
Turquoise	1955	1957	$145.00 – 165.00

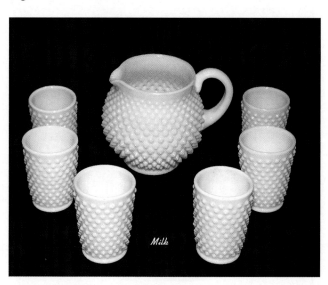

Milk

NO. 389-48 OZ. TANKARD JUG

Fenton's 48 oz. tankard-style jug entered the regular line in 1940. This slender jug is 8" tall with a crystal applied handle and a smooth round top edge. The Cranberry jug with the crimped top was not in the line.

No. 389 Tankard jug	Introduced	Discontinued	Value
Blue Opalescent	1940	1944	$400.00 – 500.00
Cranberry*	1940	1944	$500.00 – 600.00
Crystal	1940	1942	$50.00 – 60.00
French Opalescent	1940	1944	$250.00 – 275.00
Green Opalescent	1940	1941	$450.00 – 500.00
Topaz Opalescent	1941	1944	$400.00 – 450.00

*With crimped top, $1,400.00 – 1,600.00.

Topaz Opalescent

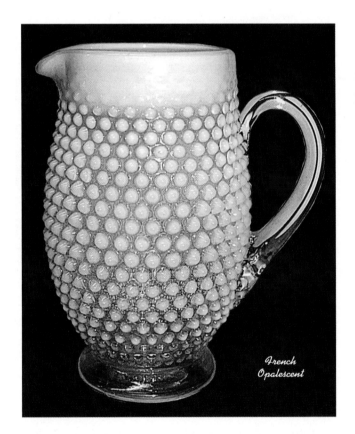

French Opalescent

Cranberry

NO. 3764-54 OZ. JUG

Fenton's No. 3764-54 oz. jug was originally made in Milk beginning in 1958. This jug is 8" tall and has a pie crust crimped top edge. Another color produced for the regular line was amber. It was made for the last six months of 1959. This pitcher was made for Levay in 1980 in Blue Opalescent with a mother-of-pearl iridescence (IQ) as part of the No. 3860 pitcher and bowl set. The No. 3938-12" bowl completed the set. Blue Opalescent and Aqua Opalescent Carnival (IO) jugs were made for Levay in 1982 as part of the No. 3908, 5-piece water set. Four No. 3949-9 oz. tumblers were included with this set. In 1988, this style pitcher was the centerpiece of a 7-piece Pink Opalescent (UO) water set made for the Collector's Extravaganza limited edition assortment. Gold Pearl (GP) pitchers were used in Fenton's 1992 limited edition Historic Collection as part of a five-piece No. 3908 water set. Rose Magnolia (RV) jugs were made in the first half of 1993 as a part of the Historic Collection. Cranberry Opalescent was made for QVC in 2002.

No. 3764 Jug	Introduced	Discontinued	Value
Cranberry	2002	2002	$120.00 – 140.00
Milk	1958	1981	$60.00 – 70.00
Gold Pearl	1992	1992	$90.00 – 110.00
Pink Opalescent	1988	1988	$85.00 – 95.00
Rose Magnolia	1993	July 1993	$90.00 – 110.00
Topaz Opalescent	1981	1981	$300.00 – 350.00

No. 3764 Jug	Introduced	Discontinued	Value
Amber	1959	1960	$85.00 – 90.00
Aqua Opalescent Carnival	1982	1982	$125.00 – 150.00
Blue Opalescent	1982	1982	$140.00 – 160.00
Blue Opalescent with MOP Iridescence	1980	1980	$140.00 – 160.00

Amber

Topaz Opalescent

Milk

NO. 3664-70 OZ. JUG WITH ICE LIP

This No. 3664-70 oz. tall bulbous ice lip jug entered the Fenton line in 1964. The jug is 9¼" high and has a pie crust crimped top edge. It was also listed in the 1988 and 1989 Gracious Touch catalog in Sapphire Blue Opalescent (BX) and Pink Opalescent (UO). Pink Opalescent was also called Peaches 'n Cream Opalescent. Plum Opalescent was made for The Levay Distributing Company in 1984. A Black Carnival (XB) No. 3008, 7-piece water set made for QVC in 1990 included this jug. Gold Pearl jugs were a limited edition production during the first half of 1992. The Spruce Green Carnival (SJ) jug was made in August 1995 for QVC .

Plum Opalescent

No. 3664 Jug	Introduced	Discontinued	Value
Black Carnival	1990	1990	$180.00 – 220.00
Blue Slag	1988	1988	$300.00 – 340.00
Cranberry	1965	1969	$300.00 – 325.00
French Opalescent	1964	1965	$150.00 – 175.00
Gold Pearl	1992	July 1992	$95.00 – 125.00
Milk	1964	1990*	$60.00 – 75.00
Persian Blue Opalescent	July 1989	1990	$175.00 – 200.00
Pink Opalescent	1989	1990	$120.00 – 130.00
Plum Opalescent	1984	1984	$375.00 – 425.00
Purple Carnival	1977	1977	$300.00 – 350.00
Sapphire Blue Opalescent	1988	1990	$140.00 – 160.00
Spruce Green Carnival		1995	$125.00 – 150.00

*Also made from January 1991 to July 1992.

Cranberry

Blue Slag
"Almost Heaven"

NO. 3967-80 OZ. JUG

Fenton introduced this 80 oz. non ice lip jug in opalescent colors in 1941. This pitcher is 7¾" tall and has a pie crust crimped top edge. Beginning in the 1990s, several carnival and overlay colors were made for QVC. A Twilight Blue Carnival Hobnail pitcher was sold on the August 1992 show. This Family Signature piece was marked on the bottom: "Fenton 1992 — We of the Fenton family, who have owned and operated the company since its founding in 1905, are proud of our reputation as a premier producer of handcrafted glassware...." Signatures include Bill, Frank, Don, George, Randy, Mike, Shelley, and Tom Fenton. A set of four tumblers (C10596) could also be ordered. Dusty Rose Carnival pitcher and tumbler sets were available on the March 1993 QVC show. A Cobalt Overlay jug was made for the November 1998 program. A Violet Iridized Hobnail water pitcher and a set of four matching tumblers were offered on the January 2002 show.

No. 3967 80 oz. Jug	Introduced	Discontinued	Value
Blue Opalescent	1941	1955	$225.00 – 275.00
Cobalt Blue Overlay	1998	1998	$110.00 – 130.00
Cranberry	1941	1967	$300.00 – 325.00
Dusty Rose Carnival	1993	1993	$120.00 – 140.00
French Opalescent	1941	1956	$150.00 – 180.00
Milk	July 1953	1969	$85.00 – 110.00
Topaz Opalescent	1941	1944	$300.00 – 350.00
Twilight Blue Carnival	1992	1992	$120.00 – 140.00
Violet Iridescent	2002	2002	$110.00 – 125.00

Cobalt Blue Overlay

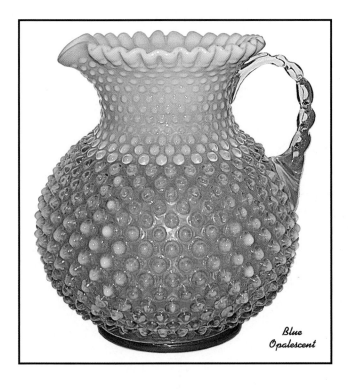

Blue Opalescent

Cranberry

NO. 3360-11" PITCHER

This 11" tall pitcher was first made for The Levay Distributing Company in Purple Carnival as part of the No. 3306, 7-piece water set. Later, it was produced for Levay in Cranberry as part of the No. 3907, 7-piece water set and in Plum Opalescent and Topaz Opalescent for use in the No. 3306, 7-piece water set. It was also made for QVC in Dusty Rose Carnival with Teal trim (DO) in 1988. In 1990, pitchers in Champagne Satin with Light Plum trim (LJ) and Shell Pink Iridescent with Salem Blue trim (YK) were made for QVC. In 1992, this pitcher was placed in the Fenton regular line in milk. The pitcher is about 7" in diameter and has an applied ribbed handle. It has a long narrow neck and a pie crust crimping on its saddle-shaped flanged rim.

No. 3360 Pitcher	Introduced	Discontinued	Value
Champagne Satin Iridescent w/light Plum trim	1990	1990	$125.00 – 150.00
Cranberry	1981	1981	$300.00 – 325.00
Dusty Rose Carnival w/Teal trim	1988	1988	$160.00 – 180.00
Milk	1992	1994	$40.00 – 55.00
Pink Opalescent	1988	1989	$125.00 – 150.00
Plum Opalescent	1984	1984	$350.00 – 400.00
Purple Carnival	1977	1977	$300.00 – 325.00

No. 3360 Pitcher	Introduced	Discontinued	Value
Shell Pink Iridescent w/Salem Blue trim 1990		1990	$140.00 – 160.00
Topaz Opalescent			$300.00 – 350.00

Champagne Satin Iridescent with Light Plum Trim

NO. 3000 PITCHER AND BOWL SET

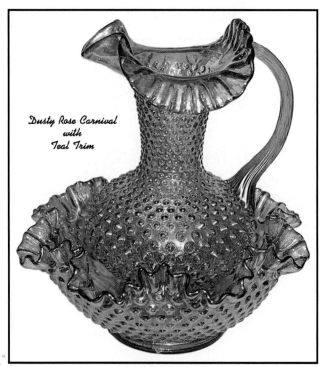

Dusty Rose Carnival with Teal Trim

Fenton's No. 3000 pitcher and bowl set is comprised of a No. 3360-11" pitcher and a No. 3938-12" double crimped bowl. The Dusty Rose Carnival (DO) and Shell Pink Iridescent (YK) sets were made for QVC and the Pink Opalescent (UO) set was in the Collector's Extravaganza assortment. The set made in Milk was in the general catalog.

No. 3000 Pitcher and bowl set	Introduced	Discontinued	Value
Dusty Rose Carnival w/Teal trim	1988	1988	$180.00 – 215.00
Milk	1992	1994	$75.00 – 95.00
Pink Opalescent	1988	1989	$160.00 – 180.00
Shell Pink Iridescent w/Salem Blue trim	1990	1990	$200.00 – 225.00

NO. 3303 PITCHER AND BOWL SET

This set consists of a No. 3664-70 oz. ice lip pitcher and a No. 3939-12" double crimped bowl. The Blue Sag set in the photo was sold through the Fenton Gift Shop in 1988. This color was dubbed "Almost Heaven" by Bill Fenton. Plum Opalescent sets were made for The Levay Distributing Company in 1984. This ware number was also used for a melon-style Gone with the Wind lamp introduced into the line in 2000.

Blue Slag
"Almost Heaven"

No. 3303 Pitcher and bowl set	Produced	Value
Blue Slag	1988	$385.00 – 425.00
Plum Opalescent	1984	$600.00 – 675.00

LECHLER MINIATURE LEMONADE SET

During the 1980s Doris Lechler of Columbus, Ohio, commissioned Fenton to produce a series of miniature collectables for her "Heirlooms of Tomorrow" collection. Among the items made were several colors of a miniature Hobnail lemonade set. A No. 3361 pitcher and either four or six No. 3341 tumblers were placed on a French Opalescent tray to make a lemonade set. Another set was made in French Opalescent. A third set was made on Cobalt Blue Overlay with a cobalt tray.

Lemonade set	Value
Cobalt Blue Overlay	$325.00 – 375.00
Cranberry	$500.00 – 550.00
French Opalescent	$275.00 – 325.00

Cranberry

Cobalt Blue Overlay

NO. 3908 WATER SET

This ware number was used for both 7- and 5-piece water sets comprised of the No. 3764 crimped top water pitcher and either four or six No. 3949-9 oz. tumblers. A 7-piece water set was made for The Levay Distributing Company in 1980 in Blue Opalescent with a mother-of-pearl iridescence (IQ). The next year this water set was made for Levay in Topaz Opalescent. In 1982, a 5-piece water set was made for Levay in Blue Opalescent. This style pitcher was not made previously in this color. Tumblers from this issue will have the Fenton oval mark embossed in the base. During this year a 5-piece water set was also made for Levay in Aqua Opalescent Carnival (IO). Two 7-piece water sets were later made for Fenton limited edition promotions. Pink Opalescent (UO) water sets were part of the Collector's Extravaganza assortment in 1988 and Rose Magnolia (RV) sets were made for the Historical Collection during the first half of 1993. A 5-piece water set was made for the 1992 Historic Collection in Gold Pearl (GP). This ware number was also used for Fenton's 10-piece octagonal punch set made in 1953.

No. 3908 Water set	Produced	Value
Aqua Opalescent Carnival	1982	$225.00 – 270.00
Blue Opalescent	1982	$240.00 – 365.00
Blue Opalescent with MOP Iridescence	1980	$340.00 – 400.00
Gold Pearl	1992	$160.00 – 190.00
Pink Opalescent	1988	$195.00 – 215.00
Rose Magnolia	1993	$200.00 – 220.00
Topaz Opalescent	1981	$525.00 – 290.00

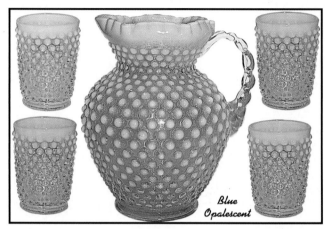

Blue Opalescent

NO. 3306 WATER SET

Plum Opalescent

This style water set was made for The Levay Distributing Company during the 1980s. The 7-piece set is made up of a No. 3360-11" pitcher and six No. 3949-9 oz. water tumblers. Topaz Opalescent sets were made in 1983 and Plum Opalescent sets were made in 1984.

No. 3306 Water set	Produced	Value
Plum Opalescent	1984	$550.00 – 600.00
Topaz Opalescent	1983	$500.00 – 550.00

NO. 3909 WATER SET

Fenton produced the No. 3909, 7-piece water set in Cranberry for The Levay Distributing Company in 1982. This set is comprised of a No. 3360-11" jug and six No. 3947 barrel-shaped tumblers.

No. 3909 Water set	Produced	Value
Cranberry	1982	$600.00 – 675.00

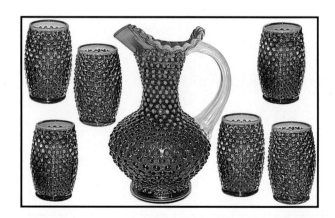

LAMPS IN THE GENERAL LINE

NO. 3305 MINI LAMP

Fenton created this small lamp by drilling a hole in the Butterfly candy base. The base was inverted and an electric light socket and stenciled parchment shade completed the lamp. The glass part of the lamp is 4" high and 4" in diameter. This lamp was not in the line for very long and is not easily found. The shade pictured is not original.

No. 3305 Lamp	Introduced	Discontinued	Value
Milk	July 1987	1988	$120.00 – 140.00

NO. 3604 BOUDOIR LAMP

This 2-piece Hobnail lamp was made during 1969 in Opal. This formula of glassware is more translucent and has better heat resistance than regular milk Hobnail. The assembled lamp is 10½" tall. The shade is connected to the base of the lamp with a curved brass hanger. Notice this elusive lamp was only made for one year.

No. 3604 Boudoir lamp	Introduced	Discontinued	Value
Opal	1969	1970	$350.00 – 400.00

NO. 3792 & NO. 3793 COURTING LAMP

Fenton's handled Hobnail courting lamp entered the line in 1965. Two versions of this lamp were produced — oil and electric. Oil lamps have ware number 3792 and electric lamps use the ware number 3793. The lamp is 9½" tall and about 6" in diameter. The shade has a pie crust crimped top edge.

No. 3792, 3793 Courting lamp	Introduced	Discontinued	Value
Colonial Amber	1965	1969	$55.00 – 60.00
Colonial Blue	1965	1968	$75.00 – 85.00
Colonial Green	1965	1968	$55.00 – 60.00
Milk	1965	1972	$90.00 – 125.00

Milk

Colonial Blue

NO. 3998 HURRICANE LAMP

Peach Blow

Fenton's No. 3998, 2-piece hurricane lamp is 8¼" tall and 6¼" in diameter. The chimney is 6" high, is covered with hobs, and has a pie crust crimped top edge. The handled base is plain. Pastel colors have matching color bases. Milk and Peach Blow lamps have a milk base.

No. 3998 Hurricane lamp	Introduced	Discontinued	Value
Blue Pastel	1954	1955	$100.00 – 1.0.00
Green Pastel	1954	1956	$90.00 – 110.00
Milk	1952	1970	$40.00 – 45.00
Peach Blow	July 1952	1954	$110.00 – 135.00
Rose Pastel	1954	1955	$90.00 – 100.00

NO. 3713-11" HURRICANE LAMP

This 11" tall electric lamp has a 7½" tall Hobnail shade with a double crimped top edge. The base of the lamp is antique brass. It has been designed to have the appearance of an old oil lamp. Since it was only made for two years, this lamp is elusive.

No. 3713	Introduced	Discontinued	Value
Hurricane lamp			
Milk	1979	1981	$150.00 – 190.00

NO. 3307-15" STUDENT LAMP

This 15" tall Cranberry electric lamp entered the Fenton line in 1984. The shade is 7½" in diameter and has a pie crust crimped top. The round base has a brass finish with a soft patina.

No. 3307	Introduced	Discontinued	Value
Student lamp			
Cranberry	1984	1989	$175.00 – 200.00

NO. 1150-18" STUDENT LAMP

A new Cranberry Hobnail 18" tall student lamp entered the Fenton general line in 2002. The shade is 7½" in diameter and has a crimped top. The base is embossed brass with a concave octagonal-shaped bottom.

No. 1150 Student lamp	Introduced	Discontinued	Value
Cranberry	2002	2003	$175.00 – 200.00

NO. 3707-19" STUDENT LAMP

Cranberry

Fenton's No. 3707 Hobnail electric student lamp entered the line in milk in 1968. This lamp is 19" high and has a 7½" diameter shade with a piecrust crimped top. A Hobnail fount divides the brass stem. The scalloped foot of the brass stem rests upon a square marble base.

No. 3707 Student lamp	Introduced	Discontinued	Value
Cranberry	1968	1975	$250.00 – 300.00
Milk	1966	1977	$200.00 – 225.00

NO. 3807-21" STUDENT LAMP

This Hobnail 21" tall electric student lamp entered the Fenton line at the beginning of the 1970s. The shade has 12 panels, a ribbed neck, and a double crimped top. The stem and shade support are brass. The stem is separated into two parts by a Hobnail glass fount with six panels. The bottom of the lamp has four feet that rest upon a square marble base. This ware number was also used for a 4-quart, 15-piece punch set marketed during the 1950s.

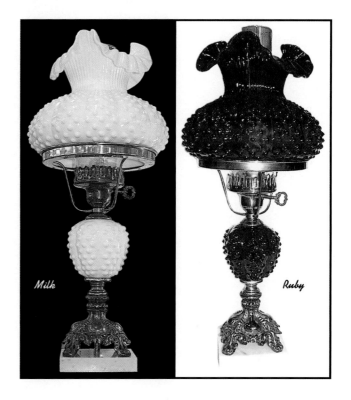

No. 3807 Student lamp	Introduced	Discontinued	Value
Decorated Roses	1974	1976	$225.00 – 275.00
Milk	1971	1990*	$200.00 – 225.00
Ruby	1972	1975	$125.00 – 150.00

*Also produced from January 1991 until July 1992.

NO. 1174-22½" STUDENT LAMP

Fenton's No. 1174-22½" Hobnail student lamp was made for the general line in Cranberry and Milk. The shade is 10" wide and has a crimped top. The lamp is adorned with prisms that hang from the bottom of the shade support. This style lamp was made in Opaline Iridescent for QVC in 1997.

No. 1174 Student lamp	Introduced	Discontinued	Value
Cranberry	1993	1994*	$225.00 – 250.00
Milk	1993	1994	$175.00 – 200.00
Opaline Iridescent	1997	1997	$250.00 – 275.00

*Also made from 1995 through 1998.

NO. 3808-22" GWTW LAMP

Fenton made a 22" tall Hobnail Gone with the Wind style lamp with paneled globes in milk. The shade is about 8" in diameter and the top is double crimped. This lamp was produced in milk almost every year between 1976 and 1998. This lamp has the same ware number as the square cup and saucer made in the 1950s.

No. 3808-22" GWTW lamp	Introduced	Discontinued	Value
Milk	1976	1998	$200.00 – 250.00

NO. 3304-25" GWTW LAMP

Fenton produced the No. 3308 Cranberry Hobnail Gone with the Wind style lamp continuously for about 15 years before it was discontinued at the end of 1998. In 2002, after a a few years without a GWTW lamp in this color, Fenton introduced a new version of this style lamp. This lamp has a different style of antique brass hardware. The glass globes are 8" in diameter and the shade has a double crimped top. This lamp was still available in Fenton's 2005 general catalog.

No. 3304-25" GWTW lamp	Introduced	Discontinued	Value
Cranberry	2002		$350.00 – 375.00

NO. 3303-25" GWTW LAMP

Fenton introduced a new 25" tall Hobnail paneled-style Gone with the Wind type lamp with the dawn of the new century. This lamp featured heavy antique looking brass hardware. The globes have eight panels and are 8" in diameter. The shade has a crimped top edge. This ware number was also used for a Plum Opalescent pitcher and bowl set produced for The Levay Distributing Company in 1984.

No. 3303-25" GWTW lamp	Introduced	Discontinued	Value
Champagne	2000	2001	$250.00 – 275.00
Cranberry	2001	2002	UND
Pink Chiffon Opalescent	2001	2003	$250.00 – 275.00
Willow Green Opalescent	2001	2003	$250.00 – 275.00

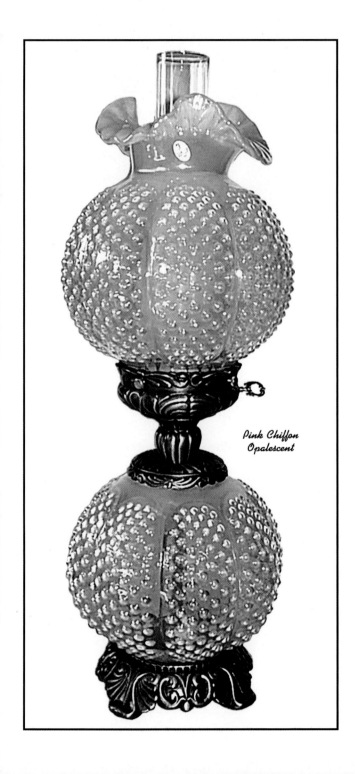

Pink Chiffon Opalescent

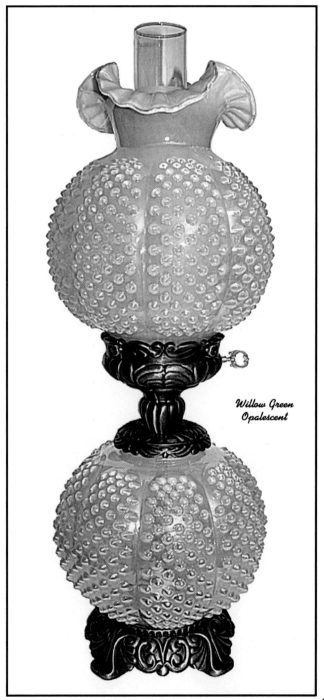

Willow Green Opalescent

NO. 3308-25" GWTW LAMP

This 25" tall Gone with the Wind style electric lamp was made in Cranberry beginning in 1984. The round, ball-shaped Hobnail globes are 8" in diameter. The shade has a double crimped top edge. Pink Opalescent lamps (A3308-UO) were made for Fenton's limited edition Collector's Extravaganza offering in 1988.

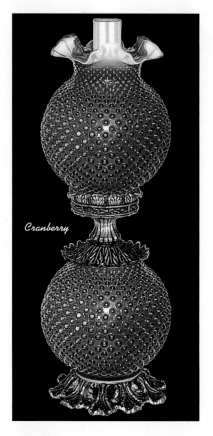

Cranberry

No. 3308-25" GWTW lamp	Introduced	Discontinued	Value
Cranberry	1984	1999	$300.00 – 350.00
Pink Opalescent	1988	1989	$250.00 – 275.00

NO. 3907-26" PILLAR LAMP

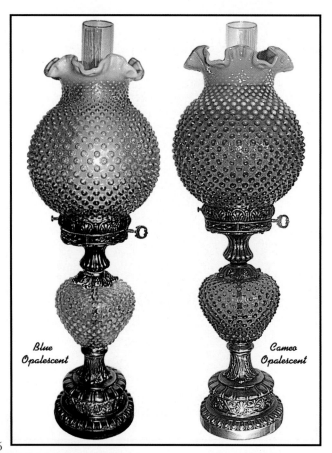

Blue Opalescent

Cameo Opalescent

Fenton's 26" tall Hobnail pillar lamp entered the general line in Blue Opalescent in mid-1978. The lamp shade is 8" in diameter and has a double crimped top.

No. 3907-26" Pillar lamp	Introduced	Discontinued	Value
Blue Opalescent	July 1978	1981	$360.00 – 400.00
Cameo Opalescent	July 1979	1983	$250.00 – 300.00
Cranberry	1977	1996	$275.00 – 325.00
Milk	1992	1993	$175.00 – 225.00

LAMP SHAPES NOT IN THE GENERAL LINE

Many Hobnail lamps were assembled by independent manufacturers. These retailers often bought glass, wood, and metal lamp parts from various sources. They assembled these parts to produce a finished lamp and sold the resulting products under their brand names.

This Green Opalescent nightlight was made by combining a handled brass base with a drilled Hobnail 6" double crimped bonbon. $85.00 – 125.00.

To produce this small nightlight, a handled brass base was attached through a hole drilled in a Hobnail 6" flared bonbon. $65.00 – 75.00.

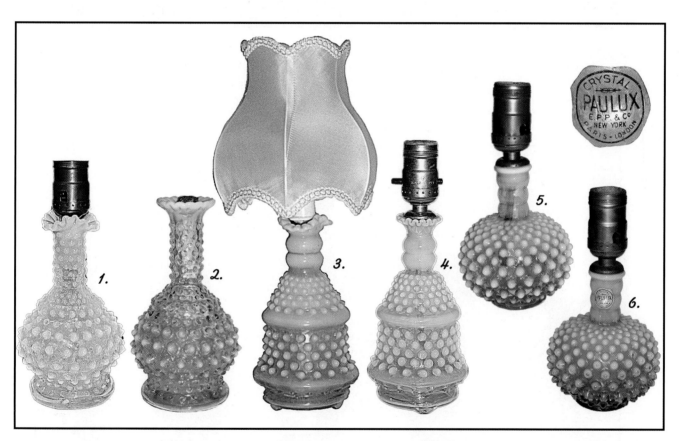

The above lamp bases were made by Fenton for Edward P. Paul and Company. They were sold under the "Paulux" label. Lamp bases on the far right were made from old Wrisley cologne bottle molds. This is one explanation for the appearance of these bottoms in colors that were not originally made for Wrisley. A close-up of an original label is pictured at the top right of the photo.

E. P. Lamp	Value
1. Topaz Opalescent	$55.00 – 65.00
2. Blue Opalescent	$45.00 – 55.00
3. Blue Opalescent	$85.00 – 100.00
4. French Opalescent	$35.00 – 45.00
5. Green Opalescent	$55.00 – 65.00
6. Blue Opalescent	$45.00 – 55.00

Lamp	Value	Lamp	Value
1. Blue Opalescent	$125.00 – 150.00	4. Topaz Opalescent	$140.00 – 160.00
2. Milk, handled hurricane	$70.00 – 80.00	5. Green Opalescent	$100.00 – 125.00
3. Blue Opalescent	$125.00 – 150.00	6. French Opalescent	$40.00 – 45.00

Lamp	Value	Lamp	Value
1. Ruby Overlay courting lamp	$150.00 – 200.00	4. Cranberry handled lamp	$150.00 – 175.00
2. Cranberry finger lamp	$280.00 – 310.00	5. Cranberry lamp from	
3. Cranberry pitcher lamp	$160.00 – 180.00	candleholder	$80.00 – 90.00

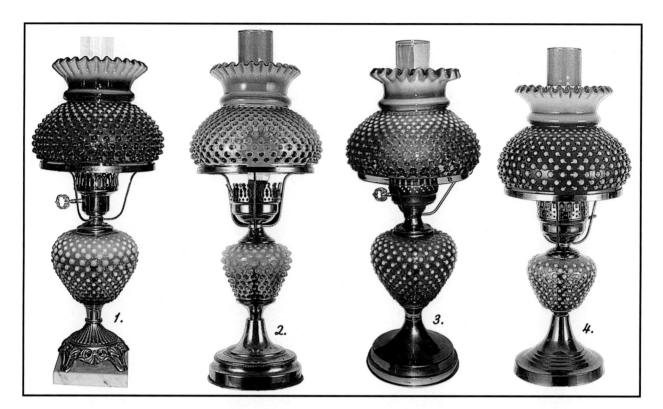

Lamp	Value
1. Cranberry 20" electric student lamp with glass fount and marble base.	$300.00 – 325.00
2. Blue Opalescent electric student lamp with glass fount and brass base.	$375.00 – 425.00
3. Cranberry electric student lamp with brass base and three arms supporting shade.	$300.00 – 325.00
4. Cranberry electric student lamp with glass fount and brass base.	$300.00 – 325.00

Lamp	Value
1. Cranberry electric double student lamp with single glass fount and brass base.	$450.00 – 500.00
2. Cranberry weighted electric student lamp with glass fount and brass base.	$350.00 – 400.00
3. Amber electric double student lamp with glass fount and marble base.	$100.00 – 125.00
4. Cranberry electric double student lamp with glass fount and marble base.	$425.00 – 475.00

Lamp	Value
1. Cranberry electric lamp with a special rose bowl glass fount and marble base.	$275.00 – 300.00
2. Honey Amber Overlay electric student lamp with glass fount and brass base.	$100.00 – 125.00
3. Cranberry 22" tall electric lamp with brass base and large glass fount.	$300.00 – 350.00
4. Cranberry electric lamp made with GWTW-style shade on the bottom.	$150.00 – 175.00

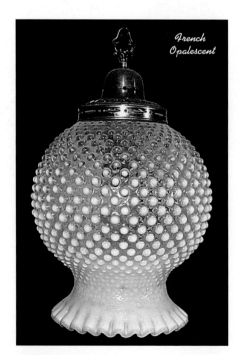

Lamp	Value
French Opalescent hanging shade, 10" diameter	$125.00 – 150.00

Lamp

1. Peach Blow double floor lamp with milk fount and brass stand.
2. Cranberry offset floor lamp with brass stand and eagle finial.
3. Cranberry double floor lamp with Cranberry fount and brass stand.
4. Cranberry floor lamp with brass stand.

Value

$200.00 – 225.00
$275.00 – 325.00
$400.00 – 450.00
$150.00 – 170.00

NO. 9201-36" BANQUET LAMP

This 36" tall Hobnail banquet lamp was made for The Levay Distributing Company in Cranberry Opalescent in 1981. Production was very limited and not many of these lamps will be found.

No. 9201 Lamp	Produced	Value
Cranberry	1981	$400.00 – 450.00

CHANDELIER

Numerous chandelier style hanging fixtures were produced from Hobnail parts. Some were made from one shape part, but others will have several different shapes of Hobnail parts incorporated into the design. The most commonly seen color is Cranberry, but other color fixtures such as Topaz Opalescent, French Opalescent, and Blue Opalescent may be found.

Topaz Opalescent

Chandelier	Value
Blue Opalescent	$350.00 – 400.00
Cranberry	$400.00 – 500.00
French Opalescent	$200.00 – 250.00
Topaz Opalescent	$400.00 – 500.00

MISCELLANEOUS ITEMS

NO. 3808 SQUARE CUP AND SAUCER

This shape cup and saucer is part of a square line of Hobnail dinnerware that Fenton introduced into the regular line in 1951. The same ware number was used for a 22" GWTW lamp that entered the line in 1976.

No. 3808	Introduced	Discontinued	Value
Cup & saucer			
Blue Opalescent	1951	1954	$85.00 – 100.00
French Opalescent	1951	1955	$35.00 – 40.00

NO. 3647 EGG CUP

Introduced into the general line in January 1970, Fenton's Milk Hobnail egg cup was produced for only 2 years. Therefore, this piece is seldom found on the secondary market. The egg cup is 4" tall and 3¾" in diameter. There are six scallops around the top edge and the sides have six panels. A ruby egg cup was produced for the National Fenton Glass Society. This egg cup has the Fenton logo and is signed by Nancy Fenton.

No. 3647	Introduced	Discontinued	Value
Egg cup			
Milk	1970	1972	$95.00 – 110.00

NO. 3904 NAPKIN RING SET

Hobnail napkin rings were made in Milk. They were sold as a set of four packaged in a gift box. They are priced individually below. This ware number was also used for a 3-piece console set sold during the 1950s consisting of a pair of No. 3974 candleholders and a No. 3924 bowl.

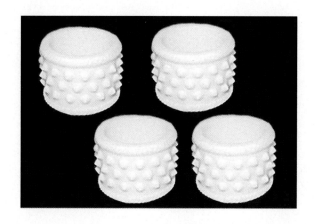

No. 3904	Introduced	Discontinued	Value
Napkin ring			
Milk	1976	1978	$25.00 – 30.00

NO. 3867 LAVABO

A three-piece lavabo was made in Milk, Turquoise, and several overlay colors from the mid-1950s until the mid-1960s. Milk is the color seen most frequently. Wild Rose is the most elusive. The covered urn is 10" high and 6" wide. It has a brass spigot near the bottom of the urn. The basin is 9" wide and 5½" deep. Pictured is a set mounted on a walnut backboard and another set with mirrored advertising.

No. 3867 Lavabo	Introduced	Discontinued	Value
Honey Amber	1962	1967	$180.00 – 200.00
Opaque Blue Overlay	1962	1964	$200.00 – 225.00
Milk	July 1955	1977	$125.00 – 140.00
Turquoise	July 1955	1957	$170.00 – 200.00
Wild Rose	1962	1963	$225.00 – 250.00

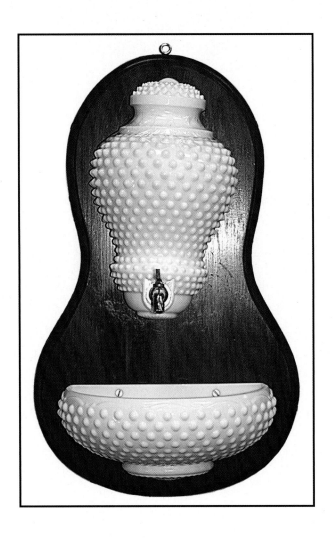

NO. 3612 SPOON HOLDER

Fenton produced a Milk Hobnail spoon holder for two years during the late 1960s. This spoon holder is 7¼" long and has hobs on both the sides and bottom.

No. 3612 Spoon holder	Introduced	Discontinued	Value
Milk	1967	1969	$85.00 – 110.00

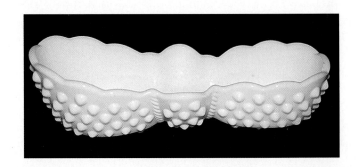

NO. 3795 TOOTHPICK HOLDER

This 3-toed toothpick holder was made in numerous colors for the general line, the Fenton Gift Shop, and special order customers. The toothpick is 3" high and 2" in diameter. It has a scalloped top edge and six rows of hobs on the side. Aqua Opalescent Carnival, Blue Opalescent, and Topaz Opalescent colors were made for The Levay Distributing Company during the early 1980s. Topaz Opalescent was made for Levay during two separate times — in 1980 and again in 1983. Pink Opalescent was made in 1988 as a part of Fenton's special Collector's Extravaganza assortment.

No. 3795 Toothpick holder	Introduced	Discontinued	Value
Amber	1966	1976	$8.00 – 10.00
Aqua Opalescent Carnival	1982		$20.00 – 25.00

No. 3795 Toothpick holder	Introduced	Discontinued	Value
Black			$10.00 – 12.00
Blue Opalescent	1982	1982	$20.00 – 25.00
Blue Satin Opal	1980	1980	$10.00 – 12.00
Carnival	1980	1981	$14.00 – 16.00
Colonial Blue	1966	1976	$12.00 – 14.00
Colonial Green	1966	1976	$8.00 – 10.00
Crystal	1968	1969	$4.00 – 6.00
Decorated Blue Bell	1972	July 1972	$22.00 – 27.00
Milk	1966	1985	$10.00 – 14.00
Orange	1966	1976	$8.00 – 10.00
Pekin Blue II	1968	1968	$12.00 – 14.00
Pink Opalescent	1988	1989	$10.00 – 12.00
Pink Satin Opal	1981	1981	$10.00 – 12.00
Topaz Opalescent	1980*	1980	$27.00 – 32.00

*Also made for Levay in 1983.

Colonial Blue

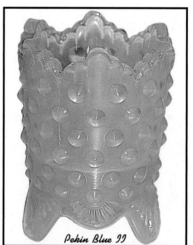

Pekin Blue II

NO. 3895 TOOTHPICK/CANDLEHOLDER

Fenton's No. 3895-2¾" tall toothpick holder was also promoted as a candleholder. This toothpick holder was in the general line in Milk during the 1970s. It is 1¾" in diameter and has concave sides. A crudely made import may be found that closely resembles this toothpick.

No. 3895 Toothpick holder	Introduced	Discontinued	Value
Milk	1971	July 1976	$20.00 – 22.00

PLATES, TIDBITS, AND TRAYS

ROUND CRIMPED PLATES

Fenton's 6" plate was introduced in opalescent colors in 1940 as a flat variation of the 6" bonbon. This small plate has a plain center and a slightly upward flared pie crust crimped edge.

No. 389-6" Plate	Introduced	Discontinued	Value
Blue Opalescent	1940	1952	$14.00 – 16.00
Cranberry	1940	1952	$18.00 – 20.00
French Opalescent	1940	1952	$8.00 – 10.00
Green Opalescent	1940	1941	$22.00 – 27.00
Rose Overlay	1943	1945	$27.00 – 30.00
Topaz Opalescent	1941	1944	$30.00 – 35.00

An 8½" diameter plate with a pie crust crimped edge was made in milk for a short time during the mid-1950s. This plate has a plain center on the bottom side. There are also seven rows of hobs on the underside of the plate. This plate is elusive.

No. 3912 8½" Plate	Introduced	Discontinued	Value
Milk	1955	1957	$25.00 – 28.00

Topaz Opalescent 13 1/2" Plate

Round 9¾" diameter crimped edge dinner plates were made for Fenton's Gracious Touch division in 1989. The colors produced were Peaches 'n Cream Opalescent (UO) and Sapphire Blue Opalescent (BX).

No. 3312 9¾" Plate	Produced	Value
Peaches 'n Cream Opalescent	1989	$12.00 – 14.00

Topaz Opalescent 8" Plate

No. 3312-9¾" Plate	Produced	Value
Sapphire Blue Opalescent	1989	$16.00 – 18.00

Fenton's 8" diameter plate with a crimped edge was made in several colors. This plate has a plain center on the bottom with seven rows of hobs radiating toward the outside edge. French Opalescent and Topaz Opalescent plates were only made for a short time and are not often seen. Although they were made for over 10 years, plates in Milk are found infrequently.

No. 3816 8" Plate	Introduced	Discontinued	Value
French Opalescent	1956	1957	$12.00 – 15.00
Milk	1956	1968	$16.00 – 19.00
Topaz Opalescent	July 1959	1960	$40.00 – 45.00

Fenton's round 13½" diameter salver with a pie crust crimped edge was introduced into the line in mid-1959. Topaz Opalescent salvers were only made for six months. Milk plates were made through the mid-1960s. Notice the small plain center of this plate. A small number of Plum Opalescent plates were produced for a special order customer.

No. 3714 13½" Plate	Introduced	Discontinued	Value
Milk	July 1959	1967	$45.00 – 55.00
Plum Opalescent	2000	2000	$75.00 – 85.00
Topaz Opalescent	July 1959	1960	$80.00 – 95.00

ROUND SMOOTH EDGE PLATES

Round 8" diameter plain edge luncheon plates were intro-
duced in the early 1940s with the advent of the Hobnail line.
This style plate is much more common than the crimped edge
plates. These plates have a plain center. Many people confuse
Hocking's Moonstone pattern plates with Fenton's French
Opalescent plates. Hocking's plates have rays in the center.
Peaches 'n Cream Opalescent (UO) and Sapphire Blue
Opalescent (BX) plates were sold in sets of four through Fen-
ton's Gracious Touch division.

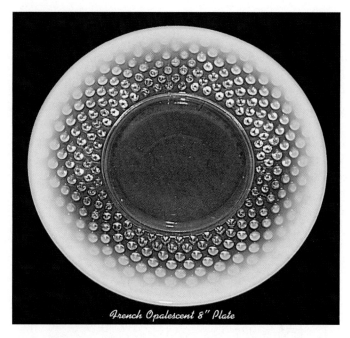
French Opalescent 8" Plate

No. 3918 8" Plate	Introduced	Discontinued	Value
Blue Opalescent	1940	1955	$18.00 – 22.00
Crystal	1940	1942	$3.00 – 5.00
French Opalescent	1940	1957	$12.00 – 15.00
Peaches 'n Cream Opalescent	1988	1990	$12.00 – 14.00
Sapphire Blue Opalescent	1988	1990	$16.00 – 18.00
Topaz Opalescent	1942	1944	$40.00 – 45.00

Fenton made a round plain edge 16" torte plate for use as
the underplate for the No. 3827 punch bowl. This punch set
was introduced into the line in the fall of 1950. Colors made
were Blue Opalescent, French Opalescent, and Milk. This
plate has an indented plain area in the center in which the bowl
rests. There are 13 rows of hobs on the underside of the plate.

No. 3917-16" Torte plate	Introduced	Discontinued	Value
Blue Opalescent	Sept. 1950	1955	$100.00 – 120.00
French Opalescent	Sept. 1950	1955	$45.00 – 50.00
Milk	Sept. 1950	1969	$55.00 – 60.00

NO. 389 CRESCENT TRAY

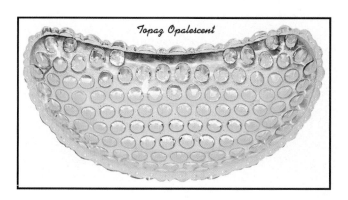
Topaz Opalescent

This small 6½" long, oval kidney-shaped plate was made
briefly during two different eras. It was first made in Blue
Opalescent, French Opalescent, and Topaz Opalescent during
the early 1940s. It was made for another two years at the end
of the decade in Blue Opalescent and French Opalescent.

No. 389 Crescent tray	Introduced	Discontinued	Value
Blue Opalescent	1942	1943*	$50.00 – 65.00
French Opalescent	1942	1943*	$35.00 – 40.00
Topaz Opalescent	1942	1943	$90.00 – 125.00

*Reissued in 1948 and 1949.

SQUARE PLATES

Square Hobnail 6½" plates may be found in French Opalescent and Blue Opalescent. Square dinnerware was introduced into the Fenton general line in the fall of 1950. These plates have 12 rows of hobs on the undersides and are 5½" wide from side to side. The diagonal measurement is about 6½".

French Opalescent Square 6 1/2" Plate

No. 3819-6½" square plate	Introduced	Discontinued	Value
Blue Opalescent	Sept. 1950	1954	$30.00 – 35.00
French Opalescent	Sept. 1950	1955	$20.00 – 25.00

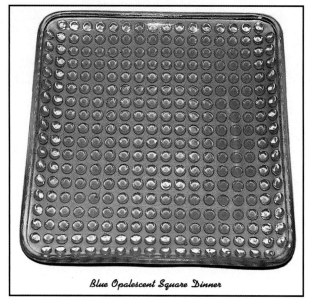

Blue Opalescent Square Dinner

Square dinner plates measure 11½" diagonally. They have 18 rows of hobs on the undersides. Square dinnerware was not a huge marketing success for Fenton; therefore, square dinner plates are elusive.

No. 3910-11" square plate	Introduced	Discontinued	Value
Blue Opalescent	Sept. 1950	1955	$110.00 – 125.00
French Opalescent	Sept. 1950	1955	$40.00 – 45.00

OVAL TRAY WITH CHROME HANDLE

This tray is commonly found in milk, but is elusive in French Opalescent. Fenton used this 7½" long by 3¾" wide handled tray to produce several condiment sets. It was used to hold the star-shaped sugar and creamer. It was also used in combination with two marmalade jars to make a jam and jelly set. Two oil bottles placed on this tray created an oil and vinegar set. An oil bottle and mustard were also sold with this tray as another condiment selection. For more information about these sets, see the Condiment Sets section of this book.

Milk

Oval handled tray	Introduced	Discontinued	Value
French Opalescent	1955	1956	$45.00 – 55.00
Milk	1955	1984	$10.00 – 12.00

NO. 3791 CHROME HANDLED SANDWICH TRAY

Fenton introduced the No. 3714-13½" diameter plate in July 1959. The pie crust crimped plates were sometimes drilled and fitted with chrome handles with oval tops. These converted plates were sold as sandwich trays. Colors produced were Milk and Topaz Opalescent. Since they were only made for six months, Topaz Opalescent trays are not easily found.

Milk

No. 3791-13½" Sandwich tray	Introduced	Discontinued	Value
Milk	July 1959	1974	$25.00 – 35.00
Topaz Opalescent	July 1959	1960	$85.00 – 90.00

NO. 3709 2-TIER SERVER

A milk 2-tier server was introduced into the Fenton general line in 1970. The bottom tier of the server was composed of a drilled 12" diameter shallow cupped bowl that was also used with the No. 3703 chip 'n dip set. The top part of the server was made from the 3-part, No. 3607-7½" diameter relish. The two pieces were connected with a chrome handle that produced a server about 10" tall.

No. 3709 2-Tier server	Introduced	Discontinued	Value
Milk	1970	1980	$40.00 – 50.00

NO. 389-10½" FAN TRAY

Fenton's large fan tray entered the line in 1941. The original colors were Blue Opalescent, French Opalescent, and Topaz Opalescent. The tray is 10½" long and 7" wide. It has nine scallops along the top of the longest side. The underside of the tray has 15 rows of hobs. Violet trays were made for the Fenton Gift Shop in 2002.

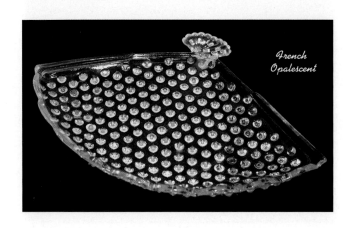

French Opalescent

No. 389-10½" Fan tray	Introduced	Discontinued	Value
Blue Opalescent	1941	1951	$40.00 – 45.00
French Opalescent	1941	1951	$30.00 – 35.00
Topaz Opalescent	1941	1944	$55.00 – 60.00
Violet	2002	2002	$20.00 – 25.00

NO. 3879-7¾" DIVIDED TRAY WITH CHROME HANDLE

This round tray with a center chrome handle entered the Fenton line in the fall of 1950. The tray is 7¾" in diameter and has a center division on the top side. The flared side of the tray is 1" high and has three rows of hobs. The underside of the tray has 16 rows of hobs. This tray was used to hold the oil bottle, shakers, creamer, sugar, and mustard in the No. 3809 condiment set.

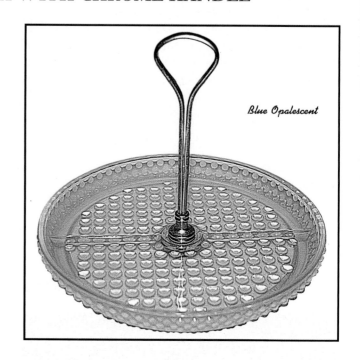

Blue Opalescent

No. 3879-7¾" Handled tray	Introduced	Discontinued	Value
Blue Opalescent	Sept. 1950	1954	$85.00 – 100.00
French Opalescent	Sept. 1950	1954	$55.00 – 60.00
Milk	Sept. 1950	1959	$35.00 – 45.00

NO. 3794, 2-TIER CHROME HANDLED TIDBIT

Milk

Fenton's No. 3794, 2-tier tidbit was unveiled in July 1959. This tidbit consists of a round, crimped edge, 13½" diameter plate and a round, 8" diameter crimped edge plate. These two plates are drilled in the center and are connected with a chrome handle. Notice the Topaz Opalescent tidbit was only made for six months. This color is elusive.

No. 3794, 2-tier handled tray	Introduced	Discontinued	Value
Crystal	1968	1969	$15.00 – 20.00
Milk	July 1959	1984	$45.00 – 50.00
Topaz Opalescent	July 1959	1960	$120.00 – 140.00

NO. 389, 2-TIER TIDBIT

This square tidbit server was introduced into the regular Fenton line in October 1950. It was produced by drilling a hole in the center of a square dinner plate for the bottom tier. The top tray was fashioned from the smaller bread and butter plate. A chrome handle with a round top linked the two plates to produce the tidbit. These tidbits disappeared from the price lists by mid-1951.

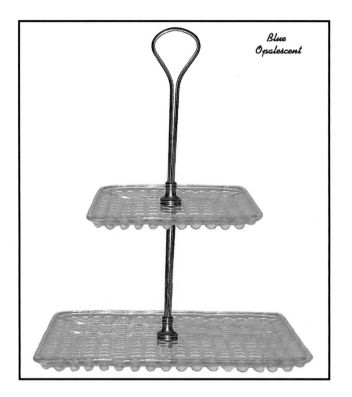

Blue Opalescent

No. 389, 2-tier tidbit tray	Introduced	Discontinued	Value
Blue Opalescent	Sept. 1950	July 1951	$185.00 – 200.00
French Opalescent	Sept. 1950	July 1951	$100.00 – 125.00

NO. 3913-13" FOOTED CAKE PLATE

Fenton's Hobnail footed cake plate was introduced into the regular line in July 1941. Inaugural colors were Blue Opalescent, French Opalescent, and Topaz Opalescent. This piece disappeared from the line during the mid-1940s and was reintroduced in 1948. Although the cake plate measures about 12½" in diameter, it has been listed in Fenton catalogs at both 12" and 13" sizes. Woodland Frost (FM), a French Opalescent satin finished version of this cake plate, was presented in the Christmas 2001 supplement. In 2002, this French Opalescent Iridescent (C3913-FM) cake plate was made exclusively for a Country Living QVC show.

No. 3913-13" Cake plate	Introduced	Discontinued	Value
Blue Opalescent	July 1941	1944*	$125.00 – 145.00
Crystal	1968	1969	$12.00 – 15.00
French Opalescent	July 1941	1944**	$80.00 – 95.00
French Opalescent Iridescent	August 2002	2002	$35.00 – 40.00
Milk	1956	July 1989***	$35.00 – 40.00
Topaz Opalescent	July 1941	1944†	$145.00 – 185.00
Turquoise	1955	1958	$75.00 – 85.00
Willow Green Opalescent	2001	2002	$35.00 – 40.00
Woodland Frost	July 2001	2002	$30.00 – 35.00

*Also made from January 1948 through December 1954.
**Also made from January 1948 through December 1955.
***Also made from January 1991 through December 1993.
†Also made from January 1959 through December 1959.

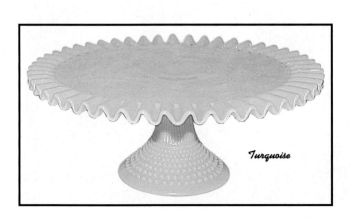

Turquoise

PUNCH SETS

NO. 3722, 7-QUART PUNCH BOWL

This large 7-quart pie crust crimped top punch bowl was combined with a base and different numbers of cups to produce several different punch sets. The bowl is 15" in diameter and 7½" high. This bowl was originally made for the general line in milk during 1958. It was reissued in milk in 1991 and 1992. This later issue will have the embossed Fenton logo. The bowl is designed to rest upon the No. 3778 base. The base is 8¼" in diameter and 4" high. The ware number for this base was also used for an 8" diameter ashtray/chip 'n dip candle bowl. No. 3847 punch cups were sold with this bowl. The cups are 2¼" high and 3" in diameter (not including the handle). The two sizes of sets sold originally include:

1. No. 3712, 15-piece — a No. 3722 bowl, No. 3778 base, 12 No. 3847 cups, and a No. 9527 crystal ladle.
2. No. 3718, 21-piece — a No. 3722 bowl, No. 3778 base, 18 No. 3847 cups, and a No. 9527 crystal ladle.

Later, in the early 1980s, the No. 3712, 15-piece punch set was made for The Levay Distributing Company. Colors produced for Levay were Topaz Opalescent and Blue Opalescent. A limited number of sets were also produced for Fenton special offerings. During the last half of 1985, the No. 3712 set was made in Green Opalescent for the Connoisseur Collection. In 1988, this set was made in Pink Opalescent (UO) for the Collector's Extravaganza. Persian Blue (XC) sets were made in 1989. Rose Magnolia (RV) sets were part of the 1993

Historical Collection. Hunter Green Carnival (GZ) 14-piece sets (no ladle) were made for QVC in 1991.

Item	Value in Milk
Punch bowl	$275.00 – 325.00
Base	$30.00 – 45.00
Cup	$18.00 – 20.00
Ladle	$25.00 – 35.00
Punch set, 15-piece	$500.00 – 550.00
Punch set, 21-piece	$700.00 – 800.00

No. 3712 Punch set	Introduced	Discontinued	Value
Blue Opalescent	1982	1982	$500.00 – 550.00
Green Carnival	1991	1991	$550.00 – 650.00
Green Opalescent	July 1985	1986	$450.00 – 500.00
Milk	1958	1967*	$500.00 – 550.00
Persian Blue Opalescent	July 1989	1990	$400.00 – 500.00
Pink Opalescent	1988	1989	$400.00 – 450.00
Rose Magnolia	1993	July 1993	$450.00 – 550.00
Topaz Opalescent	1980	1980	$600.00 – 700.00

*Reissued in 1991 and 1992.

NO. 389 CRIMPED PUNCH SET

Fenton introduced three different styles of punch sets into the general line in the fall of 1950. This crimped punch bowl was included in a 15-piece punch set. The bowl is 9½" in diameter and 4" high. This set was composed of 12-No. 3847 cups, a No. 3917-16" torte underplate, and a ladle. The punch cups are priced on page 174 and the underplate is priced on page 167.

French Opalescent

No. 389 Crimped punch bowl	Introduced	Discontinued	Value
Blue Opalescent	Sept. 1950	July 1952	$250.00 – 300.00
French Opalescent	Sept. 1950	July 1952	$200.00 – 250.00
Milk	Sept. 1950	July 1952	$200.00 – 250.00

NO. 3827 PUNCH BOWL

Milk

This punch bowl is 11" in diameter and 5¼" high. It was introduced into the Fenton line in the fall of 1950. It completes a 15-piece punch set that consists of this bowl, a 16" torte underplate, a crystal or milk ladle, and 12 No. 3847 punch cups.

No. 3827 Punch bowl	Introduced	Discontinued	Value
Blue Opalescent	Sept. 1950	1955	$250.00 – 275.00
French Opalescent	Sept. 1950	1955	$200.00 – 250.00
Milk	Sept. 1950	July 1959	$225.00 – 250.00

No. 3807-15-piece Punch set	
Blue Opalescent	$550.00 – 600.00
French Opalescent	$325.00 – 425.00
Milk	$495.00 – 525.00

NO. 389 HANDLED PUNCH BOWL

Of the three styles of punch bowls introduced in the fall of 1950, Fenton's handled punch bowl was made for the shortest period. It was out of the line by the beginning of 1952. This bowl has an applied handle and is 11" in diameter. Blue opalescent bowls may be found with either blue or crystal handles. This bowl was sold as part of a punch set that included a 16" torte underplate and 12 punch cups.

No. 389 Handled punch bowl	Introduced	Discontinued	Value
Blue Opalescent	Sept. 1950	1952	$400.00 – 600.00
French Opalescent	Sept. 1950	1952	$300.00 – 400.00
Milk	Sept. 1950	1952	$500.00 – 600.00

15-piece Handled punch set	Value
Blue Opalescent	$700.00 – 820.00
French Opalescent	$475.00 – 600.00

15-piece Handled punch set	Value
Milk	$750.00 – 850.00

Milk

NO. 3820 OCTAGONAL PUNCH BOWL

This flared, 8-sided punch bowl was introduced in July 1953. The bowl is 6¼" high and 11¼" in diameter. It was part of a 14-piece punch set (No. 3911) that consisted of a milk ladle and 12 octagonal punch cups. The milk ladle was ware number 9520. This set was also sold with eight cups. The ware number for this selection was 3908.

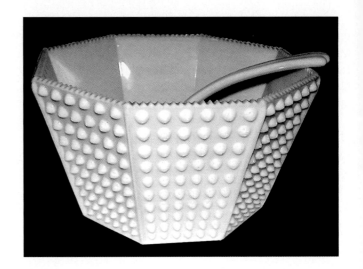

No. 3820 Octagonal punch bowl	Introduced	Discontinued	Value
Milk	July 1953	1958	$300.00 – 350.00

No. 3911-14-piece Octagonal punch set			
Milk			$550.00 – 630.00

NO. 3840 OCTAGONAL PUNCH CUP

Octagonal shaped punch cups were made to be used with the octagonal shaped punch bowl shown above. Sets included 12 punch cups.

No. 3840 Octagonal punch cup	Introduced	Discontinued	Value
Milk	July 1953	1958	$22.00 – 24.00

NO. 3847 PUNCH CUP

Fenton's No. 3847 round punch cup was used with all the punch sets except the octagonal set. The cups measure 2¼" high and 3" in diameter (not including the handle).

No. 3847 Punch cup	Introduced	Discontinued	Value
Blue Opalescent	Sept. 1950	1955	$18.00 – 20.00
French Opalescent	Sept. 1950	1955	$10.00 – 14.00
Green Carnival	1991	1991	$30.00 – 35.00
Green Opalescent	July 1985	1986	$12.00 – 15.00
Milk	Sept. 1950	1966	$18.00 – 20.00
Persian Blue Opalescent	July 1989	1990	$12.00 – 15.00
Pink Opalescent	1988	1989	$12.00 – 15.00
Rose Magnolia	1993	July 1993	$12.00 – 15.00
Topaz Opalescent	1980	1980	$30.00 – 35.00

Blue Opalescent

NO. 3611 CHAMPAGNE PUNCH SET

Champagne punch sets were made for The Levay Distributing Company in Blue Opalescent and Aqua Opalescent Carnival during 1982. These sets consisted of a punch bowl, a low flat base, and eight sherbets. The bowl is 12½" in diameter and has a crimped top edge. The sherbets are 3¾" in diameter and 4" tall.

No. 3611 Champagne punch set	Produced	Value
Aqua Opalescent Carnival	1982	$400.00 – 450.00
Blue Opalescent	1982	$450.00 – 500.00

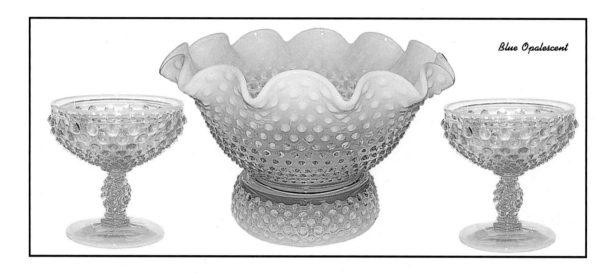

Blue Opalescent

SHAKERS

NO. 3806 FLAT SALT & PEPPER

Fenton introduced flat salt and pepper shakers into the general line during the fall of 1949. These shakers are 3" high and 1½" in diameter. They have slightly rounded chrome lids. The first colors made were Blue Opalescent and French Opalescent. Milk shakers were made beginning in 1950. Later, in the 1960s and 1970s a milk shaker was paired with a black shaker to produce a salt and pepper pair. Pink Opalescent and Sapphire Blue Opalescent shakers were made for Fenton's Gracious Touch division in the late 1980s. Sapphire Blue Opalescent shakers were also made for the June 1990 QVC program.

Cranberry

No. 3806 Flat shakers	Introduced	Discontinued	Value
Amber	1959	1960	$12.00 – 15.00
Blue Opalescent	Sept. 1949	1955*	$35.00 – 45.00
Cranberry	July 1954	1968	$85.00 – 100.00
French Opalescent	Sept. 1949	1965	$35.00 – 40.00
Milk	1950	1985**	$12.00 – 15.00
Pink Opalescent	1988	1990	$20.00 – 25.00
Plum Opalescent	1998	1998	$85.00 – 100.00
Sapphire Blue Opalescent	1988	1990	$30.00 – 35.00
Topaz Opalescent	1960	1961	$85.00 – 95.00
Turquoise	1955	1957	$25.00 – 35.00

*Reissued from 1959 to 1964.

**Also made from 1991 through 1995.

NO. 389 FOOTED SALT & PEPPER

Footed Hobnail salt and pepper shakers were introduced into the Fenton general line in opalescent colors in 1940. They are 3½" tall. The side of the shaker and the top of the foot have hobs. These shakers may be found with either metal or plastic lids. These shakers were also used in the early 5-piece condiment set with the fan tray, mustard, and oil bottle.

No. 389 Footed shakers	Introduced	Discontinued	Value
Blue Opalescent	1940	1944	$55.00 – 75.00
French Opalescent	1940	1944	$45.00 – 60.00
Green Opalescent	1940	1941	$200.00 – 250.00
Topaz Opalescent	1941	1944	$100.00 – 125.00

Topaz Opalescent

Blue Opalescent

NO. 3609 SHAKER

These shakers are 3¾" tall and 2" in diameter. The foot is scalloped and has an embossed design near the edge. The side of the shaker is straight and has nine rows of hobs. The chrome lid is slightly curved. Crystal and Milk colors were in the general line. Topaz Opalescent shakers were made for The Levay Distributing Company.

No. 3609 Footed shakers	Introduced	Discontinued	Value
Crystal	1968	1969	$8.00 – 10.00
Milk	1966	1990	$20.00 – 25.00
Topaz Opalescent	1983	1983	$65.00 – 75.00

Topaz Opalescent

NO. 3602 KITCHEN SALT & PEPPER

These large range shakers are 4¼" tall and 2" in diameter. There are 11 rows of hobs on the side. These shakers have slightly rounded chrome lids. Shakers were sold either as an all Milk pair, or as a black and Milk pair. Black and Milk sets were sold from 1962 through December 1965.

No. 3602 Kitchen shakers	Introduced	Discontinued	Value
Black and Milk	1962	1965	$27.00 – 35.00
Milk	1962	1979	$25.00 – 32.00

Black & Milk Salt & Pepper

NO. 3797 CINNAMON OR SUGAR SHAKER

This large footed shaker was designed to be used for dispensing sugar or cinnamon. It is 4¾" tall and 2½" in diameter. The foot of the shaker is scalloped and has an embossed design near the edge. It has a slightly rounded chrome lid. This shaker was only in the regular line in Milk for one year. Although it is much larger, this shaker is similar in shape to the No. 3609 salt and pepper shaker. The two shakers are shown together in the photo for a size comparison.

No. 3797 Kitchen shakers	Introduced	Discontinued	Value
Milk	1968	1969	$120.00 – 140.00

VANITY ITEMS

VANITY ITEMS MADE FOR WRISLEY

Fenton began a long romance with the Hobnail pattern during the mid-1930s with the production of a lamp fount that was sold to lamp manufacturers. Over the next several years, from 1936 to 1938, reproductions of barber bottles were made from old molds for the L. G. Wright Company. Beginning in 1938, a modified 5½" tall barber bottle with a shorter neck and a slightly wider opening to fit a wooden stopper was sold to Wrisley of Chicago for use as a perfume bottle. A smaller No. 389 cologne bottle was also sold to Wrisley. Two sizes of French Opalescent puff boxes (4½" diameter and 3½" diameter) were also provided to Wrisley. The colognes and puff boxes were topped with wooden closures that were not made by Fenton. The bottles were often filled with bath salts and the puff boxes normally contained dusting powder. Later, the greater economies of mass-produced, machine-made glassware caused Fenton to lose this contract with Wrisley. Close examination of a bottle will reveal the maker. Fenton bottles were made from a 6-part mold. The machine-made bottles were produced from a four part mold. The earlier Fenton cologne bottles were fitted with a wooden stopper. The machine-made bottles were fitted with a cork-encased glass stopper. Examples of the two colors of bottles that Fenton made for Wrisley are pictured below. Other colors of bottles will sometimes be found. One explanation for the existence of bottles found in other colors is that these bottles were also produced as lamp bases for the E. P. Paul Company. Over the years the lamp fixture has become separated from the bottle.

Item	French Opalescent	Cranberry Opalescent
No. 289 Cologne with wooden stopper	$18.00 – 25.00	$85.00 – 100.00
No. 389 Cologne with wooden stopper	$30.00 – 35.00	N/A
Puff box with wooden lid	$22.00 – 27.00	N/A

No. 289 Colognes and Puff Box Made For Wrisley

FO Puff Box with Original Wooden Lid

FO Cologne with Original Stopper

No. 389 FO Cologne with Original Stopper

CR Cologne with Original Stopper

FO Cologne Filled with Original Cologne

COVERED BATH SALTS JAR OR GINGER JAR

This small 4½" tall French Opalescent jar was produced in the late 1930s for Wrisley of Chicago. It may sometimes be found with an original "Bath Salts" label still intact on the bottom. The jar was sold complete with an opal glass lid.

Bath Salts jar	Produced	Value
French Opalescent	1930s	$30.00 – 35.00

NO. 1230 ATOMIZER BASE FOR DEVILBISS

Green Opalescent

The Devilbiss Manufacturing Company of Toledo, Ohio, incorporated spray technology into fragrance bottles called perfumizers. Devilbiss decorated and applied the spray parts to glass blanks produced by many of the leading glass houses in the world. Hobnail atomizers were fashioned from cologne bottles utilizing cologne molds from the Fenton regular line. The Hobnail perfumizer was in the Devilbiss line in 1941. This 2¼ oz. bottle was produced in Cranberry, French Opalescent, Blue Opalescent, Green Opalescent, and Topaz Opalescent.

No. 1230 Atomizer	Produced	Value
Blue Opalescent	1941	$40.00 – 50.00
Cranberry	1941	$90.00 – 110.00
Green Opalescent	1941	$80.00 – 90.00
French Opalescent	1941	$25.00 – 35.00
Topaz Opalescent	1941	$90.00 – 110.00

NO. 3865 VANITY BOTTLE

Vanity bottles entered the Fenton general line in 1940. Two different styles of bottles and two different shapes of stoppers were used with these bottles. Early cologne bottles in Crystal, Blue Opalescent, Green Opalescent, and Topaz Opalescent were pressed from a No. 389 miniature vase mold. This shape is illustrated by the two colognes at the left of the photo below. Early colors such as Cranberry or Rose Overlay that had to be blown were made from a different shape blown mold. Examples of the mold-blown shape are the two colognes at the right of the photo. In the early 1950s Fenton began producing all these bottles from the blown mold. Thus, Blue Opalescent and French Opalescent bottles may be found in either shape. Early bottles in Green Opalescent and Topaz Opalescent were only made from the pressed mold. Colors of bottles produced later, such as Milk and Turquoise, will only be found in the mold-blown shape.

Both the flat and pointed stoppers are illustrated in the photo. Stoppers made until about 1947 were the flat style. Colors of the early flat stoppers for the Blue, French, Green, and Topaz Opalescent bottles should match the color of the bottle. Cranberry, Crystal, and Rose Overlay bottles used crystal stoppers. Beginning in 1947, Fenton started using the pointed stoppers in all cologne bottles. Crystal stoppers were used in all colors of these later bottles except for milk and turquoise. Milk and turquoise bottles were made after Fenton converted to the pointed shape stopper. Therefore, they will only have pointed stoppers and the color of the stopper should match the color of the bottle.

No. 3865 Vanity bottle	Introduced	Discontinued	Value
Blue Opalescent	1940	1954	$50.00 – 60.00
Cranberry	1940	1957	$80.00 – 90.00
Crystal			$10.00 – 20.00
French Opalescent	1940	1954	$35.00 – 45.00
Green Opalescent	1940	1941	$100.00 – 125.00
Milk	1955	1965	$45.00 – 55.00
Rose Overlay	1943		$100.00 – 125.00
Ruby Overlay			$100.00 – 125.00
Topaz Opalescent	1941	1944	$140.00 – 150.00
Turquoise	1956	1957	$55.00 – 65.00

Green Opalescent   Topaz Opalescent   Cranberry   Blue Opalescent

NO. 3885 PUFF BOX

Two different styles of powder lids will be found. The early lids were slightly curved and had no defined finial. These lids should match the color of the puff box bottom except for Cranberry and Rose Overlay. These two colors have crystal lids. Green Opalescent and Topaz Opalescent have only flat lids that match the color of the bottom. Lids produced after 1947 have a pointed hobnail finial. Therefore, Blue Opalescent and French Opalescent jars will be found with both styles of lids — lids with a finial and the plainer curved lids. Ruby Overlay jars have a crystal lid with a finial. Milk and Turquoise jars have finial style lids in colors that match the bottom.

This same ware number was also used for a milk footed candy jar made in the 1970s.

No. 3885 **Puff box**	Introduced	Discontinued	Value
Blue Opalescent	1940	1954	$55.00 – 60.00
Cranberry	1940	1957	$75.00 – 80.00
Crystal			$12.00 – 15.00
French Opalescent	1940	1954	$35.00 – 45.00
Green Opalescent	1940	1941	$140.00 – 165.00
Milk	1955	1965	$55.00 – 65.00
Rose Overlay	1943		$90.00 – 100.00
Ruby Overlay			$75.00 – 85.00
Topaz Opalescent	1941	1944	$125.00 – 150.00
Turquoise	1956	1957	$50.00 – 60.00

Blue Opalescent

Ruby Overlay

NO. 3775 VANITY TRAY

From 1960 through 1964, a Milk oval handled vanity tray was sold as an optional accessory for the 3-piece No. 3805 cologne set. This tray is 12½" long and 7" wide. Since many cologne sets were sold without trays, these trays are scarce. This vanity tray shares the 3775 ware number with a 4" candleholder marketed during the 1970s.

No. 3775 **Vanity tray**	Introduced	Discontinued	Value
Milk	1955	1965	$175.00 – 200.00

NO. 3805 VANITY SET

The No. 389, 3-piece vanity set consists of two cologne bottles and a puff box. These sets were sold as described on the previous pages under the Vanity Bottle (page 180) and Puff Box (page 181) headings. After July 1952, these 3-piece sets were designated as ware No. 3805. Milk sets were sold with an optional oval tray from 1960 through 1964. This tray is pictured on page 181 and the set is shown on the tray in the photo below. Other sets are sometimes sold with the 10½" fan tray. However, there is no catalog evidence that these sets were ever sold this way originally.

No. 3805 Vanity set	Introduced	Discontinued	Value
Blue Opalescent	1940	1954	$155.00 – 185.00
Cranberry	1940	1957	$245.00 – 260.00
Crystal			$32.00 – 50.00
French Opalescent	1940	1954	$105.00 – 135.00
Green Opalescent	1940	1941	$340.00 – 415.00
Milk w/tray	1955	1965	$295.00 – 325.00
Rose Overlay	1943		$290.00 – 350.00
Ruby Overlay			$275.00 – 315.00
Topaz Opalescent	1941	1944	$405.00 – 450.00
Turquoise	1956	1957	$170.00 – 195.00

Milk

Blue Opalescent

Ruby Overlay

NO. C3386 VANITY BOXTLE

This 3-piece combination powder box and cologne bottle vanity boxtle was made for QVC. It is 7" tall and 4½" in diameter. The Pink Chiffon Iridescent (XT) boxtle was introduced on the August 2000 show. The Willow Green Opalescent (GY) boxtle was made as a part of the Museum Collection for the December 2002 show. The Blue Topaz Opalescent (I2) boxtle was a part of the Museum Collection offered on the May 2003 show.

Willow Green Opalescent

No. C3386 Boxtle	Produced	Value
Blue Satin Opalescent		$60.00 – 70.00
Blue Topaz Opalescent	2003	$80.00 – 90.00
Pink Chiffon Iridescent	2000	$80.00 – 90.00
Willow Green Opalescent	2002	$80.00 – 90.00

NO. 3986 VANITY BOXTLE

Blue Opalescent

Fenton's original 3-piece combination powder box and cologne bottle vanity boxtle was introduced into the regular line in 1953. The colors produced were Blue Opalescent, French Opalescent, and Milk. The opalescent colors were only made for one year and the Milk version was made for two years. The French Opalescent boxtle was made again in 1982, as a limited edition of 800 pieces for Cosmetics 'N Glass. In 2003, this boxtle was made as a special order in Topaz Opalescent. A few of these Topaz Opalescent boxtles were produced with a satin finish. Both of these later issues will have the Fenton logo embossed on the bottom.

No. 3986 Boxtle	Introduced	Discontinued	Value
Blue Opalescent	1953	1954	$400.00 – 425.00
*French Opalescent	1953	1954	$250.00 – 275.00
Milk	1953	1955	$185.00 – 200.00
Topaz Opalescent	2003	2003	$150.00

*French Opalescent 1982 issue, $150.00 – 175.00.

VASES – FLAT

NO. 389-3" ROSE BOWL

Fenton's smallest rose bowl is about 3¼" in diameter and 3" high. It has a plain bottom and eight rows of hobs on the side. The top has an 8-point crimp. This style rose bowl was only made for a few years in the early 1950s. All colors are elusive.

Cranberry

No. 389-3" Rose bowl	Introduced	Discontinued	Value
Blue Opalescent	Sept. 1949	1951	$80.00 – 90.00
Cranberry	Sept. 1949	1951	$90.00 – 125.00
French Opalescent	Sept. 1949	1951	$25.00 – 28.00

NO. 3853-3" VASE

The double crimped version of the 3" vase was introduced at the same time as the rose bowl shape above. However, this shape was made in far more colors than the rose bowl. It was also made for a longer time and continued in production after the conversion to ware numbers. The vase is about 3¼" tall and 3½" in diameter. The Topaz Overlay vase listed was produced as a sample.

Lime Green Opalescent

No. 3853-3" DC vase	Introduced	Discontinued	Value
Black	1970	1971	$16.00 – 18.00
Burmese	1994	1994	$30.00 – 35.00
Blue Opalescent	Sept. 1949	1955	$32.00 – 37.00
Chocolate	1982	1982	$18.00 – 22.00
Colonial Amber	1968	1981	$7.00 – 9.00
Colonial Blue	1968	1978	$10.00 – 12.00
Colonial Green	1968	1977	$6.00 – 8.00
Cranberry	Sept. 1949	July 1956	$70.00 – 80.00
French Opalescent	Sept. 1949	1956	$10.00 – 12.00
Lime Green Opalescent	1952	1955	$50.00 – 75.00
Milk	1950	1985	$7.00 – 9.00
Orange	1968	1978	$10.00 – 12.00
Peach Blow	July 1952	1956	$25.00 – 32.00
Pekin Blue II	1968	1968	$15.00 – 20.00
Ruby	1972	1985	$14.00 – 16.00
Topaz Overlay			$50.00 – 55.00

NO. 389-4" MINIATURE VASE

This 4" tall miniature vase was made in fan, flared, hat, cupped crimped, oval, cupped flared, and triangular shapes. After the introduction of ware numbers in July 1952, this vase was made with an 8-point crimp. This shape is detailed at the bottom of this page. All shapes for Green Opalescent were discontinued by the fall of 1941. All shapes of Topaz Opalescent were discontinued by 1944. Rose Overlay and Orchid Opalescent were made during the mid-1940s. The exact dates are uncertain.

No. 389-4" Miniature vase	Introduced	Discontinued	Value
Blue Opalescent	1940	1952	$18.00 – 25.00
Cranberry	1940	1951	$30.00 – 35.00
French Opalescent	1940	1952	$14.00 – 16.00
Green Opalescent	1940	1941	$30.00 – 35.00
Rose Overlay	1943	1945	$20.00 – 25.00
Topaz Opalescent	1941	1944	$32.00 – 40.00
Violet Opalescent	1942	1945	$28.00 – 32.00
Wisteria Opalescent	1943	1945	$28.00 – 32.00

Rose Overlay Fan Shape   *Blue Opalescent Cupped Shape*   *Cranberry Hat Shape*   *Blue Opalescent Cupped Flared Shape*

NO. 3855 MINIATURE VASE

This vase is about 4" tall and 2¼" in diameter. It has an 8-point crimp around the top edge. Blue Opalescent, Cranberry, and French Opalescent crimped miniature vases entered the Fenton line in 1940 and were discontinued in the mid-1950s. Peach Blow and Lime Green Opalescent vases were only made for a few years and are not plentiful.

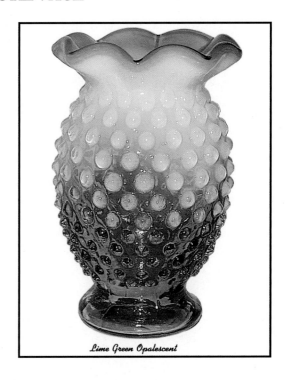

Lime Green Opalescent

No. 3855-4" Crimped vase	Introduced	Discontinued	Value
Blue Opalescent	1940	1955	$15.00 – 18.00
Cranberry	1940	1957	$30.00 – 35.00
French Opalescent	1940	July 1956	$14.00 – 16.00
Lime Green Opalescent	1952	July 1955	$50.00 – 75.00
Milk	1950	1969	$15.00 – 18.00
Peach Blow	July 1952	1956	$20.00 – 25.00

NO. 389-4½" VASE

This 4½" tall vase was in the general line in cupped square, cupped flared, and double crimped shapes. The vase was introduced in 1940 in opalescent colors. Topaz Opalescent replaced Green Opalescent during the fall of 1941. Rose Overlay vases were made in the mid-1940s. The double crimped shape of this vase continued in the line after the introduction of ware numbers in mid-1952. This shape is shown at the bottom of this page.

No. 389-4½" Vase	Introduced	Discontinued	Value
Blue Opalescent	1940	July 1952	$22.00 – 27.00
Cranberry	1940	1949	$45.00 – 55.00
French Opalescent	1940	July 1952	$18.00 – 20.00
Green Opalescent	1940	1941	$40.00 – 45.00
Rose Overlay	1943	1945	$20.00 – 30.00
Topaz Opalescent	1941	1944	$40.00 – 50.00

Green Opalescent — Flared Crimped

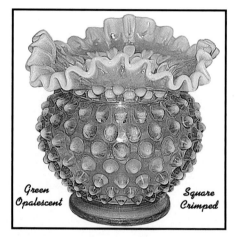

Green Opalescent — Square Crimped

NO. 3854-4½" DC VASE OR ROSE BOWL

The double crimped version of this vase is about 4½" high and 5½" in diameter. This was one of the more popular styles and vases were produced in many colors. Topaz Opalescent vases were reissued in 1959. They were made again in 1980 for The Levay Distributing Company. These later vases have the oval Fenton logo.

No. 3854-4½" DC vase	Introduced	Discontinued	Value
Amber	1959	July 1959*	$7.00 – 9.00
Blue Opalescent	1940	July 1955	$20.00 – 24.00
Blue Pastel	1954	1955	$20.00 – 27.00
Cameo Opalescent	1979	1982	$14.00 – 16.00
Carnival	1980	1981	$25.00 – 30.00
Colonial Blue	1975	1980	$12.00 – 14.00
Colonial Green	1969	1977	$8.00 – 10.00
Cranberry	1940	1978	$40.00 – 50.00
French Opalescent	1940	July 1956	$18.00 – 20.00
Green Pastel	1954	1956	$20.00 – 22.00
Lime Green Opal	1952	1955	$35.00 – 40.00
Milk	1950	1990	$9.00 – 11.00
Orange	1969	1978	$12.00 – 14.00
Peach Blow	July 1952	1957	$30.00 – 35.00
Pink Opalescent	1988	1989	$18.00 – 22.00
Rose Magnolia	1993	1993	$20.00 – 22.00
Rose Pastel	1954	1957	$20.00 – 22.00

No. 3854-4½" DC vase	Introduced	Discontinued	Value
Ruby	1976	1983**	$18.00 – 20.00
Springtime Green	1977	1979	$10.00 – 12.00
Topaz Opalescent	1959	1961***	$40.00 – 50.00
Turquoise	1955	1959	$25.00 – 32.00

*Reissued in Colonial Amber from 1969 through 1980.
**Also made in the last half of 1987.
***Also made for Levay in 1980.

Lime Green Opalescent

NO. 389-4½" ROSE BOWL

Fenton produced a rose bowl with an 8-point crimp from the 4½" vase mold. The vase was made in opalescent colors and was discontinued by 1944.

No. 389-4½" Rose bowl	Introduced	Discontinued	Value
Blue Opalescent	1940	1944	$40.00 – 45.00
Cranberry	1940	1944	$50.00 – 60.00
French Opalescent	1940	1944	$25.00 – 30.00
Green Opalescent	1940	1941	$65.00 – 85.00
Rose Overlay	1943	1945	$60.00 – 70.00
Topaz Opalescent	1941	1944	$70.00 – 80.00

Green Opalescent

NO. 3861-4¼" ROSE BOWL

Violet Opalescent

This small rose bowl with a 6-point crimp was first made in Topaz Opalescent for The Levay Distributing Company in 1980. Later in the decade it was made in Pink Opalescent as part of a Hobnail assortment for the limited edition Collector's Extravaganza. In the mid-1990s this rose bowl was in the general line in Cranberry. Violet Opalescent rose bowls were made for QVC in 2002, and Cobalt Opalescent rose bowls were made for the August 2004 program.

No. 3861-4½" Rose bowl	Produced	Value
Cobalt Opalescent	2004	$35.00 – 45.00
Cranberry	1995	$35.00 – 45.00
Topaz Opalescent	1980	$45.00 – 55.00
Pink Opalescent	1988	$27.00 – 30.00
Violet Opalescent	2002	$35.00 – 40.00

NO. 3323-4½" ROSE BOWL

This 4¼" tall and 4" diameter rose bowl with an 8-point crimp was made for The Levay Distributing Company in the 1980s. The bottom of the bowl has an embossed Fenton oval logo. There are 10 rows of hobs on the side of the bowl.

No. 3323-4½" Rose bowl	Produced	Value
Plum Opalescent	1984	$85.00 – 95.00
Topaz Opalescent	1983	$50.00 – 60.00

Plum Opalescent

NO. 3649-4½" VASE

This bulbous 4½" double crimped vase was in a small assortment of Cranberry Hobnail that returned to the Fenton general line in 2001. This vase was in the line for two years.

No. 3649-4½" Vase	Introduced	Discontinued	Value
Cranberry	2001	2003	$25.00 – 30.00

NO. 3669-4½" VASE

This vase was part of an 8-piece assortment of Pink Chiffon Opalescent Hobnail that debuted in the Fenton general line in 2001. This 4½" high cupped crimped vase remained in production in that color for two years. The vase is marked with the Fenton oval logo on the bottom. It is 4¾" in diameter and has 10 rows of hobs.

No. 3669-4½" Vase	Introduced	Discontinued	Value
Jade			$20.00 – 25.00
Pink Chiffon Opalescent	2001	2003	$18.00 – 22.00

NO. CV234-4½" DC CRANBERRY SPIRAL OPTIC VASE

This Cranberry Spiral Optic Hobnail double crimped vase was made for QVC. The vase is 4½" tall and was produced for the August 1998 QVC show.

No. CV234-4½" Vase	Produced	Value
Cranberry	1998	$30.00 – 35.00

NO. 389-5" VASE

This 5" bulbous vase was made with various crimpings. These include cupped flared, square, triangle, tulip, and double crimped. The double crimped style of this vase continued in production after the introduction of ware numbers in mid-1952. Therefore, this style of vase is identified as a No. 3850-5" DC vase. Double crimped vases made from this mold that were produced after this date are listed and priced below. Other crimped shapes as well as all the crimped shapes of Green Opalescent, Rose Overlay, and Wisteria Opalescent vases are priced here.

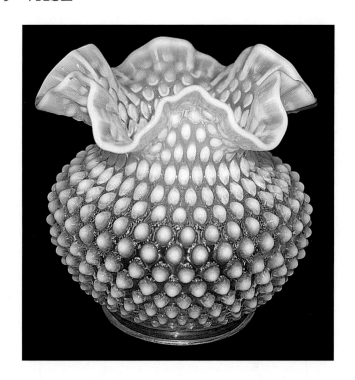

No. 389-5" Vase	Introduced	Discontinued	Value
Blue Opalescent	1940	1952	$25.00 – 30.00
Cranberry	1940	1944	$60.00 – 75.00
French Opalescent	1940	1951	$20.00 – 25.00
Green Opalescent	1940	1941	$50.00 – 60.00
Rose Overlay	1943	1945	$25.00 – 35.00
Topaz Opalescent	1941	1944	$50.00 – 60.00
Wisteria Opalescent	1943	1945	$60.00 – 80.00

NO. 3850-5" DC VASE

This popular double crimped 5" vase was made in numerous colors. It was made originally in opalescent colors and entered the regular line in 1940 along with the other various crimpings which are detailed above. After July 1952 this shape vase assumed ware number 3850. The Orange Opalescent color was produced as a sample.

Dusty Rose

No. 3850-5" DC vase	Introduced	Discontinued	Value
Apple Green Overlay	1961	1962	$30.00 – 35.00
Black			$20.00 – 25.00
Blue Opalescent	1940	1955	$25.00 – 30.00
Coral	1961	1962	$35.00 – 45.00
Cranberry	1940	1978	$60.00 – 70.00
Dusty Rose	1984	1985	$18.00 – 20.00
Federal Blue	1984	1985	$18.00 – 20.00
French Opalescent	1940	1955	$20.00 – 28.00
Honey Amber	1961	1963	$25.00 – 27.00
Lime Green Opal	1952	1955	$65.00 – 75.00
Milk	1956	1984	$12.00 – 14.00
Opaque Blue Overlay	1962	1963	$40.00 – 50.00
Orange Opalescent			$90.00 – 110.00
Peach Blow	July 1952	1956	$40.00 – 50.00
Powder Blue Overlay	1961	1962	$30.00 – 35.00
Ruby Overlay	1968	1969	$35.00 – 45.00
Topaz Opalescent	1959	1961	$50.00 – 60.00
Turquoise	1955	1957	$40.00 – 45.00
Wild Rose	1961	1963	$40.00 – 50.00

NO. 389-5" ROSE BOWL

This cupped vase, more commonly called a rose bowl, is 5" high and 5" in diameter. This large size rose bowl was only in the line in the early years of Hobnail production. The smaller rose bowls are found more frequently.

Blue Opalescent

No. 389-5" Rose bowl	Introduced	Discontinued	Value
Blue Opalescent	1940	1944	$45.00 – 55.00
Cranberry	1940	1944	$85.00 – 100.00
French Opalescent	1940	1944	$100.00 – 125.00
Green Opalescent	1940	1941	$70.00 – 90.00
Rose Overlay	1943	1945	$75.00 – 95.00
Topaz Opalescent	1941	1944	$90.00 – 110.00

NO. 3350-5" VASE

Champagne

This 5" high vase was made with a 6-point crimp. It was in the general line in Champagne. Iridescent Willow Green Opalescent (GY) and Iridescent Plum Opalescent (IP) were made for QVC. This latter color came with a tea light and was marketed as a candle bowl.

No. 3350-5" Vase	Introduced	Discontinued	Value
Champagne	2000	2001	$40.00 – 45.00
Iridescent Plum Opalescent	2001	2001	$45.00 – 50.00
Iridescent Willow Green Opalescent	2000	2000	$40.00 – 45.00

NO. 3326-5" VASE

A new double crimped 5" vase in Cranberry Opalescent entered the Fenton line in 2002. This vase has the Fenton logo embossed into the base. It remained in production for three years.

No. 3326-5" Vase	Introduced	Discontinued	Value
Cranberry	2002	2005	$50.00 – 60.00

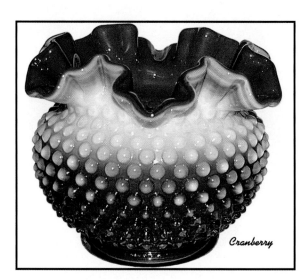

Cranberry

NO. 389-5½" VASE

Fenton's 5½" tall vase was introduced in the early 1940s. Styles produced included crimped, flared, square, triangle, and tulip. The original colors of this shape vase were discontinued in the early 1950s. Double crimped styles were produced in new colors after the introduction of ware numbers.

No. 389-5½" Vase	Introduced	Discontinued	Value
Blue Opalescent	1941	1951	$28.00 – 32.00
Cranberry	1941	1951	$45.00 – 55.00
French Opalescent	1941	1951	$25.00 – 30.00
Rose Overlay	1943	1945	$30.00 – 40.00
Topaz Opalescent	1941	1944	$50.00 – 60.00
Violet Opalescent	1942	1945	$60.00 – 70.00

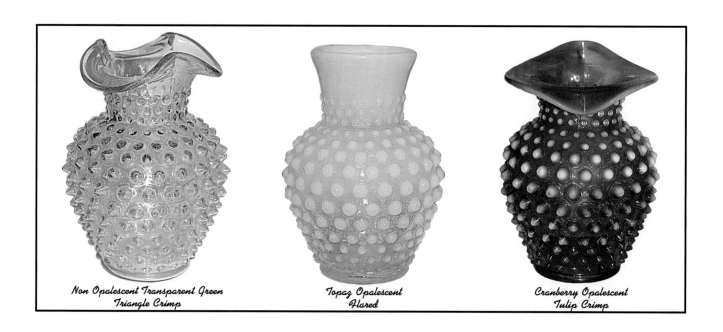

Non Opalescent Transparent Green Triangle Crimp   *Topaz Opalescent Flared*   *Cranberry Opalescent Tulip Crimp*

NO. 3656-5½" VASE

Milk

Fenton revived a double crimped version of the 5½" tall urn-shaped vase in the early 1960s. This shape vase had been out of production for almost a decade. New colors included Milk and overlay colors. The Empress Rose Iridescent Overlay with Violet trim (CH) vase was made for QVC in late 1999.

No. 3656-5½" Vase	Introduced	Discontinued	Value
Empress Rose Iridescent Overlay w/Violet trim	1999	1999	$30.00 – 35.00
Honey Amber	1962	1964	$27.00 – 32.00
Milk	1962	1974	$15.00 – 18.00
Opaque Blue Overlay	1962	1964	$35.00 – 50.00
Wild Rose	1961	1963	$45.00 – 55.00

NO. 3022-5½" ROSE BOWL

This cupped 5½" diameter rose bowl has a waved design among the hobs. The top two rows of hobs have a flat ground surface. The bowl is 4¼" high. This rose bowl was in the line in milk and Cobalt Marigold during the late 1980s.

No. 3022-5½" Rose bowl	Introduced	Discontinued	Value
Cobalt Marigold	1987	1988	$28.00 – 32.00
Milk	1987	1989	$20.00 – 25.00

Cobalt Marigold

NO. 3750-6" HANDKERCHIEF VASE

Fenton introduced this 6" swung handkerchief vase into the general line in July 1960. The vase was made in three opalescent colors and Milk. All of the opalescent colors were discontinued by the end of 1961, but the Milk vase continued in production through 1978.

No. 3750-6" Vase	Introduced	Discontinued	Value
Blue Opalescent	July 1960	1962	$50.00 – 60.00
Green Opalescent	July 1960	July 1961	$60.00 – 70.00
Milk	July 1960	1979	$25.00 – 30.00
Plum Opalescent	July 1960	1962	$85.00 – 95.00

Blue Opalescent

Green Opalescent

NO. 389-6" VASE

Early crimp styles for this 6" tall flat vase were double crimped, flared, square, and triangle. All of the shapes except double crimped were discontinued by July 1952, when ware numbers were instituted. The double crimped version of this vase went on to become the No. 3856-6" vase. See the list below for pricing of this style of crimping.

French Opalescent — Flared Shape

No. 389-6" Vase	Introduced	Discontinued	Value
Blue Opalescent	1940	1952	$27.00 – 32.00
Cranberry	1940	1957	$75.00 – 85.00
French Opalescent	1940	1952	$25.00 – 30.00
Green Opalescent	1940	1941	$75.00 – 85.00
Rose Overlay	1943	1945	$50.00 – 60.00
Topaz Opalescent	1941	1944	$70.00 – 75.00

NO. 3856-6" VASE

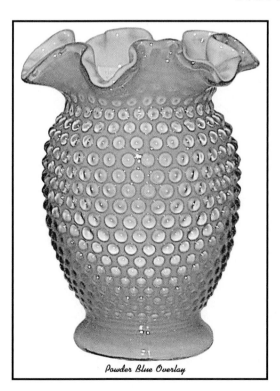

Powder Blue Overlay

This 6" tall double crimped vase was made in Milk and numerous opalescent and overlay colors. The shape was discontinued from the regular line in the mid-1970s. Recently, vases have be made in this shape again. Cranberry Opalescent was part of the original offering and was reissued in 2002. Topaz Blue Overlay vases were also available in 2002. These newer vases have the Fenton logo embossed on the bottom.

No. 3856-6" Vase	Introduced	Discontinued	Value
Apple Green Overlay	1961	1962	$30.00 – 35.00
Blue Opalescent	1940	1955	$27.00 – 32.00
Coral	1961	1962	$40.00 – 50.00
Cranberry	1940	1957*	$65.00 – 75.00
French Opalescent	1940	1954	$25.00 – 30.00
Honey Amber	1961	1963	$30.00 – 40.00
Lime Green Opal	1952	1953	$80.00 – 90.00
Milk	1951	1974	$12.00 – 14.00
Opaque Blue Overlay	1962	1963	$45.00 – 55.00
Peach Blow	July 1952	1956	$45.00 – 55.00
Powder Blue Overlay	1961	1962	$30.00 – 35.00
Topaz Blue Overlay	2002	2003	$25.00 – 30.00
Wild Rose	1961	1963	$45.00 – 55.00

*Also made from 2002 through 2004.

NO. 3954-6" VASE

When this double crimped vase was first introduced, it was listed as a 7" vase. In later years, it was called a 6" vase. Actually, the vase measures about 7" tall and is 5" in diameter. This vase was only in the general line in Milk.

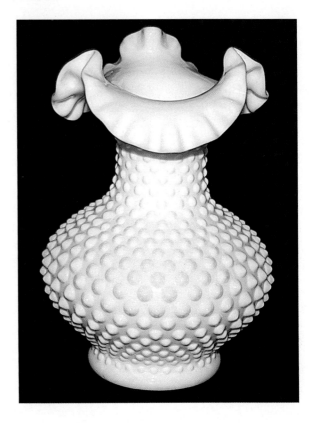

No. 3954-6" Vase	Introduced	Discontinued	Value
Milk	1972	1990	$18.00 – 20.00

NO. CV273 CRANBERRY SPIRAL OPTIC TULIP VASE

This tulip crimped Cranberry Spiral Optic vase is 6½" tall. The vase was produced for the August 1999 QVC show.

No. CV273-7" Vase	Produced	Value
Cranberry	1999	$85.00 – 95.00

NO. 3362-6½" JACK-IN-THE-PULPIT VASE

In 1981, this 6½" tall Jack-in-the-Pulpit style vase was made in Cranberry for The Levay Distributing Company. During 1988, Pink Opalescent vases were made for Fenton's Collector's Extravaganza collection.

No. 3362-6½" Vase	Produced	Value
Cranberry	1981	$70.00 – 80.00
Pink Opalescent	1988	$35.00 – 45.00

NO. 3052-7" CRANBERRY SPIRAL OPTIC VASE

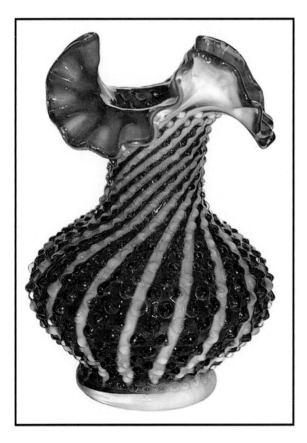

Fenton made this triangular crimped 7" tall Cranberry Spiral Optic vase for QVC. The vase was featured on the January 1992 show.

No. 3052-7" Vase	Produced	Value
Cranberry	1992	$85.00 – 95.00

NO. 1155-7½" VASE

This 7½" tall, 6-point crimped vase was part of an assortment of Cranberry Opalescent Hobnail that entered the Fenton general line in 1996. This vase has the Fenton logo embossed on the bottom.

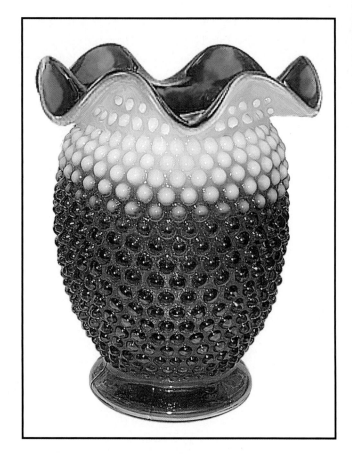

No. 1155-7½" Vase	Introduced	Discontinued	Value
Cranberry	1996	1997	$50.00 – 55.00

NO. 3356-8" TULIP VASE

Jade

This flat, 8" tall tulip crimped vase first entered the Fenton line in milk during the reintroduction of Milk Hobnail in 1992. The vase was made later for two years in Ruby Carnival. Rose Magnolia vases were produced briefly as part of the special 1993 Historic Collection. The jade vase in the photo was produced as a special order item in the mid-1990s.

No. 3356-8" Tulip vase	Introduced	Discontinued	Value
Cranberry	1995	1998	$70.00 – 75.00
Jade	1995	1995	$30.00 – 40.00
Milk	1991	1994	$25.00 – 30.00
Rose Magnolia	1993	July 1993	$35.00 – 40.00
Ruby Carnival	1992	1994	$55.00 – 60.00

NO. 389-8" VASE

During the early years of production, this vase had various crimpings. Cupped crimped, cupped flared, triangle, square, and double crimped shapes may be found. The double crimped shape evolved into the ware No. 3858-8" vase shown at the bottom of this page.

No. 389-8" Vase	Introduced	Discontinued	Value
Blue Opalescent	1941		$65.00 – 70.00
Cranberry	1941		$125.00 – 150.00
French Opalescent	1941	1949	$45.00 – 50.00
Green Opalescent	1940	1941	$120.00 – 140.00
Topaz Opalescent	1941	1944	$220.00 – 240.00

Blue Opalescent Flared Crimped Style   *Cranberry Opalescent Flared Style*

NO. 3858-8" DC VASE

Coral

This 8" tall, 6¼" diameter double crimped vase is found commonly in Blue, Cranberry, and French Opalescent colors. It is a little more elusive in the other opalescent and overlay colors. This Cranberry Opalescent vase was reissued in 2002. This new issue only remained in the line for one year.

No. 3858-8" DC vase	Introduced	Discontinued	Value
Apple Green Overlay	1961	1962	$45.00 – 55.00
Blue Opalescent	1943	1955	$65.00 – 70.00
Coral	1961	1962	$55.00 – 65.00
Cranberry	1941	1973*	$95.00 – 125.00
Cranberry Opal Satin			$55.00 – 65.00
French Opalescent	1941	1954	$45.00 – 50.00
Honey Amber	1961	1963	$40.00 – 50.00
Lime Green Opal	1952	1954	$125.00 – 150.00
Milk	1961	1974	$20.00 – 25.00
Powder Blue Overlay	1961	1962	$50.00 – 60.00
Wild Rose	1961	1963	$70.00 – 80.00

*Reissued in 2002.

NO. 3859-8" DC VASE

This large, 8¼" tall, 9" diameter flat vase is usually found in the double crimped style. However, other crimpings were made during the 1940s. Occasionally a vase will be found with square, triangular, or flared crimping. See page 199 for these additional shapes. Topaz Opalescent, Lime Green Opalescent, and Milk colors are the most difficult to find.

No. 3859-8" DC vase	Introduced	Discontinued	Value
Cranberry	1953	July 1961	$200.00 – 225.00
Lime Green Opal	1953	1954	$250.00 – 275.00
Milk	1953	1967	$55.00 – 65.00
Topaz Opalescent	1959	July 1960	$225.00 – 250.00

Milk

Cranberry Opalescent

NO. CV415-8" VASE

Sunset Iridescent Overlay

This 8¼" tall Sunset Overlay Hobnail vase was made for QVC. It has a double crimped edge with a black glass crest. It was sold on the May 2002 program. It came complete with the Museum Collection backstamp and certificate.

No. CV415-8" Vase	Produced	Value
Sunset Iridescent Overlay	2002	$85.00 – 95.00

NO. 389-8½" VASE

This large flat vase was made with several styles of crimpings. Styles produced were double crimped, flip, flared, square, and triangular. Flip style vases are especially hard to find. Double crimped vases in several colors were made in the 1950s and 1960s. For more information see page 198.

No. 389-8½" Vase	Introduced	Discontinued	Value
Blue Opalescent	1941	1944	$160.00 – 190.00
Cranberry	1941	1944	$300.00 – 345.00
French Opalescent	1941	1951	$90.00 – 110.00
Topaz Opalescent	1941	1944	$250.00 – 300.00

No. 389-8½" Flip vase	Introduced	Discontinued	Value
Blue Opalescent	1941	1944	$340.00 – 375.00
Cranberry	1941	1944	$400.00 – 500.00
French Opalescent	1941	1951	$125.00 – 150.00
Topaz Opalescent	1941	1944	$350.00 – 450.00

Blue Opalescent Triangle Vase

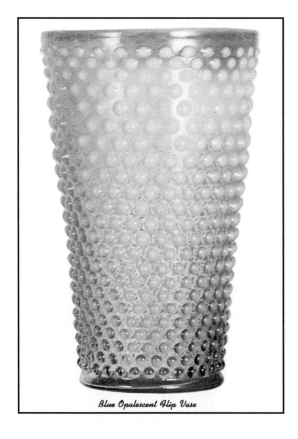

Blue Opalescent Flip Vase

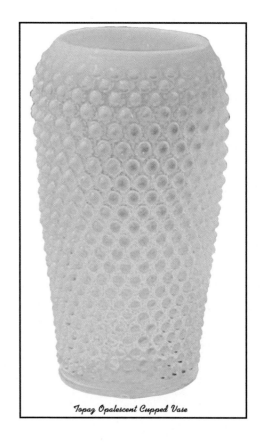

Topaz Opalescent Cupped Vase

NO. 3752-11" DC VASE

This style of 11" tall double crimped vase with an elongated neck was introduced into the Fenton line in the early 1960s. The vase was made in numerous transparent, opalescent, and overlay colors. Vases in sample colors such as Peach Blow and Orange Opalescent also exist. Cranberry Opalescent vases that were discontinued in the late 1970s were reissued in 2001. These new vases remained in production for two years. Other recent colors have been Champagne (PY), Pink Chiffon Opalescent (YS), and Willow Green Opalescent (GY).

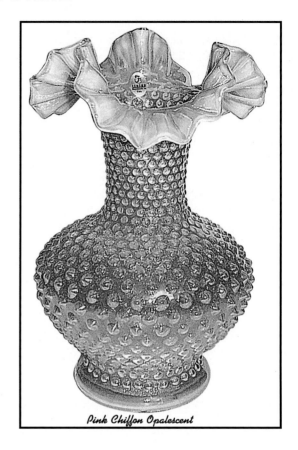

Pink Chiffon Opalescent

No. 3752-11" Vase	Introduced	Discontinued	Value
Apple Green Overlay	1961	July 1962	$90.00 – 110.00
Burmese	1971	1972	$150.00 – 180.00
Champagne	2000	2001	$50.00 – 60.00
Colonial Amber	1977	July 1978	$20.00 – 30.00
Colonial Blue	1977	1978	$35.00 – 45.00
Coral	1961	July 1962	$125.00 – 150.00
Cranberry	1969	1979*	$125.00 – 145.00
Honey Amber	1961	1963	$85.00 – 95.00
Milk	1958	1990**	$28.00 – 32.00
Opaque Blue Overlay	1962	1964	$125.00 – 175.00
Orange	1977	1978	$35.00 – 45.00
Orange Opalescent			$200.00 – 225.00
Peach Blow			$140.00 – 160.00
Pink Chiffon Opalescent	2001	2003	$50.00 – 55.00
Powder Blue Overlay	1961	1962	$90.00 – 110.00
Ruby	1977	1980	$35.00 – 45.00
Ruby Overlay	1968	1969	$125.00 – 150.00
Springtime Green	1977	July 1978	$35.00 – 45.00
Wild Rose	1961	1963	$125.00 – 150.00
Willow Green Opalescent	2001	2003	$50.00 – 60.00

*Reissued in 2001 and 2002.

**Also made from 1991 – 1994.

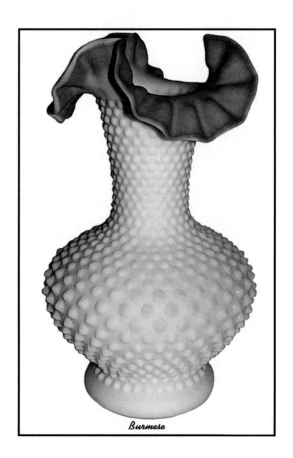

Burmese

NO. 3758 MEDIUM SWUNG VASE

Fenton's medium swung vases are about 12" tall and have a 2½" diameter base. These vases entered the Fenton line in Milk and several opalescent colors in July 1959. Green Opalescent and Topaz Opalescent vases were only made for one year. Later, in 1980, Carnival vases were made for one year.

No. 3758 Med. swung vase	Introduced	Discontinued	Value
Blue Opalescent	July 1959	July 1962	$75.00 – 90.00
Carnival	1980	1981	$45.00 – 55.00
Green Opalescent	July 1959	1961	$100.00 – 125.00
Milk	July 1959	1981	$15.00 – 20.00
Plum Opalescent	July 1959	1964	$120.00 – 140.00
Topaz Opalescent	July 1959	July 1960	$140.00 – 160.00

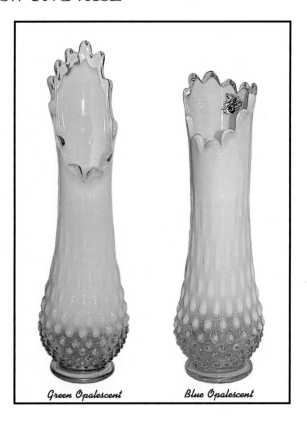

Green Opalescent   *Blue Opalescent*

NO. 3759 TALL SWUNG VASE

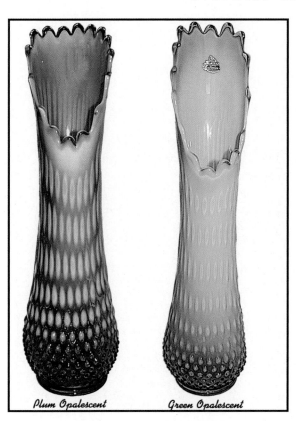

Plum Opalescent   *Green Opalescent*

Hobnail No. 3759 tall swung vases are about 16" to 18" tall. These vases have 3¼" diameter bases and bodies that are about 4" in diameter. Topaz and Blue Opalescent vases are elusive.

No. 3759 Tall swung vase	Introduced	Discontinued	Value
Blue Opalescent	July 1959	1961	$100.00 – 125.00
Green Opalescent	July 1959	1961	$150.00 – 185.00
Milk	July 1959	1977	$35.00 – 40.00
Plum Opalescent	July 1959	July 1962	$225.00 – 250.00
Topaz Opalescent	July 1959	July 1960	$190.00 – 220.00

NO. CV192-11" CRANBERRY SPIRAL OPTIC VASE

This Cranberry Opalescent Spiral Optic 10½" tall vase was made for QVC in October 1997. The vase is 6½" in diameter and has a triangular crimped top.

No. CV192-11" Vase	Produced	Value
Cranberry	1997	$140.00 – 160.00

NO. 3760 PITCHER VASE

This handled pitcher vase is about 14" to 16" tall and 8" in diameter. The handle is applied. Plum Opalescent pieces were only made for a few years and are scarce.

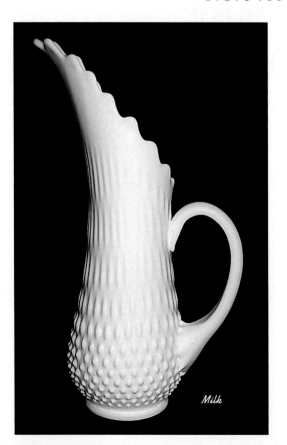

No. 3760 Pitcher vase	Introduced	Discontinued	Value
Milk	1960	1977	$65.00 – 75.00
Plum Opalescent	1960	1963	$300.00 – 350.00

VASES – FOOTED

NO. 3953-4" FAN VASE

Fenton's 4" high footed fan vase was made in several opaque and opalescent colors. The vase has a plain round foot. Pastel colors were made for the shortest time and are the most elusive. The double crimped version of this vase is shown below.

No. 3953-4" Fan vase	Introduced	Discontinued	Value
Blue Opalescent	1949	1955	$22.00 – 25.00
Blue Pastel	1954	1955	$18.00 – 22.00
French Opalescent	1948	1956	$18.00 – 20.00
Green Pastel	1954	1956	$18.00 – 22.00
Milk	1950	1972	$8.00 – 9.00
Rose Pastel	1954	1957	$18.00 – 20.00
Topaz Opalescent Iridescent	1975	1975	$30.00 – 35.00
Turquoise	1955	1959	$18.00 – 22.00

Milk

NO. 3952-4" FOOTED DC VASE

This small footed double crimped vase was made in a multitude of colors. The shape was introduced into the line in 1948 and various colors of the vase were still being made in the late 1980s. The vase is about 3¾" in diameter and has a plain round foot. The fan-shaped crimping of this vase is pictured at the top of this page.

No. 3952-4" Footed DC vase	Introduced	Discontinued	Value
Blue Opalescent	1948	1955*	$22.00 – 25.00

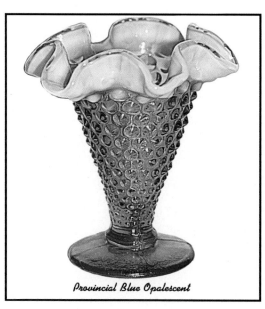

Provincial Blue Opalescent

No. 3952-4" Footed DC vase	Introduced	Discontinued	Value
Blue Pastel	1954	1955	$18.00 – 22.00
Blue Royale	1987	1989	$18.00 – 22.00
Burmese	1994	1994	$25.00 – 35.00
Colonial Amber	1965	1978**	$7.00 – 9.00
Colonial Blue	1965	1979	$12.00 – 14.00
Colonial Green	1965	1977	$6.00 – 8.00
Dusty Rose	1987	1989	$12.00 – 14.00
French Opalescent	1948	1956	$12.00 – 15.00
Green Opalescent	1960	July 1961	$20.00 – 22.00
Green Pastel	1954	1956	$12.00 – 14.00
Milk	1950	1985	$6.00 – 8.00
Minted Cream	1987	1988	$12.00 – 14.00
Orange	1965	1978	$11.00 – 13.00
Peaches 'n Cream	1987	1989	$12.00 – 14.00
Plum	1984	1984	$16.00 – 18.00
Provincial Blue Opalescent	1987	1989	$18.00 – 20.00
Rose Pastel	1954	1957	$14.00 – 16.00
Teal Royale	1988	1989	$14.00 – 16.00
Topaz Opalescent Iridescent	1975	1975	$30.00 – 35.00
Turquoise	1955	1959	$16.00 – 18.00

*Reissued from 1959 through 1963.

**Also made in amber in 1987.

NO. 3726 IVY BALL

Fenton's No. 3726 ivy ball is 4¾" tall and 3" in diameter. It is footed with a thick ribbed stem. The top edge is scalloped. This piece entered the regular Fenton line in Milk and Topaz Opalescent in July 1959. Topaz Opalescent vases were only made for a short time and are elusive.

No. 3726 Ivy ball	Introduced	Discontinued	Value
Milk	July 1959	1969	$15.00 – 18.00
Topaz Opalescent	July 1959	1961	$65.00 – 85.00

Milk

NO. 3757 FOOTED IVY VASE

This Milk Hobnail footed ivy vase is 5¾" tall and 4¼" in diameter. The plain foot is connected to the body of the ivy bowl by a long ribbed stem. The top of the body has a cupped ribbon crimped edge.

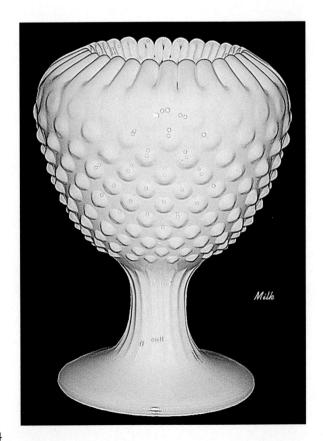

Milk

No. 3757 Ivy vase	Introduced	Discontinued	Value
Milk	1957	1969	$18.00 – 22.00

NO. 3653-5", 3-TOED VASE

This 3-toed cupped vase is 5" high and and about 3½" in diameter. It is 3-footed and was made in transparent Colonial colors during the late 1960s and early 1970s.

No. 3653-5", 3-Toed vase	Introduced	Discontinued	Value
Colonial Amber	1965	July 1971	$9.00 – 12.00
Colonial Blue	1965	1970	$16.00 – 18.00
Colonial Green	1965	1971	$10.00 – 12.00
Orange	1965	1970	$12.00 – 14.00

NO. 3654-5", 3-TOED VASE

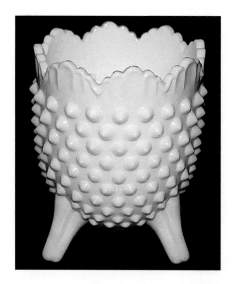

This Milk 3-toed vase is 5" tall and 3¾" in diameter. The top edge is scalloped and there are eight rows of hobs on the sides.

No. 3654-5", 3-Toed vase	Introduced	Discontinued	Value
Milk	1963	1980	$12.00 – 14.00

NO. 3655-5" VASE

This 5" footed cone-shaped vase was in the general line in Milk. The top edge and footed base are scalloped.

No. 3655-5" Footed vase	Introduced	Discontinued	Value
Milk	1962	1977	$12.00 – 14.00

NO. 389-6" HAND VASE

Fenton produced this hand vase in opalescent colors during the early 1940s. The vase is 6" tall and has a flared top. This vase is also known in Blue Opalescent with a triangular crimped top. Hand vases with several styles of crimped tops have been made recently. These have an embossed Fenton logo.

No. 389-6" Hand vase	Introduced	Discontinued	Value
Blue Opalescent	1942	1943	$125.00 – 150.00
French Opalescent	1942	1943	$90.00 – 110.00
Topaz Opalescent	1942	1943	$160.00 – 190.00

NO. CV287-6" CORNUCOPIA HAND VASE

A Gold Carnival Hobnail cornucopia hand vase was made for QVC in November 1999. The cornucopia of the vase features a hand-crimped edge. The vase measures 6" high and has 12 crimps around the top edge.

No. CV287 Cornucopia vase	Produced	Value
Gold Carnival	1999	$45.00 – 55.00

NO. 3951-6" HANDKERCHIEF VASE

This small footed handkerchief vase was made in Milk. It was also decorated with the hand-painted Holly decoration for a brief time. The vase is 6" tall and has six elongated panels. The foot is scalloped and has hobs on the top.

No. 3951-6" Vase	Introduced	Discontinued	Value
Milk	1972	1974	$30.00 – 35.00
Decorated Holly	July 1973	1974	$45.00 – 55.00

NO. 389-6¼" FOOTED VASE

Fenton's 6¼" footed vase was introduced into the line in 1941. Various crimpings include cupped, cupped flared, fan flared, and triangular. Some styles of vases may be found with either a scalloped or pie crust crimped edge. The double crimped style and fan-shaped vases continued in production after the introduction of ware numbers. This style vase is shown at the bottom of this page and the top of page 208.

No. 389-6¼" Footed vase	Introduced	Discontinued	Value
Blue Opalescent	1941	1949	$30.00 – 35.00
French Opalescent	1941	1949	$25.00 – 30.00
Topaz Opalescent	1941	1944	$70.00 – 80.00
Violet Opalescent	1942	1945	$70.00 – 80.00

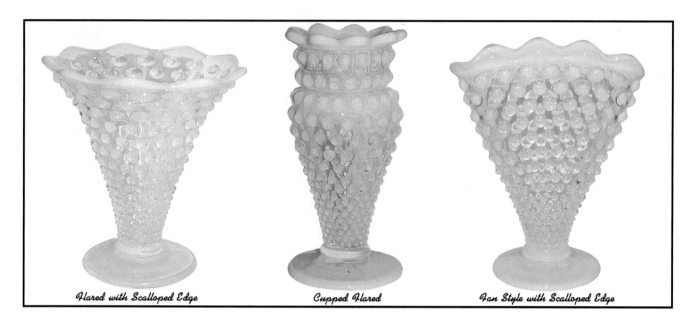

Flared with Scalloped Edge   *Cupped Flared*   *Fan Style with Scalloped Edge*

NO. 3956-6¼" FOOTED DC VASE

This double crimped 6¼" vase is found frequently in all colors. Topaz Opalescent vases are the most difficult to locate. Glossy Opaque vases were available through several sources in the 1970s. Floral arrangements were sold in these vases in the general line at various times. The vases were offered in a special promotion to florists through floral supply wholesaler A. L. Randall of Chicago. Some vases were also sold through the Fenton Gift Shop.

Glossy Blue

No. 3956-6¼" Footed DC vase	Introduced	Discontinued	Value
Blue (Glossy)			$18.00 – 20.00
Blue Opalescent	1941	1955	$30.00 – 35.00
Custard (Glossy)			$15.00 – 18.00
French Opalescent	1941	1956	$25.00 – 30.00
Lime (Glossy)			$18.00 – 20.00
Milk	July 1953	July 1978	$14.00 – 16.00
Topaz Opalescent	1959	1960*	$70.00 – 80.00

*Also made from 1941 – 1944.

NO. 3957-6¼" FOOTED FAN VASE

This footed fan-shaped vase is 6¼" tall. The round foot is plain. The 6" wide top edge of the vase is pie crust crimped. The opalescent colors were made from the early 1940s and some of these colors will be found with a scalloped top edge. A fan vase with a scalloped top is shown in the top photo on page 207.

Milk

No. 3957-6¼" Footed fan vase	Introduced	Discontinued	Value
Blue Opalescent	1941	1955	$35.00 – 38.00
French Opalescent	1941	1956	$27.00 – 32.00
Milk	July 1953	1972	$14.00 – 16.00

NO. 389-6½" SCALLOPED VASE

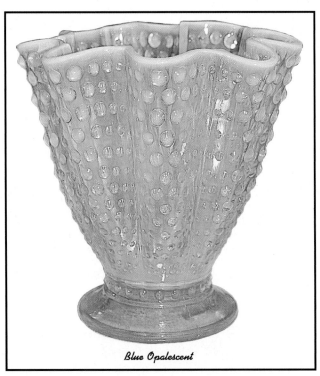

Blue Opalescent

This early 1940s, 6½" tall scalloped vase was made in opalescent colors in fan and flared shapes. The fan style is slightly more common than the flared shaped. Both styles of this vase are more elusive than the larger 9" size.

No. 389-6½" Footed fan vase	Introduced	Discontinued	Value
Blue Opalescent	1942	1944	$40.00 – 50.00
French Opalescent	1942	1944	$30.00 – 35.00
Topaz Opalescent	1942	1944	$60.00 – 70.00

No. 389-6½" Footed swung vase	Introduced	Discontinued	Value
Blue Opalescent	1942	1944	$50.00 – 60.00
French Opalescent	1942	1944	$40.00 – 45.00
Topaz Opalescent	1942	1944	$70.00 – 90.00

NO. 3651-6½" HANDKERCHIEF VASE

Fenton's No. 3651 footed handkerchief vase is 6" tall and about 3" in diameter. This vase has a round foot with three rows of hobs. There are also three rows of hobs around the bottom of the body of the vase. This vase was only in the line in Milk.

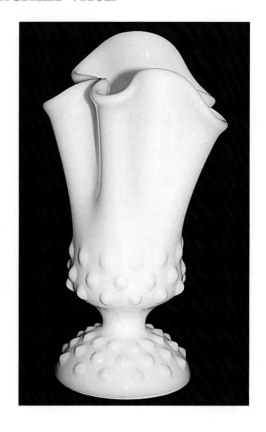

No. 3651-6½" Vase	Introduced	Discontinued	Value
Milk	1968	1971	$27.00 – 32.00

NO. 3657-7" VASE

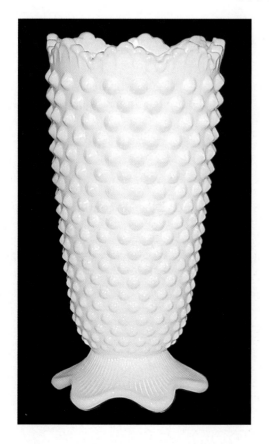

This is the medium size vase in Fenton's set of three cone-shaped vases that were made in Milk. The vase is 7" tall and 3¼" in diameter. There are eight scallops around the top edge and the foot has six scallops.

No. 3657-7" Vase	Introduced	Discontinued	Value
Milk	1962	1977	$20.00 – 22.00

NO. 389-8" FOOTED VASE

During the 1940s this 8" footed vase was made in double crimped, fan, square, and triangle shapes. After the introduction of ware numbers in July 1952, the styles that continued in production were double crimped and fan. The following two listings detail those shapes.

Blue Opalescent Triangle Vase

No. 389-8" Footed vase	Introduced	Discontinued	Value
Blue Opalescent	1943	1949	$55.00 – 60.00
French Opalescent	1943	1949	$40.00 – 45.00
Topaz Opalescent	1943	1944	$200.00 – 275.00
Violet Opalescent	1942	1945	$80.00 – 90.00

NO. 3958-8" FOOTED DC VASE

This double crimped 8" footed vase was introduced into the Fenton line in opalescent colors in 1943. Milk vases were added in 1956. This vase has a plain round foot and is about 6½" in diameter.

No. 3958-8" Footed vase	Introduced	Discontinued	Value
Blue Opalescent	1943	1955	$65.00 – 75.00
French Opalescent	1943	1956	$40.00 – 45.00
Milk	1956	1978	$16.00 – 20.00
Topaz Opalescent	1943	1944	$200.00 – 275.00

NO. 3959-8" FOOTED FAN VASE

This large footed fan vase is 8" tall and flares 8" wide. It has a plain round 4" diameter foot and the top edge of the vase is pie crust crimped. Opalescent colors were introduced in the 1940s and Milk entered the line in 1956.

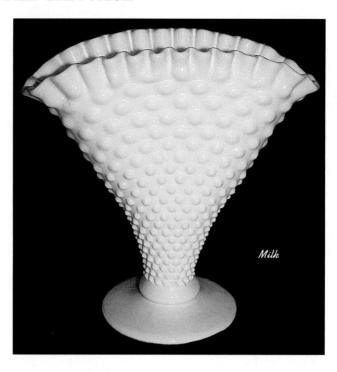

No. 3959-8" Footed vase	Introduced	Discontinued	Value
Blue Opalescent	1943	1955	$65.00 – 75.00
French Opalescent	1943	1956	$40.00 – 45.00
Milk	1956	1972	$16.00 – 20.00
Topaz Opalescent	1943	1944	$200.00 – 275.00

NO. 3756-8" BUD VASE

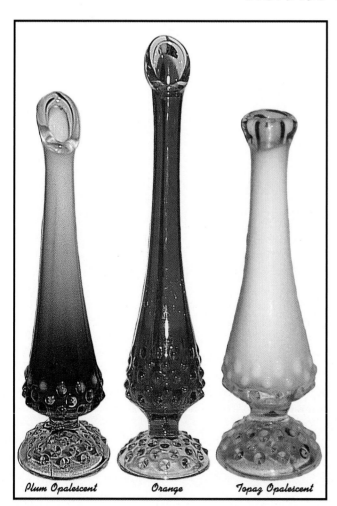

Plum Opalescent   Orange   Topaz Opalescent

Fenton's No. 3756 swung bud vase is 8" tall This vase entered the line in the mid-1950s and has been made in numerous colors since then. The vase has a round foot with three rows of hobs. There are four rows of hobs around the bottom of the vase body.

No. 3756-8" Bud vase	Introduced	Discontinued	Value
Amber	1959	July 1959*	$14.00 – 16.00
Blue Opalescent	July 1959	1965	$20.00 – 22.00
Carnival	1980	1981	$25.00 – 30.00
Colonial Amber	1967	1981	$14.00 – 16.00
Colonial Blue	1967	1981	$10.00 – 14.00
Colonial Green	1967	1977	$14.00 – 16.00
Crystal	July 1968	1969	$60.00 – 8.00
Decorated Blue Bell	1971	July 1972	$25.00 – 30.00
Green Opalescent	July 1959	July 1961	$30.00 – 40.00
Milk	1957	1985	$12.00 – 14.00
Orange	1967	1978	$14.00 – 16.00
Plum Opalescent	July 1959	1964	$65.00 – 70.00
Ruby	1976	1986	$14.00 – 18.00
Springtime Green	1977	1979	$14.00 – 18.00
Topaz Opalescent	1959	July 1961	$45.00 – 60.00

*Reissued as Colonial Amber from 1967 – 1981.

NO. CV321-8½" FAN VASE

This paneled fan vase is slightly over 8" tall and 7½" in diameter. The vase has a scalloped top edge and a plain cone-shaped foot. There are 12 V-shaped panels around the outside. This large vase was made for QVC in Champagne Opalescent Iridescent (PY) and Plum Opalescent Iridescent (IP). This vase is similar to the No. 3852 fan vase made in milk for the general line.

Plum Opalescent Iridescent

No. CV321-8½" Footed fan vase	Produced	Value
Champagne Opalescent Iridescent	October 2000	$60.00 – 70.00
Plum Opalescent Iridescent	November 2001	$70.00 – 80.00

NO. 3852-8½" FAN VASE

Milk

This large scalloped milk fan vase entered the Fenton line in 1971. It is similar to the fan vase above that was made for QVC. The most obvious difference is the lack of a collar between the foot and the body of the vase. This vase is 7" long and 3" wide at the top. The foot is plain and round. The body of the vase has 12 panels that are covered with hobs. The top edge has 12 scallops.

No. 3852-8½" Footed vase	Introduced	Discontinued	Value
Decorated			
Blue Bell	1972	1973	$140.00 – 160.00
Milk	1971	1973	$140.00 – 160.00

NO. 389-8½" SCALLOPED VASE

This 8" tall swung flared vase was made in the early 1940s in opalescent colors. The vase has eight scalloped panels. The small foot is round and plain. This shape is more elusive than the fan-shaped version of this vase, pictured below.

Blue Opalescent

No. 389-8½" Scalloped vase	Introduced	Discontinued	Value
Blue Opalescent	1941	1944	$90.00 – 100.00
French Opalescent	1941	1944	$55.00 – 65.00
Topaz Opalescent	1941	1944	$150.00 – 185.00

NO. 389-9" SCALLOPED FAN VASE

This scalloped vase is 8" tall, 10" long, and about 2¾" wide. The vase has eight scalloped panels and a scalloped top edge. It was produced in opalescent colors during the early 1940s.

No. 389-9" Scalloped fan vase	Introduced	Discontinued	Value
Blue Opalescent	1941	1944	$80.00 – 90.00
French Opalescent	1941	1944	$50.00 – 60.00
Topaz Opalescent	1941	1944	$150.00 – 160.00

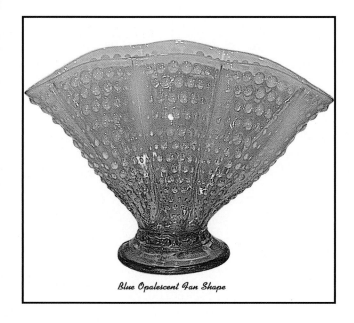

Blue Opalescent Fan Shape

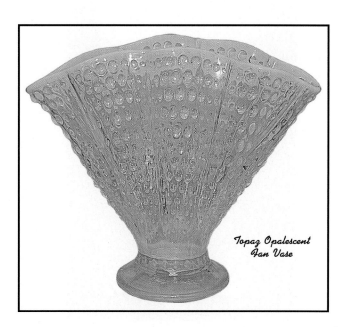

Topaz Opalescent Fan Vase

NO. 3755-9" VASE

This 9" tall swung vase was in the Fenton line in Milk and Plum Opalescent during the early 1960s. This ware number was also used for a tall swung vase produced during the 1970s and 1980s.

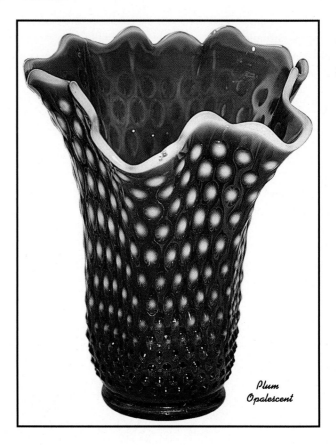

Plum Opalescent

No. 3755-9" Vase	Introduced	Discontinued	Value
Milk	1960	1963	$25.00 – 30.00
Plum Opalescent	1960	July 1961	$165.00 – 175.00

NO. 3659-9" VASE

This vase was in the Fenton line in Milk. It is the largest of a series of three sizes of cone-shaped vases. The vase has eight scallops around the top edge and a scalloped foot.

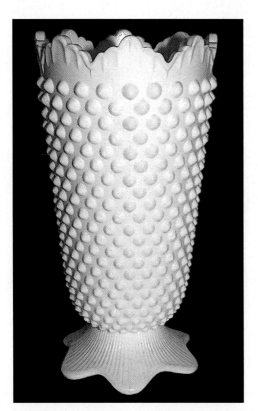

No. 3659-9" Footed vase	Introduced	Discontinued	Value
Milk	1962	1974	$25.00 – 35.00

NO. 3950-10" BUD VASE

This 10" tall swung bud vase entered the line in Milk during the early 1970s. It was hand painted with the Holly and Roses decorations during the mid-1970s. The vase is scalloped with six panels. There are four rows of hobs around the bottom of the body of the vase. The foot is also scalloped with six panels. There are two rows of hobs on the foot.

Decorated Roses on Milk

No. 3950-10" Bud vase	Introduced	Discontinued	Value
Blue Opalescent	July 1978	1982	$35.00 – 40.00
Burmese			UND
Cameo Opalescent	July 1979	July 1982	$24.00 – 30.00
Decorated Holly	July 1974	July 1975	$30.00 – 35.00
Decorated Roses	July 1974	July 1976	$32.00 – 35.00
Milk	1972	1990*	$20.00 – 22.00

*Also made from 1991 through 1992.

NO. 389-10" FLARED VASE

This elusive 10" tall bottle shaped vase was produced during the early 1940s. The vase looks similar to a decanter without a handle. The top edge is round and flared.

Cranberry

No. 389-10" Flared vase	Introduced	Discontinued	Value
Blue Opalescent	1941	1943	$150.00 – 185.00
Cranberry	1941	1944	$200.00 – 225.00
French Opalescent	1941	1943	$100.00 – 125.00
Topaz Opalescent	1941	1943	$200.00 – 225.00

NO. 3855-10" HANDKERCHIEF VASE

This 10" tall, 4¾" diameter, footed, swung handkerchief vase was made in milk. It was in the general line for only 18 months. It has a round 3¼" diameter base. The vertical ribs from the stem extend out on to the inside of the base. The rest of the base is plain. This piece uses the same ware number as the 8-point crimped miniature vase produced in the 1950s and 1960s.

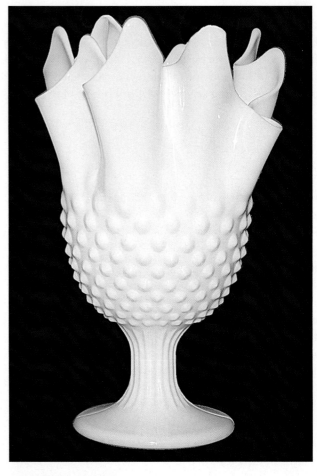

No. 3855-10" Vase	Introduced	Discontinued	Value
Milk	1977	July 1978	$35.00 – 45.00

NO. 3658-12", 3-FOOTED VASE

This 3-footed tall vase was made in milk for two years near the end of the 1960s. Although it was listed as a 12" vase it only actually measures about 9" high. It is 5" in diameter. The top of the vase has eight scallops.

No. 3658-12", 3-Footed Vase	Introduced	Discontinued	Value
Milk	1967	1969	$140.00 – 165.00

NO. 3753 FOOTED SWUNG VASE

This medium-sized, footed swung vase was made in several colors. It is commonly found in Milk and in the transparent colors from the late 1960s. Topaz Opalescent vases are elusive. Although it is listed as a 12" vase, vases may vary in height from about 12" to 14" tall. The vase has a 3¼" diameter foot and a vertical ribbed stem.

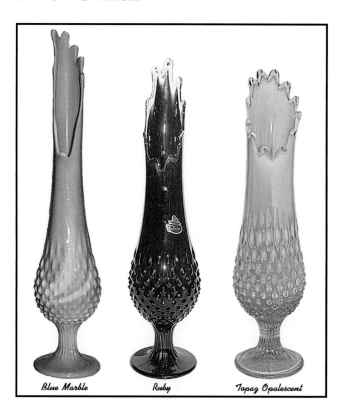

No. 3753-12" Footed swung vase	Introduced	Discontinued	Value
Blue Marble	1970	1973	$30.00 – 35.00
Colonial Amber	1968	1971*	$24.00 – 30.00
Colonial Blue	1968	1971**	$35.00 – 40.00
Colonial Green	1968	1971	$10.00 – 12.00
Crystal	1968	1969	$22.00 – 25.00
Decorated Blue Bell	1971	1972	$65.00 – 75.00
Milk	July 1959	1985	$20.00 – 22.00
Orange	1968	1971	$35.00 – 45.00
Ruby	1972	1980	$45.00 – 55.00
Topaz Opalescent	July 1959	July 1960	$125.00 – 150.00

*Also made from 1979 through May 1980.
**Also made in 1979.

Blue Marble Ruby Topaz Opalescent

NO. 3755 TALL SWUNG VASE

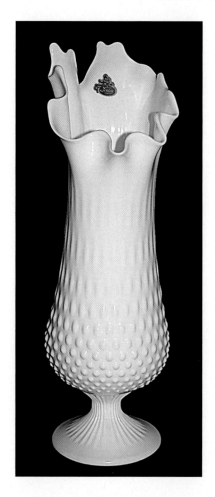

This swung handkerchief vase was made in milk. It is in excess of 14" tall and is about 4¾" in diameter. It has a round 4" diameter base. The vertical ribs from the stem extend out on to the top of the foot. The rest of the foot is plain. This ware number was also used for a 9" swung vase produced in the 1960s.

No. 3755 Tall swung vase	Introduced	Discontinued	Value
Milk	1971	1988	$25.00 – 30.00

NO. 3652-24" TALL SWUNG VASE

These tall swung footed vases vary in height from about 20" to 24" tall. They are about 4¼" in diameter and have a 4¼" diameter foot. The vases have a vertical ribbed stem that extends onto the foot. This style vase was introduced into the Fenton line in Milk and transparent Colonial colors during the mid-1960s. The Pekin Blue II vase in the photo was made around 1968.

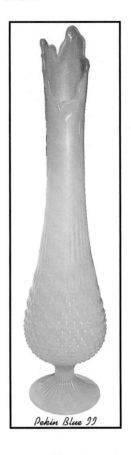

Pekin Blue II

No. 3652-24" Swung vase	Introduced	Discontinued	Value
Colonial Amber	1965	1978	$30.00 – 40.00
Colonial Blue	1965	1978	$50.00 – 60.00
Colonial Green	1965	1977	$30.00 – 40.00
Milk	1965	1981	$40.00 – 50.00
Orange	1965	July 1975	$55.00 – 65.00
Pekin Blue II	1968	1968	$90.00 – 110.00

LAMP SHADE STYLE VASE

Cranberry

This large 12" diameter vase is an example of a lamp shade style vase. Although they were not in the general line, these uncut lamp shades can be found on occasion.

Lamp shade-style vase	Value
Cranberry	$185.00 – 200.00

BIBLIOGRAPHY

BOOKS

Griffith, Shirley. *A Pictorial Review of Fenton's White Hobnail Milk Glass*. Warren, Ohio: Shirley Griffith, 1994.

Heacock, William. *Fenton Glass, The Second Twenty-five Years*. Marietta, Ohio: O-val Advertising Corp., 1980.

———. *Fenton Glass, The Third Twenty-five Years*. Marietta, Ohio: O-val Advertising Corp., 1989.

Newbound, Betty and Bill. *The Collector's Encyclopedia of Milk Glass, Identification and Values*. Paducah, Kentucky: Collector Books, 1995.

Palmer, Michael and Lori. *The Charleton Line: AWCO's Decorations on Fenton, Cambridge, Consolidated, Westmoreland, Duncan and Miller, Heisey, Imperial, Limoges and Others*. Atglen, PA: Schiffer Publishing, Ltd., 2002.

CATALOGS

DeVilbiss Company. *Devilbiss Perfume Atomizers*. Toledo, Ohio: The Devilbiss Company, 1939 – 1955.

Randall, A. L. *Fenton for Flowers*. Chicago, Illinois: A. L. Randall Company, 1970 – 1980.

Fenton Art Glass Company. Fenton general catalogs and supplements. Williamstown, West Virginia: Fenton Art Glass Company, 1940 – 2005.

NEWSLETTERS

Fenton Art Glass. *Glass Messenger*. Williamstown, West Virginia: Fenton Art Glass Company, 2000 – 2005.

Pacific Northwest Fenton Association. *The Fenton Nor'wester*. Tillamook, Oregon: P. N. W. F. A., 1992 – 2005.

WEBSITES

Fenton Fanatics website, www.fentonfan.com
Fenton Art Glass website, www.fentonartglass.com

INDEX

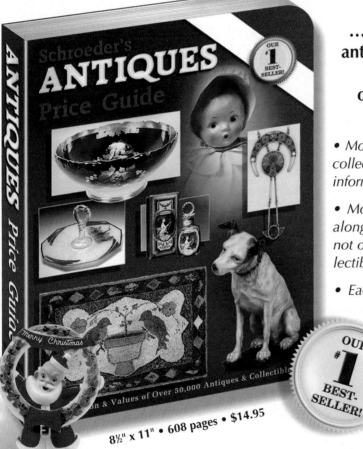